T.S. Eliot

THE WASTE LAND AND OTHER POEMS

T.S. Eliot

THE WASTE LAND AND OTHER POEMS

[Edited with Introduction, Author's Information, Complete Text, Summary and Analysis and Study Questions]

Aditya Nandwani
B.A. English (Hons) , Delhi University;
M.A. (English), IGNOU; Print Journalism (English) YMCA

ANMOL PUBLICATIONS PVT. LTD.
NEW DELHI - 110 002 (INDIA)

ANMOL PUBLICATIONS PVT. LTD.

H.O.: 4374/4B, Ansari Road, Darya Ganj,
New Delhi-110 002 (India)
Ph.: 23278000, 23261597

B.O.: No. 1015, Ist Main Road, BSK IIIrd Stage
IIIrd Phase, IIIrd Block
Bangalore - 560 085 (India)
Visit us at: www.anmolpublications.com

The Waste Land and Other Poems

First Published, 2009

PRINTED IN INDIA

Printed at Balaji Offset Press, Delhi.

Contents

Preface

Thomas Stearns Eliot (1888-1965), American-English poet, playwright, and critic, a leader of the modernist movement in literature. Eliot was awarded the Nobel Prize for literature in 1948. His most famous work is THE WASTE LAND, written when he was 34. On one level this highly complex poem describes cultural and spiritual crisis.

Eliot attended Smith Academy in St. Louis and Milton Academy in Massachusetts. In 1906 he went to Harvard, where he contributed poetry to Harvard Advocate. After receiving his B.A. in 1909, Eliot spent a year in France, attending Henri Bergson's lectures at the Sorbonne and studying poetry with the novelist and poet Henri Alain-Fournier.

Author

Chapter 1

Introduction

The Waste Land is a highly influential 434-line modernist poem by T. S. Eliot. Despite the alleged obscurity of the poem its shifts between satire and prophecy, its abrupt and unannounced changes of speaker, location and time, its elegiac but intimidating summoning up of a vast and dissonant range of cultures and literatures – the poem has nonetheless become a familiar touchstone of modern literature. Among its famous phrases are "April is the cruellest month" (its first line); "I will show you fear in a handful of dust"; and the Sanskrit "Shantih shantih shantih" (its last line).

Writing

Eliot probably worked on what was to become The Waste Land for several years preceding its first publication in 1922. In a letter to John Quinn dated 9 May 1921, Eliot wrote that he had "a long poem in mind and partly on paper which I am wishful to finish."

Richard Aldington, in his memoirs, relates that "a year or so" before Eliot read him the manuscript draft of The Waste Land in London, Eliot visited him in the country. While walking through a graveyard, they started discussing Thomas Gray's Elegy Written in a Country Churchyard. Aldington writes: "I was surprised to find that Eliot admired something so popular, and then went on to say that if a contemporary poet, conscious of his limitations as Gray evidently was, would concentrate all his gifts on one such poem he might achieve a similar success." Eliot, having been diagnosed with some form of nervous disorder, had been recommended rest, and applied for three months' leave from the bank where he was employed; the reason stated on his staff card was "nervous breakdown". He and his wife Vivien travelled to the coastal resort of Margate for a period cf convale cence. While there, Eliot worked on the poem, and possibly showed an early version to Ezra Pound when, after a brief return to London, the Eliots travelled to Paris in November 1921 and were guests of Pound. Eliot was en route to Lausanne, Switzerland, for treatment by Doctor Roger Vittoz, who had been recommended to him by Ottoline Morrell; Vivien was to stay at a sanatorium just outside Paris. In Lausanne, Eliot produced a 19-page version of the poem. He returned from Lausanne in early January 1922. Pound then made detailed editorial comments and significant cuts to the manuscript. Eliot would later dedicate the poem to Pound.

The Manuscript Drafts

Eliot sent the manuscript drafts of the poem to John Quinn in October 1922; they reached Quinn in New York in January 1923. Upon Quinn's death they were inherited by his sister, Julia Anderson. Years later, in the early 1950s, Mrs Anderson's daughter, Mary Conroy, found the documents in storage. In 1958 she sold them privately to the New York Public Library.

It was not until April 1968 that the existence and whereabouts of the manuscript drafts were made known to Valerie Eliot, the poet's second wife and widow. In 1971, Faber and Faber published a "facsimile and transcript" of the original drafts, edited and annotated by Valerie Eliot. The full poem prior to the Pound editorial changes is contained in the facsimile.

Editing

Ezra Pound in 1913. In 1922 he helped Eliot with the editing of The Waste Land. The drafts of the poem reveal that it originally contained almost twice as much material as the final published version. The significant cuts are in part due to Ezra Pound's suggested changes, although Eliot himself is also responsible for removing large sections.

The now famous opening lines of the poem – 'April is the cruellest month, breeding/Lilacs out of the dead land,...' – did not appear until the top of the second page of the typescript. The first page of the typescript contained 54 lines in the sort of street voice that we hear again at the end of the second section, 'A Game of Chess.' This page appears to have been lightly crossed out in pencil by Eliot himself.

Although there are several signs of similar adjustments made by Eliot, and a number of significant comments by Vivien, the most significant editorial input is clearly that of Pound, who recommended many cuts to the poem.

'The typist home at teatime' section was originally in entirely regular stanzas of iambic pentameter, with a rhyme scheme of abab – the same form as Gray's Elegy, which was in Eliot's thoughts around this time. Pound's note against this section of the draft is "verse not interesting enough as verse to warrant so much of it". In the end, the regularity of the four-line stanzas was abandoned. At the beginning of 'The Fire Sermon' in one version, there was a lengthy section in heroic couplets, in imitation of Alexander Pope's The Rape of the Lock. It described one lady Fresca (who appeared in the earlier poem "Gerontion"). As Richard Ellmann describes it, "Instead of making her toilet like Pope's Belinda, Fresca is going to it, like Joyce's Bloom." The lines read:

Leaving the bubbling beverage to cool,
Fresca slips softly to the needful stool,
Where the pathetic tale of Richardson
Eases her labour till the deed is done...

Ellmann notes "Pound warned Eliot that since Pope had done the couplets better, and Joyce the defecation, there was no point in another round."

Pound also excised some shorter poems that Eliot wanted to insert between the five sections. One of these, that Eliot had entitled 'Dirge', begins

Full fathom five your Bleistein lies
Under the flatfish and the squids.
Graves' Disease in a dead Jew's eyes!
Where the crabs have eat the lids

At the request of Eliot's wife, Vivien, a line in the A Game of Chess section was removed from the poem: "And we shall play a game of chess/The ivory men make company between us/Pressing lidless eyes and waiting for a knock upon the door". This section is apparently based on their marital life, and she may have felt these lines too revealing. The "ivory men" line must have meant something to Eliot though; in 1960, thirteen years after Vivien's death, he inserted the line in a copy made for sale to aid the London Library.

In a late December 1921 letter to Eliot to celebrate the "birth" of the poem Pound wrote a bawdy poem of 48 lines entitled "Sage Homme" in which he identified Eliot as the mother of the poem but compared himself to the midwife. Some of the verses are:

E. P. hopeless and unhelped
Enthroned in the marmorean skies
His verse omits realities,
Angelic hands with mother of pearl
Retouch the strapping servant girl,
Balls and balls and balls again
Can not touch his fellow men.
His foaming and abundant cream
Has coated his world. The coat of a dream;
Or say that the upjut of sperm
Has rendered his sense pachyderm.

Publishing history

Before the editing had even begun Eliot found a publisher. Horace Liveright of the New York publishing firm of Boni and Liveright was in Paris for a number of meetings with Ezra Pound. At a dinner on 3 January 1922 he made offers for works by Pound, James Joyce and Eliot. Eliot was to get a royality of 15% for a book version of the poem planned for autumn publication.

To maximize his income and reach a broader audience, Eliot also sought a deal with magazines. Being the London correspondent for The Dial magazine and a college friend of its co-owner and co-editor, Scofield Thayer, the Dial was an ideal choice. Even though the Dial offered $150 for the poem (25% more than its standard rate) Eliot was offended that a year's work would be valued so low, especially since another contributor was found to have been given an exceptional compensation for a short story. The deal with the Dial almost fell through (other magazines considered were the Little Review and Vanity Fair) but with Pound's efforts eventually a deal was worked out where, in addition to the $150, Eliot would be awarded the Dial magazine's second annual prize for outstanding service to letters. The prize carried an award of $2,000.

In New York in the late summer (with John Quinn, a lawyer and literary patron, representing Eliot's interests) Boni and Liveright made an agreement with The Dial where the magazine would be the first to publish the poem in the US by agreeing to purchase 350 copies of the book at discount from Boni and Liveright. Boni and Liveright would use the publicity of the award of the Dial's prize to Eliot to increase their initial sales. The poem was first published in the UK, without the author's notes, in the first issue (October 1922) of The Criterion, a literary magazine started and edited by Eliot. The first appearance of the poem in the US was in the November 1922 issue of The Dial magazine (actually published in late October). In December 1922, the poem was published in the US in book form by Boni and Liveright, the first publication to print the notes. In September 1923, the Hogarth Press, a private press run by Eliot's friends Leonard and Virginia Woolf, published the first UK book edition of The Waste Land in an edition of about 450 copies, the type handset by Virginia Woolf.

The publication history of The Waste Land (as well as other pieces of Eliot's poetry and prose) has been documented by Donald Gallup. Eliot, whose 1922 salary at Lloyds Bank was £500 made approximately $2,800 with the Dial, Boni and Liveright and Hogarth Press publications.

The title

Eliot originally considered titling the poem He do the Police in Different Voices. In the version of the poem Eliot brought back from Switzerland, the first two sections of the poem – 'The Burial of the Dead' and 'A Game of Chess' – appeared under this title. This strange phrase is taken from Charles Dickens' novel Our Mutual Friend, in which the widow Betty Higden, says of her adopted foundling son Sloppy: "You mightn't think it, but Sloppy is a beautiful reader of a newspaper. He do the Police in different voices." This would help the reader to understand that, while there are many different voices (speakers) in the poem, there is one central consciousness. What was lost by the rejection of this title Eliot might have felt compelled to restore by commenting on the commonalities of his characters in his note about Tiresias.

In the end, the title Eliot chose was The Waste Land. In his first note to the poem he attributes the title to Jessie L. Weston's book on the Grail legend, From Ritual to Romance. The allusion is to the wounding of the Fisher King and the subsequent sterility of his lands. To restore the King and make his lands fertile again the Grail questor must ask "What ails you?"

The poem's title is often mistakenly given as "Waste Land" (as used by Weston) or "Wasteland", dropping the article. However, in a letter to Ezra Pound, Eliot politely insisted that the title include the article.

Structure

The epigraph and dedication to The Waste Land showing some of the languages that Eliot used in the poem: Latin, Greek, English and Italian.

The poem is preceded by a Latin and Greek epigraph from The Satyricon of Petronius. In English, it reads: "I saw with my own eyes the Sibyl at Cumae hanging in a jar, and when the boys said to her, Sibyl, what do you want? she replied I want to die." (Petronius cast the question and answer in Greek). Following the epigraph is a dedication (added in a 1925 republication) that reads "For Ezra Pound: il miglior fabbro" Here Eliot is both quoting line 117 of Canto XXVI of Dante's Purgatorio, the second cantica of The Divine Comedy, where

Dante defines the troubadour Arnaldo Daniello as "the best smith of the mother tongue" and also Pound's title of chapter 2 of his The Spirit of Romance where he translated the phrase as "the better craftsman." This dedication was originally written in ink by Eliot in the 1922 Boni & Liveright paperback edition of the poem presented to Pound; it was subsequently included in future editions.

The five parts of The Waste Land are entitled:

- The Burial of the Dead
- A Game of Chess
- The Fire Sermon
- Death by Water
- What the Thunder Said

The first four sections of the poem correspond to the Greek classical elements of Earth, Air (voices – the draft title for this section was "In the Cage", an image of hanging in air; also, the element of Air is generally thought to be aligned with the intellect and the mind), Fire, and Water (the draft of the poem had additional water imagery in a fishing voyage.) The title of the fifth section could be a reference to the fifth element of Aether, which is included in many mystical traditions (one line here mentions aetherial rumours)citation needed.

The text of the poem is followed by several pages of notes, purporting to explain his metaphors, references, and allusions. Some of these notes are helpful in interpreting the poem, but some are arguably even more puzzling, and many of the most opaque passages are left unannotated. The notes were added after Eliot's publisher requested something longer to justify printing The Waste Land in a separate book.

There is some question as to whether Eliot originally intended The Waste Land to be a collection of individual poems (additional poems were supplied to Pound for his comments on including them) or to be considered one poem with five sections.

Style

The style of the work in part grows out of Eliot's interest in exploring the possibilities of dramatic monologue. This interest dates back at least as far as The Love Song of J. Alfred Prufrock. Eliot also enjoyed the music hall, and something of the flavour of this popular form of entertainment gets into the poem. It follows the pattern of the musical fugue, in which many voices enter throughout the piece re-stating the themescitation needed.

Above all perhaps it is the disjointed nature of the poem, the way it jumps from one adopted manner to another, the way it moves between different voices and makes use of phrases in foreign languages, that is the most distinctive feature of the poem's style. Interestingly, at the same time as Eliot was writing The Waste Land, Robert Bridges was working on the first of his Neo-Miltonic Syllabics, a poem called 'Poor Poll', which also includes lines in several different languages.

Sources

Sources from which Eliot quotes or to which he alludes include the works of: Homer, Sophocles, Petronius, Virgil, Ovid, Saint Augustine of Hippo, Dante Alighieri, William Shakespeare, Edmund Spenser, Gérard de Nerval, Thomas Kyd, Geoffrey Chaucer, Thomas Middleton, John Webster, Joseph Conrad, John Milton, Andrew Marvell, Charles Baudelaire, Richard Wagner, Oliver Goldsmith, Hermann Hesse, Aldous Huxley, Paul Verlaine, Walt Whitman and Bram Stoker. Eliot also makes extensive use of Scriptural writings including the Bible, the Book of Common Prayer, the Hindu Brihad-Aranyaka-Upanishad, and the Buddha's Fire Sermon, and of cultural and anthropological studies such as Sir James Frazer's The Golden Bough and Jessie Weston's From Ritual to Romance (particularly its study of the Wasteland motif in Celtic mythology).

Critical Reception

The poem's initial reception was mixed; though many hailed its portrayal of universal despair and ingenious technique, others, such as F. L. Lucas, detested the poem from the first, while Charles Powell commented "so much waste paper". Edmund Wilson's influential piece for The New Republic, "The Poetry of Drought," which many critics have noted is unusually generous in arguing that the poem has an effective cohesive structure, emphasizes autobiographical and emotional elements:

Not only is life sterile and futile, but men have tasted its sterility and futility a thousand times before. T. S. Eliot, walking the desert of London, feels profoundly that the desert has always been there. Like Tiresias, he has sat below the wall of Thebes; like Buddha, he has seen the world as an arid conflagration; like the Sibyl, he has known everything and known everything in vain.

Critic Harold Bloom has observed that the forerunners for The Waste Land are Alfred Lord Tennyson's Maud: A Monodrama and particularly Walt Whitman's elegy, When Lilacs Last in the Dooryard Bloom'd. The major images of Eliot's poem are found in Whitman's ode: the lilacs that begin Eliot's poem, the "unreal city," the duplication of the self, the "dear brother," the "murmur of maternal lamentation," the image of faces peering at us, and the hermit thrush's song.

Chapter 2

T.S. Eliot's Life and Career

Eliot, T. S. (26 Sept. 1888-4 Jan. 1965), poet, critic, and editor, was born Thomas Stearns Eliot in St. Louis, Missouri, the son of Henry Ware Eliot, president of the Hydraulic-Press Brick Company, and Charlotte Champe Stearns, a former teacher, an energetic social work volunteer at the Humanity Club of St. Louis, and an amateur poet with a taste for Emerson. Eliot was the youngest of seven children, born when his parents were prosperous and secure in their mid-forties (his father had recovered from an earlier business failure) and his siblings were half grown. Afflicted with a congenital double hernia, he was in the constant eye of his mother and five older sisters. His paternal grandfather, William Greenleaf Eliot, had been a protégé of William Ellery Channing, the dean of American Unitarianism.

William Eliot graduated from Harvard Divinity School, then moved toward the frontier. He founded the Unitarian church in St. Louis and soon became a pillar of the then southwestern city's religious and civic life. Because of William's ties to St. Louis, the Eliot family chose to remain in their urban Locust Street home long after the area had run down and their peers had moved to the suburbs. Left in the care of his Irish nurse, Annie Dunne, who sometimes took him to Catholic Mass, Eliot knew both the city's muddy streets and its exclusive drawing rooms.

He attended Smith Academy in St. Louis until he was sixteen. During his last year at Smith he visited the 1904 St. Louis World's Fair and was so taken with the fair's native villages that he wrote short stories about primitive life for the

Smith Academy Record. In 1905 he departed for a year at Milton Academy outside of Boston, preparatory to following his older brother Henry to Harvard.

Eliot's attending Harvard seems to have been a foregone conclusion. His father and mother, jealously guarding their connection to Boston's Unitarian establishment, brought the family back to the north shore every summer, and in 1896 built a substantial house at Eastern Point, in Gloucester, Massachusetts. As a boy, Eliot foraged for crabs and became an accomplished sailor, trading the Mississippi River in the warm months for the rocky shoals of Cape Ann. Later he said that he gave up a sense of belonging to either region, that he always felt like a New Englander in the Southwest, and a Southwesterner in New England.Despite his feelings of alienation from both of the regions he called home, Eliot impressed many classmates with his social ease when he began his studies at Harvard in the fall of 1906.

Like his brother Henry before him, Eliot lived his freshman year in a fashionable private dormitory in a posh neighborhood around Mt. Auburn Street known as the "Gold Coast." He joined a number of clubs, including the literary Signet. And he began a romantic attachment to Emily Hale, a refined Bostonian who once played Mrs. Elton opposite his Mr. Woodhouse in an amateur production of Emma. Among his teachers, Eliot was drawn to the forceful moralizing of Irving Babbitt and the stylish skepticism of George Santayana, both of whom reinforced his distaste for the reform-minded, progressive university shaped by Eliot's cousin, Charles William Eliot. His attitudes, however, did not prevent him from taking advantage of the elective system that President Eliot had introduced. As a freshman, his courses were so eclectic that he soon wound up on academic probation. He recovered and persisted, attaining a B.A. in an elective programme best described as comparative literature in three years, and an M.A. in English literature in the fourth.

In December 1908 a book Eliot found in the Harvard Union library changed his life: Arthur Symons's The Symbolist Movement in Literature introduced him to the poetry of Jules

Laforgue, and Laforgue's combination of ironic elegance and psychological nuance gave his juvenile literary efforts a voice. By 1909-1910 his poetic vocation had been confirmed: he joined the board and was briefly secretary of Harvard's literary magazine, the Advocate, and he could recommend to his classmate William Tinckom-Fernandez the last word in French sophistication—the Vers Libre of Paul Fort and Francis Jammes. (Tinckom-Fernandez returned the favour by introducing Eliot to Francis Thompson's "Hound of Heaven" and John Davidson's "Thirty Bob a Week," poems Eliot took to heart, and to the verse of Ezra Pound, which Eliot had no time for.) On the Advocate, Eliot started a lifelong friendship with Conrad Aiken.

In May 1910 a suspected case of scarlet fever almost prevented Eliot's graduation. By fall, though, he was well enough to undertake a postgraduate year in Paris. He lived at 151 bis rue St. Jacques, close to the Sorbonne, and struck up a warm friendship with a fellow lodger, Jean Verdenal, a medical student who later died in the battle of the Dardenelles and to whom Eliot dedicated "The Love Song of J. Alfred Prufrock." With Verdenal, he entered the intellectual life of France then swirling, Eliot later recalled, around the figures of Émile Durkheim, Paul Janet, Rémy de Gourmont, Pablo Picasso, and Henri Bergson. Eliot attended Bergson's lectures at the College de France and was temporarily converted to Bergson's philosophical interest in the progressive evolution of consciousness. In a manner characteristic of a lifetime of conflicting attitudes, though, Eliot also gravitated toward the politically conservative (indeed monarchistic), neoclassical, and Catholic writing of Charles Maurras. Warring opposites, these enthusiasms worked together to foster a professional interest in philosophy and propelled Eliot back to a doctoral programme at Harvard the next year.

In 1910 and 1911 Eliot copied into a leather notebook the poems that would establish his reputation: "The Love Song of J. Alfred Prufrock," "Portrait of a Lady," "La Figlia Che Piange," "Preludes," and "Rhapsody on a Windy Night." Combining some of the robustness of Robert Browning's monologues with the incantatory elegance of symbolist verse, and compacting Laforgue's poetry of alienation with the moral earnestness of what Eliot once called "Boston doubt," these poems explore the subtleties of the unconscious with a caustic wit. Their effect was both unique and compelling, and their assurance staggered his contemporaries who were privileged to read them in manuscript. Aiken, for example, marveled at "how sharp and complete and sui generis the whole thing was, from the outset. The wholeness is there, from the very beginning."

In the fall of 1911, though, Eliot was as preoccupied with ideas as with literature. A student in what has been called the golden age of Harvard philosophy, he worked amid a group that included Santayana, William James, the visiting Bertrand Russell, and Josiah Royce. Under Royce's direction, Eliot wrote a dissertation on Bergson's neoidealist critic F. H. Bradley and produced a searching philosophical critique of the psychology of consciousness. He also deepened his reading in anthropology and religion, and took almost as many courses in Sanskrit and Hindu thought as he did in philosophy. By 1914, when he left on a traveling fellowship to Europe, he had persuaded a number of Harvard's philosophers to regard him as a potential colleague.

Eliot spent the early summer of 1914 at a seminar in Marburg, Germany, with plans to study in the fall at Merton College, Oxford, with Harold Joachim, Bradley's colleague and successor. The impending war quickened his departure. In August he was in London with Aiken and by September Aiken had shown Eliot's manuscript poems to Pound, who, not easily impressed, was won over. Pound called on Eliot in late September and wrote to Harriet Monroe at Poetry magazine that Eliot had "actually trained himself and modernized himself on his own." The two initiated a collaboration that would change Anglo-American poetry, but not before Eliot put down deep English roots.

In early spring 1915 Eliot's old Milton Academy and Harvard friend Scofield Thayer, later editor of the Dial and then also at Oxford, introduced Eliot to Vivien Haigh-Wood, a dancer and a friend of Thayer's sister. Eliot was drawn instantly to Vivien's exceptional frankness and charmed by her family's Hampstead polish. Abandoning his habitual tentativeness with women, in June 1915 he married Vivien on impulse at the Hampstead Registry Office. His parents were shocked, and then, when they learned of Vivien's history of emotional and physical problems, profoundly disturbed. The marriage nearly caused a family break, but it also indelibly marked the beginning of Eliot's English life. Vivien refused to cross the Atlantic in wartime, and Eliot took his place in literary London. They were to have no children.

Eliot and his wife at first turned to Bertrand Russell, who shared with them both his London flat and his considerable social resources. Russell and Vivien, however, became briefly involved, and the arrangement soured. Meanwhile Eliot tried desperately to support himself by teaching school, supplemented by a heavy load of reviewing and extension lecturing. To placate his worried parents, he labored on with his Ph.D. thesis, "Experience and the Objects of Knowledge in the Philosophy of F. H. Bradley." (Eliot finished it in April 1916, but did not receive his degree because he was reluctant to undertake the trip to Massachusetts required for his dissertation defence.) As yet one more stimulating but taxing activity, he became assistant editor of the avant-garde magazine the Egoist. Then in spring 1917 he found steady employment; his knowledge of languages qualified him for a job in the foreign section of Lloyds Bank, where he evaluated a broad range of continental documents.

The job gave him the security he needed to turn back to poetry, and in 1917 he received an enormous boost from the publication of his first book, Prufrock and Other Observations, printed by the Egoist with the silent financial support of Ezra and Dorothy Pound.

For a struggling young American, Eliot had acquired extraordinary access to the British intellectual set. With Russell's help he was invited to country-house weekends where visitors ranged from political figures like Herbert Henry Asquith to a constellation of Bloomsbury writers, artists, and philosophers. At the same time Pound facilitated his entry into the international avant-garde, where Eliot mixed with a group including the aging Irish poet William Butler Yeats, the English painter and novelist Wyndham Lewis, and the Italian Futurist writer Tamaso Marinetti. More accomplished than Pound in the manners of the drawing room, Eliot gained a reputation in the world of belles-lettres as an observer who could shrewdly judge both accepted and experimental art from a platform of apparently enormous learning. It did not hurt that he calculated his interventions carefully, publishing only what was of first quality and creating around himself an aura of mystery. In 1920 he collected a second slim volume of verse, Poems, and a volume of criticism, The Sacred Wood. Both displayed a winning combination of erudition and jazzy bravura, and both built upon the understated discipline of a decade of philosophical seriousness. Eliot was meanwhile proofreading the Egoist's serial publication of Joyce's Ulysses, and, with Pound's urging, starting to think of himself as part of an experimental movement in modern art and literature.

Yet the years of Eliot's literary maturation were accompanied by increasing family worries. Eliot's father died in January 1919, producing a paroxysm of guilt in the son who had hoped he would have time to heal the bad feelings caused by his marriage and emigration. At the same time Vivien's emotional and physical health deteriorated, and the financial and emotional strain of her condition took its toll. After an extended visit in the summer of 1921 from his mother and sister Marion, Eliot suffered a nervous collapse and, on his physician's advice, took a three month's rest cure, first on the coast at Margate and then at a sanitarium Russell's friend Lady Ottoline Morell recommended at Lausanne, Switzerland.

Whether because of the breakdown or the long needed rest it imposed, Eliot broke through a severe writer's block and completed a long poem he had been working on since 1919. Assembled out of dramatic vignettes based on Eliot's London life, The Waste Land's extraordinary intensity stems from a sudden fusing of diverse materials into a rhythmic whole of great skill and daring. Though it would be forced into the mold of an academic set piece on the order of Milton's "Lycidas," The Waste Land was at first correctly perceived as a work of jazzlike syncopation—and, like 1920s jazz, essentially iconoclastic. A poem suffused with Eliot's horror of life, it was taken over by the postwar generation as a rallying cry for its sense of disillusionment. Pound, who helped pare and sharpen the poem when Eliot stopped in Paris on his way to and from Lausanne, praised it with a godparent's fervor.

As important, Eliot's old friend Thayer, by then publisher of the Dial, decided even before he had seen the finished poem to make it the centerpiece of the magazine's attempt to establish American letters in the vanguard of modern culture. To secure The Waste Land for the Dial, Thayer arranged in 1922 to award Eliot the magazine's annual prize of two thousand dollars and to trumpet The Waste Land's importance with an essay commissioned from the Dial's already influential Edmund Wilson. It did not hurt that 1922 also saw the long-heralded publication of Ulysses, or that in 1923 Eliot linked himself and Joyce with Einstein in the public mind in an essay entitled "Ulysses, Order and Myth." Meteorically, Eliot, Joyce, and, to a lesser extent, Pound were joined in a single glow—each nearly as notorious as Picasso.

The masterstroke of Eliot's career was to parlay the success of The Waste Land by means of an equally ambitious effort of a more traditional literary kind. With Jacques Riviere's La Nouvelle Revue Française in mind, in 1922 Eliot jumped at an offer from Lady Rothermere, wife of the publisher of the Daily Mail, to edit a high-profile literary journal. The first number of the Criterion appeared in October 1922. Like The Waste Land, it took the whole of European culture in its sights. The Criterion's editorial voice placed Eliot at the centre of London writing.

Eliot, however, was too consumed by domestic anxiety to appreciate his success. In 1923 Vivien nearly died, and Eliot, in despair, came close to a second breakdown. The next two years were almost as bad, until a lucky chance allowed him to escape from the demands of his job at the bank. Geoffrey Faber, of the new publishing firm of Faber and Gwyer (later Faber and Faber), saw the advantages of Eliot's dual expertise in business and letters and recruited him as literary editor. At about the same time, Eliot reached out for religious support. Having long found his family's Unitarianism unsatisfying, he turned to the Anglican church. The seeds of his future faith can be found in The Hollow Men, though the poem was read as a sequel to The Waste Land's philosophical despair when it appeared in Poems 1909-1925. In June 1927 few followers were prepared for Eliot's baptism into the Church of England. And so, within five years of his avant-garde success, Eliot provoked a second storm.

The furor grew in November 1927 when Eliot took British citizenship, and again in 1928 when he collected a group of politically conservative essays under the title of For Lancelot Andrewes, prefacing them with a declaration that he considered himself a "classicist in literature, royalist in politics, and anglo-catholic in religion." Eliot's poetry now addressed explicitly religious situations. In the late 1920s he published a series of shorter poems in Faber's Ariel series—short pieces issued in pamphlet form within striking modern covers. These included "Journey of the Magi", "A Song for Simeon", "Animula", "Marina", and 'Triumphal March". Steeped in Eliot's contemporary study of Dante and the late Shakespeare, all of them meditate on spiritual growth and anticipate the longer and more celebrated Ash-Wednesday. "Journey of the Magi" and "A Song for Simeon" are also exercises in Browningesque dramatic monologues, and speak to Eliot's desire, pronounced since 1922, to exchange the symbolist fluidity of the psychological lyric for a more traditional dramatic form.

Eliot spent much of the last half of his career writing one kind of drama or another, and attempting to reach (and bring together) a larger and more varied audience. As early as 1923 he had written parts of an experimental and striking jazz play, Sweeney Agonistes (never finished, it was published in fragments in 1932 and performed by actors in masks by London's Group Theatre in 1934). In early 1934 he composed a church pageant with accompanying choruses entitled The

Rock, performed in May and June 1934 at Sadler's Wells. Almost immediately following these performances, Bishop Bell commissioned a church drama having to do with Canterbury Cathedral, which, as Murder in the Cathedral, was performed in the Chapter House at Canterbury in June 1935 and was moved to the Mercury Theatre at Notting Hill Gate in November and eventually to the Old Vic. In the late 1930s, Eliot attempted to conflate a drama of spiritual crisis with a Noël Coward-inspired contemporary theater of social manners. Though Eliot based The Family Reunion on the plot of Aeschylus's Eumenides, he designed it to tell a story of Christian redemption.

The play opened in the West End in March 1939 and closed to mixed reviews five weeks later. Eliot was disheartened, but after the war fashioned more popular (though less powerful) combinations of the same elements to much greater success. The Cocktail Party, modernizing Euripides's Alcestis with some of the insouciance of Noël Coward, with a cast that included Alec Guinness, opened to a warm critical reception at the Edinburgh Festival in August 1949 and enjoyed popular success starting on Broadway in January 1950. Eliot's last two plays were more labored and fared less well. The Confidential Clerk had a respectable run at the Lyric Theatre in London in September 1953, and The Elder Statesman premiered at the Edinburgh Festival in August 1958 and closed after a lukewarm run in London in the fall. Eliot's reputation as a poet and man of letters, increasing incrementally from the mid-1920s, advanced and far outstripped his theatrical success.

As early as 1926 he delivered the prestigious Clark Lectures at Cambridge University, followed in 1932-1933 by the Norton Lectures at Harvard, and just about every other honour the academy or the literary world had to offer. In 1948 Eliot received the Nobel Prize for literature during a fellowship stay at the Princeton Institute for Advanced Study. By 1950 his authority had reached a level that seemed comparable in English writing to that of figures like Samuel Johnson or Samuel Taylor Coleridge.

Ironically, after 1925 Eliot's marriage steadily deteriorated, turning his public success hollow. During the tenure of his Norton year at Harvard he separated from Vivien, but would not consider divorce because of his Anglican beliefs. For most of the 1930s he secluded himself from Vivien's often histrionic attempts to embarrass him into a reconciliation, and made an anguished attempt to order his life around his editorial duties at Faber's and the Criterion and around work at his Kensington church. He also reestablished communication with Emily Hale, especially after 1934, when she began summering with relatives in the Cotswolds. Out of his thinking of "what might have been," associated with their visit to an abandoned great house, Eliot composed "Burnt Norton," published as the last poem in his Collected Poems 1909-1935. With its combination of symbolist indirection and meditative gravity, "Burnt Norton" gave Eliot the model for another decade of major verse.

In 1938 Vivien was committed to Northumberland House, a mental hospital north of London. In 1939, with the war impending, the Criterion, which had occupied itself with the deepening political crisis of Europe, ceased publication. During the Blitz, Eliot served as an air-raid warden, but spent long weekends as a guest with friends near Guildford in the country. In these circumstances, he wrote three more poems, each more somber than the last, patterned on the voice and five-part structure of "Burnt Norton."

"East Coker" was published at Easter 1940 and took its title from the village that Eliot's ancestor Andrew Eliot had departed from for America in the seventeenth century. (Eliot had visited East Coker in 1937.) "The Dry Salvages," published in 1941, reverted to Eliot's experience as a boy on the Mississippi and sailing on the Massachussetts coast. Its title refers to a set of dangerously hidden rocks near Cape Ann. "Little Gidding" was published in 1942 and had a less private subject, suitable to its larger ambitions. Little Gidding, near Cambridge, had been the site of an Anglican religious community that maintained a perilous existence for the first part of the English civil war. Paired with Eliot's experience walking the blazing streets of London during World War II, the community of Little Gidding inspired an extended meditation on the subject of the individual's duties in a world of human suffering. Its centerpiece was a sustained homage to Dante written in a form of terza rima, dramatizing Eliot's meeting with a "familiar compound ghost" he associates with Yeats and Swift.

Four Quartets, as the suite of four poems was entitled, for a period displaced The Waste Land as Eliot's most celebrated work. The British public especially responded to the topical references in the wartime poems and to the tone of Eliot's public meditation on a common disaster. Eliot's longtime readers, however, were more reticent. Some, notably F. R. Leavis, praised the philosophical suppleness of Eliot syntax, but distrusted Eliot's swerve from the authenticity of a rigorously individual voice. And, as Eliot's conservative religious and political convictions began to seem less congenial in the postwar world, other readers reacted with suspicion to his assertions of authority, obvious in Four Quartets and implicit in the earlier poetry. The result, fueled by intermittent rediscovery of Eliot's occasional anti-Semitic rhetoric, has been a progressive downward revision of his once towering reputation. After the war, Eliot wrote no more major poetry, turning entirely to his plays and to literary essays, the most important of which revisited the French symbolists and the development of language in twentieth-century poetry.

After Vivien died in January 1947, Eliot led a protected life as a flatmate of the critic John Hayward. In January 1957 he married Valerie Fletcher and attained a degree of contentedness that had eluded him all his life. He died in London and, according to his own instructions, his ashes were interred in the church of St. Michael's in East Coker. A commemorative plaque on the church wall bears his chosen epitaph—lines chosen from Four Quartets: "In my beginning is my end. In my end is my beginning."

In the decades after his death Eliot's reputation slipped further. Sometimes regarded as too academic (William Carlos Williams's view), Eliot was also frequently criticized (as he himself—perhaps just as unfairly—had criticized Milton) for a deadening neoclassicism. However, the multivarious tributes from practicing poets of many schools published during his centenary in 1988 was a strong indication of the intimidating continued presence of his poetic voice. In a period less engaged with politics and ideology than the 1980s and early 1990s, the lasting strengths of his poetic technique will likely reassert themselves. Already the strong affinities of Eliot's postsymbolist style with currently more influential poets like Wallace Stevens (Eliot's contemporary at Harvard and a fellow student of Santayana) have been reassessed, as has the tough philosophical skepticism of his prose. A master of poetic syntax, a poet who shuddered to repeat himself, a dramatist of the terrors of the inner life (and of the evasions of conscience), Eliot remains one of the twentieth century's major poets. The most important collections of Eliot's manuscripts can be found at the Houghton Library, Harvard University; the New York Public Library; and the libraries of King's and Magdalene colleges, Cambridge University.

Aside from the volumes already noted, among Eliot's numerous publications should be mentioned his extended appreciation, Dante; his free rendition of Anabasis: A Poem by St. J. Perse; the collection of his Selected Essays 1917-1932; his Norton lectures, The Use of Poetry and the Use of Criticism; his pugnacious and never reprinted Page-Barbour lectures, After Strange Gods; Essays Ancient and Modern; his metrical jeux d'esprit, Old Possum's Book of Practical Cats, popularized in the musical Cats; his studies in Christian culture, The Idea of a Christian Society and Notes towards the Definition of Culture,; and the late collections of essays On Poetry and Poets and To Criticize the Critic. Eliot's Poems Written in Early Youth were collected and printed in 1950, his Harvard Ph.D. dissertation was published in 1964 as Knowledge and Experience in the Philosophy of F. H. Bradley, and the first volume of his Letters appeared in 1988.

Although no authorized biography of Eliot has yet appeared, Peter Ackroyd, T. S. Eliot, and Lyndall Gordon, Eliot's New Life, are extremely useful, supplemented by smaller specialized studies such as John Soldo, The Tempering of T. S. Eliot, and by studies in biographical criticism such as Lyndall Gordon, Eliot's Early Years, and Ronald Bush, T. S. Eliot: A Study in Character and Style. The indispensable bibliography of Eliot's work is Donald Gallup, T. S. Eliot: A Bibliography (1947; rev. ed., 1969). Standard critical studies begin with an early group including F. O. Matthiessen, The Achievement of T. S. Eliot (1935; rev. ed., 1947); Helen Gardner, The Art of T. S. Eliot; Grover Smith, T. S. Eliot's Poetry and Plays; and Hugh Kenner, T. S. Eliot: The Invisible Poet. F. R. Leavis's early and important appreciation in New Bearings in English Poetry was expanded and qualified in essays collected in The Living Principle. Essential studies of the composition of The Waste Land and Four Quartets can be found in A. Walton Litz, ed., Eliot in His Time, and in Helen Gardner, The Composition of "Four Quartets".

Eliot attributed a great deal of his early style to the French Symbolists—Rimbaud, Baudelaire, Mallarme, and Laforgue—whom he first encountered in college, in a book by Arthur Symons called The Symbolist Movement in Literature. It is easy to understand why a young aspiring poet would want to imitate these glamorous bohemian figures, but their ultimate effect on his poetry is perhaps less profound than he claimed. While he took from them their ability to infuse poetry with high intellectualism while maintaining a sensuousness of language, Eliot also developed a great deal that was new and original. His early works, like "The Love Song of J. Alfred Prufrock" and The Waste Land, draw on a wide range of cultural reference to depict a modern world that is in ruins yet somehow beautiful and deeply meaningful.

Eliot uses techniques like pastiche and juxtaposition to make his points without having to argue them explicitly. As Ezra Pound once famously said, Eliot truly did "modernize himself." In addition to showcasing a variety of poetic innovations, Eliot's early poetry also develops a series of characters who fit the type of the modern man as described by Fitzgerald, Faulkner, and others of Eliot's contemporaries. The title character of "Prufrock" is a perfect example: solitary, neurasthenic, overly intellectual, and utterly incapable of expressing himself to the outside world. As Eliot grew older, and particularly after he converted to Christianity, his poetry changed. The later poems emphasize depth of analysis over breadth of allusion; they simultaneously become more hopeful in tone: Thus, a work such as Four Quartets explores more philosophical territory and offers propositions instead of nihilism. The experiences of living in England during World War II inform the Quartets, which address issues of time, experience, mortality, and art.

Rather than lamenting the ruin of modern culture and seeking redemption in the cultural past, as The Waste Land does, the quartets offer ways around human limits through art and spirituality. The pastiche of the earlier works is replaced by philosophy and logic, and the formal experiments of his early years are put aside in favour of a new language consciousness, which emphasizes the sounds and other physical properties of words to create musical, dramatic, and other subtle effects.

However, while Eliot's poetry underwent significance transformations over the course of his career, his poems also bear many unifying aspects: all of Eliot's poetry is marked by a conscious desire to bring together the intellectual, the aesthetic, and the emotional in a way that both honors the past and acknowledges the present. Eliot is always conscious of his own efforts, and he frequently comments on his poetic endeavors in the poems themselves. This humility, which often comes across as melancholy, makes Eliot's some of the most personal, as well as the most intellectually satisfying, poetry in the English language.

Biographical Timeline

1888	September 26: Thomas Stearns Eliot born in St. Louis, Missouri to Henry Ware and
1898	A student at Smith Academy in St. Louis
1905	To Milton Academy in Massachusetts
1906-10	Undergraduate years at Harvard. Reads Symons's The Symbolist Movement in Literature and the

poetry of Laforgue. Studies with George Santayana and Irving Babbitt.

1910-11 Having finished BA and MA degrees at Harvard, spends a year at the Sorbonne in Paris. In the summer of 1911, finishes a version of "The Love Song of J. Alfred Prufrock"

1911-14 Returns to Harvard to study philosophy as a graduate student. Begins doctoral thesis on F.H. Bradley.

1914 To England on fellowship; meets Ezra Pound.

1915 Marries Vivien Haigh-Wood on June 26th; begins publishing poems that later appear in the Prufrock volume.

1916 Eliot working as teacher at Highgate Junior School and as University Extension Lecturer.

1917 Prufrock and Other Observation published. Eliot takes a position at Lloyds Bank in the Colonial and Foreign Department.

1919 Ara Vos Prec published, with "Gerontion" and the poems later published in Poems – 1920. "Tradition and the Individual Talent" appears in The Egoist.

1920 The Sacred Wood published.

1921 Ill and exhausted, Eliot takes leave from Lloyds Bank. Recuperating at Margate and Lausanne, finishes the drafts of The Waste Land, which he then shows to Pound.

1922 The Waste Land published. First issue of Criterion appears.

1925 Poems 1909-1925 published (with "The Hollow Men"). Eliot joins the publishing house of Faber & Gwyer, leaves Lloyds bank.

1927 Enters the Church of England and assumes British citizenship

1928 For Lancelot Andrewes published.

1930 Ash-Wednesday published.

1932 Selected Essays 1917-1932

1933 Eliot's 1932-33 Norton lectures at Harvard published under the title The Use of Poetry and the Use of Criticism. At the University of Virginia, he delivers the lectures later published as After

	Strange Gods. Obtains legal separation from Vivien.
1934	The Rock: A Pageant Play performed and published.
1935	Murder in the Cathedral performed.
1936	Collected Poems 1909-1935 (first appearance of "Burnt Norton").
1939	The Family Reunion performed. The Idea of a Christian Society published. Last issue of Criterion.
1940	East Coker published.
1941	The Dry Salvages published.
1942	Little Gidding published.
1947	Vivien Eliot dies.
1948	Wins Nobel Prize for Literature. Notes Towards the Definition of Culture published.
1949	The Cocktail Party performed.
1953	The Confidential Clerk performed.
1957	Married Valerie Fletcher on January 10. On Poetry and Poets published.
1958	The Elder Statesman performed.
1963	Collected Poems 1909-1962.
1965	Dies on January 4th; his ashes to East Coker.

Selected Publications by T.S. Eliot

Prufrock and Other Observations.
Ara Vos Prec.. Republished in the US as Poems.
The Sacred Wood.
The Waste Land.
Homage to John Dryden.
Poems 1909-1925 (includes "The Hollow Men").
Sweeney Agonistes (in Criterion).
For Lancelot Andrewes.
Ash-Wednesday.
Anabasis, a Poem by St-John Perse (Eliot translation).
Selected Essays 1917-1932.
The Use of Poetry and the Use of Criticism.
After Strange Gods (1933 lectures at the University of Virginia).
The Rock: A Pageant Play.

Murder in the Cathedral.
Essays Ancient and Modern.
Collected Poems 1909-1935 (includes "Burnt Norton").
The Family Reunion.
Old Possum's Book of Practical Cats.
The Idea of a Christian Society.
East Coker.
The Dry Salvages.
Little Gidding.
Notes Towards the Definition of Culture.
The Cocktail Party.
The Complete Poems and Plays, 1909-1950.
The Confidential Clerk.
On Poetry and Poets.
The Elder Statesman.
Collected Poems, 1909-1962.

Posthumous publications: The Waste Land: A Facsimile and Transcript of the Original Drafts Including the Annotations of Ezra Pound, edited and with an introduction by Valerie Eliot.

Inventions of the March Hare: Poems 1909-1917, featuring previously unpublished works, edited by Christopher Ricks.

Chapter 3

T.S. Eliot: As a New Critic

In the twentieth century, in a new type of literary analysis, the literary work as a "separate entity divorced from extrinsic considerations" becomes the dominant concern of scholars. This "systematic and methodological formalistic approach" to literary criticism is called 'the New Criticism'. Although the New Criticism develops independently of the Russian Formalism, calling for a renewed attention to "literature as literature", distinguishing literature and other kinds of writing from each other, telling about "interrelatedness" and treating the "literary text as an object independent of its author and its historical context" are the fundamental affinities between these two movements.

The New Criticism begins with the work of I. A. Richards and T.S. Eliot before the first World War in England and is continued, in the United States during the forties, fifties and sixties, by figures such as John Crowe Ransom, W.K. Wimsatt, Cleanth Brooks and Allen Tate who come together originally at Vanderbilt University in the years following the first World War as an informal group to discuss literature. They find the necessary support for their ideas that emerge from their study and writing of lyric poetry when the poetry and critical essays of T.S.Eliot come to their attention.

Many New Critics who look to Eliot as a "guiding spirit" also look to Richards as the "trail-blazer" of the new critical theories. At Cambridge, Richards gives to his students copies of unfamiliar poems on which he asks them to comment freely and lists the responses ranging from "simple incomprehension to inhibition and sentimentality." The results of this "laboratory" experiment are exhibited in his book Practical Criticism and "the text in isolation is all that matters and the role of the critic is detailed exegesis of the words on the printed page" becomes the norm for later New Critical thinking). And the New Critics with their view that scholars should concentrate on the work itself, on the text, examining it as art revolutionise the study of literature. In this paper, first, I will tell about the views of the New Critics and then, about T.S. Eliot as a New Critic, referring to some of his well-known essays such as 'Tradition and the Individual Talent' and his famous poem The Waste Land.

As mentioned in the beginning the New Critics describe the text as an artefact that is "divorced from contexts and sites of production" and it is supposed to have "all of its essentiality contained within itself". It is the poem that explores the values and the poet's only duty is to structure the means by which the poem can exist. For the "literary appreciation" it is necessary to recognise "integrity" in text and "the text as a unified whole cannot be taken apart and put back together again, though its details can be analysed in close reading").

To look for integrity in the literary work is not something new. Before the New Critics, for example, Aristotle's Poetics suggests an "orderly arrangement of parts" that form a "beautiful whole or organism". Horace, similarly, wants the "would-be poet's subject to be simple and unified." In the late eighteenth and nineteenth centuries with the Romantic movement in Europe, analogies between the "life principle" of a work of art and that of living organisms are intensified. Coleridge declares that in a "legitimate poem the parts mutually support and explain each other." In America, Edgar Allan Poe extends Coleridge's theory and claims that short lyric poems and short tales maintain "a single, unitary effect" more successfully than can long works like Paradise Lost. Later Henry James also tells about the "intricate, necessary interrelationships of parts and the whole"

As Birch writes all that the critics needs to talk about, with regard to the "total meaning" of the text, is contained within the text and this theory of organic unity, "text-in-itself-relevance" does not permit discussion on anything other than the meaning "inherent" in the text. Robey shares the same idea and claims that:

- The only history the critic must master is the history of words. He must grasp the full historical meaning of the language used in the text, including all its associations, and of the names to which reference may be made, but only to the extent that their meaning is For Dutton, it is this view that makes New Criticism attractive among the critics (and in schoolrooms). There is no extrinsic material to be learned about authors, influences, historical movements or genres before you start reading the text. What you need here may be just a good dictionary) Whereas, some others evaluate ignoring any information not in the work itself as a guilt or a mistake since it can be helpful while interpreting the work.

The New Critics say that the chief property of poetry is "coherence" but the "harmonisation of conflicting meanings or attitudes". The wholeness of meaning is established through "internally differentiated form", "the reconciliation of diverse parts". The meaning of the text refers to the interaction of both different and similar parts. So, complexity and coherence together constitute the key considerations in the analysis of literary texts. The New Critics are also for the use of irony. As a defining characteristic of poetry, irony is closely related to "paradox" which involves the "association of conflicting elements within the same statement". But it is claimed that this use of irony (and also ambiguity and nuance) appeal only to people of a certain type of background: "sophisticated, well-read and articulate".

The author uses the text as a transparent medium for conveying his experience to the reader. It is desirable or possible for the critic to recreate in himself the "mental condition" of the author. There may be some "obstacles blocking the reader's approach to this mental condition. If you pay the right kind of attention when you are approaching the text, then, you will have no problem with your interpretation and you will be in the same mental condition with the author Otherwise you will need the help suggested by I.A.Richards in his book Practical Criticism for such a problem.

Though T.S. Eliot is seen as the father-figure of the New Criticism, in his essay 'The Frontiers of Criticism' he expresses surprise at being called the main progenitor of the New Criticism). He is not the inventor of the New Criticism but 'in criticism as in poetry he is one of the first to give expression to the spirit of his time. He provides a compelling example to others by the power and penetration of his work".

It is possible to see the theory of the New Criticism in his essays and his poetry may be referred to for practical criticism. In his influential essay, 'Tradition and the Individual Talent', he states that "criticism is as inevitable as breathing" and that "we should be none the worse for articulating what passes in our minds when we read a book and feel an emotion about it". In his essay, 'The Function of Criticism', he refers to criticism as the "commentation and exposition of works of art by means of written words" and he adds that the aim of criticism is to be the "elucidation of works of art and the correction of taste"). Here, the critic aims to "refine the reader's sensibility by increasing his understanding" through elucidation). Eliot in 'Tradition and the Individual Talent' says that "honest criticism and sensitive appreciation are directed not upon the poet but upon the poetry" and criticism for him, too, means to examine the work of art by turning all the attention on to it.

However, in 'The Frontiers of Criticism', he claims that analyzing a work in isolation, without reference to the author or to his other work, has the "merits of sincerity and single-mindedness" but, it also has the danger of making us think that the poem has only one meaning that is given by the critic or that this meaning is what the poet means to mean. So, commenting on the work and making it clear by giving details may help the reader to interpret that work and may 'correct the taste' but, this also means to direct the reader's attention towards the point the critic wants. For instance, in The Waste

Land there are some notes used to identify some of Eliot's sources or to suggest relationships between images or allusions. This prevents the reader from free interpretation. But, for such poems it may also be useful only to show the richness of them through such explanations to those who are not "sophisticated, well-read and articulate" enough. Otherwise it is not necessary for a reader to be in the some 'mental condition' with the poet while reading his work.

Eliot tries to rebut the Romantic emphasis on the 'originality' and 'personality' of the poet as the most important feature of literature. As Kantarcýoðlu writes:

- For Eliot the most philosophical literary form is poetry; and the essence of poetry is emotion. However, the emotion expressed in poetry should not be personal and be transformed into aesthetic,or objective emotions by the poet who is capable of escaping from personality.... The poet should have a mature mind in order to express his personal feelings in a traditional form. A mature mind is a neutral medium which can reconcile the opposite experiences of man in a synthesis.

In 'Tradition and the Individual Talent', Eliot likens the mind of the poet to the shred of platinum, as a catalyst, causes the combination of gases but is not affected, remains neutral and unchanged. Similarly, the poet tells about the man's experience but he keeps himself out of the poem. As Eliot says, the progress of the artist is a "continual self-sacrifice, a continual extinction of personality". It is not necessary for a poet to write about his own experiences. For Eliot, the business of the poet is to use the ordinary emotions for his poetry, not to find new ones; and "emotions which he has never experienced will serve his turn as well as those familiar to him"

For Eliot, "no poet, no artist of any art has his complete meaning alone. His significance, his appreciation is the appreciation of his relation to the dead poets and artists." He uses the past poets as judging criteria and adds that the poet must be set among the dead for contrast and comparison). But, unlike the Neoclassic evaluation of the dead poets, he is not for mere imitation. Learning about one poet, one period, or about one's own literature is not enough. He claims that it is the poet's responsibility to read all the poets from Homer down to the present and to develop "consciousness of the past". Eliot believes that the poet must develop a "historical sense" to appreciate both the pastness and the presence of tradition. This means that tradition is not a mere repetition of the old but both unity and alteration.

Every work of literature "both relates to the past and also alters art to be contemporary"). In 'Tradition and the Individual Talent', Eliot argues that if a work does not have something new, then it is not a work of art. In 'The Social Function of Poetry, he stresses the fact that "the language and culture of a nation get corrupt when the poets of that nation stop creating" (Kantarcýoðlu 167). In the Waste Land, Eliot uses the verb "foresuffer" in the line "And I Tiresias have foressuffered all."Though the use of the prefix 'fore-' to a verb is limited to a small group of items, such as foresee, foreknow, foretell and forewarn, he adds a new one to that group and this strikes us as a novelty, and as a surprising extension of expressive possibilities of the language. Eliot's "foresuffered" is not just a new word, but the "encapsulation of a newly formulated idea that it is possible to anticipate mystically the suffering of the future.

I can connect
Nothing with nothing
The broken fingernails or dirty hands
My people humble people who expect
Nothing.

In these lines from the Waste Land (III.301-305) the meaning is intensified through the repetition of the word "nothing" and these plain lines reflect barrenness and emptiness of the modern world impressively.

Eliot, in his poem Little Gidding defines poetry as follows:

What we call the beginning is often the end
And to make an end is to make a beginning,
The end is where we start from.

....

And every phrase and every sentence is an end and a beginning

Every poem an epitaph: So, for him, there must be an integrity within a work of art and every part has a significant role to constitute this wholeness. He states that "words, phrases, sentences, images rhythm and meter and rhyme and intonation and the music it creates, in short, all the elements dance to the rhythm of the same music in concentric spheres, as a component, the words are important in his own works, too. Also, his use of distorted quotations is something that Eliot adds to literature. Through them, he fuses together examples from the past in his poems, which means for him "richness and density". For instance, the beginning of The Waste Land refers to Satyricon of Petronius (1st century A.D.) which tells about the prophetic old woman of Greek mythology and her wish for death, the title of the first part," The Burial of The Dead" comes from the Anglican church, in a part from Wagner's Opera a sailor" recalls the girl he has left behind" "Good-night, ladies, good-night, sweet ladies, good-night, good-night" are the mad Ophelia's departing words in Hamlet, and also the lines "But at my back in a cold blast I hear/The rattle of the bones, and chuckle spread from ear to ear" show an ironic distortion of Andrew Marvell's famous lines from To His Coy Mistress: "But at my back I always hear/Time's winged chariot hurrying near".Such examples exhibit his poetic theory based on the quest for a "shared tradition" that can reflect the past and the present of the whole Euopean culture and may also be the examples for "objective correlative" which is the only way of expressing emotion in the form of art for Eliot. The use of "a set of objects, a situation, a chain of events that will be the formula of a particular emotion" is important for Eliot because it is possible to "express human experience with all its dimensions objectively" through this technique. And, this is the most suitable form of escaping from personality while writing.

Eliot as Critic

Although best known as a poet, Eliot also made significant

contributions to the field of literary criticism. In particular, Eliot strongly influenced the school of New Criticism. While somewhat self-deprecating and minimizing of his work as a critic—he once said his criticism was merely a "by-product" of his "private poetry-workshop"—Eliot is considered by some to be one of the greatest literary critics of the 20th century. The critic William Empson once said, "I do not know for certain how much of my own mind invented, let alone how much of it is a reaction against him or indeed a consequence of misreading him. He is a very penetrating influence, perhaps not unlike the east wind."

In his critical essay "Tradition and the Individual Talent," Eliot argues that art must be understood not in a vacuum, but in the context of previous pieces of art: "In a peculiar sense an artist or poet... must inevitably be judged by the standards of the past." This essay was one of the most important works of the school of New Criticism. Specifically, it introduced the idea that the value of one work of art must be viewed in the context of all previous work—a "simultaneous order" or works. It has also been argued that "Tradition and the Individual Talent" served to keep out the public at large from engaging in literature (or having literature in engage in them): "T. S. Eliot's insistence in essays such as 'Tradition and the Individual Talent' that the young poet need only assimilate the (all-male) canon of established authors contributed to public definitions of literary modernism that would exclude mass culture." Conversely, Eliot's work regarding music—particularly his article "Marie Lloyd"—may have actually helped lead to the idea that popular culture could be the subject of criticism.

Also extremely important to New Criticism was the idea—as articulated in Eliot's essay "Hamlet and His Problems"—of an "objective correlative," which posits a connection among the words of the text and events, states of mind, and experiences. This notion concedes that a poem means what it says, but suggests that there can be a non-subjective judgment based on different readers' different—but perhaps corollary—interpretations of a work.

More generally, New Critics took a cue from Eliot in

regards to his "'classical' ideals and his religious thought; his attention to the poetry and drama of the early seventeenth century; his deprecation of the Romantics, especially Shelley; his proposition that good poems constitute 'not a turning loose of emotion but an escape from emotion; and his insistence that 'poets...at present must be difficult.'"

Eliot's essays were also a major factor in the revival of interest in the metaphysical poets. Eliot was particularly favorable to the metaphysical poets' ability to show experience as both psychological and sensual, while at the same time infusing this portrayal with—in Eliot's view—wit and uniqueness. Eliot's essay "The Metaphysical Poets," along with giving new significance and attention to metaphysical poetry, introduced his now well known definition of "unified sensibility,"which is considered by some to mean the same thing as the term "metaphysical."

Some have argued that Eliot can be best understood as critic through his poetry—that one reflects the other and that Eliot has a unique perspective as a poet-critic. In his "Four Quartets," a series of poems, is self-aware in a way that "open the poem up to modern critical movements in which understanding is made contingent on the perspective in which it is installed." Eliot's self-examination through poetry reflects his belief in the objective correlative. Eliot's 1922 poem The Waste Land—which at the time of its publication, many critics believed to be a joke or hoax—also can be better understood in light of his work as a critic. Eliot had argued that a poet must write "programmatic criticism" or the idea that a poet should write to advance his own interests than to advance "historical scholarship". Viewed from Eliot's own critical lens, The Waste Land likely shows his personal distaste for World War I rather than an objective historical understanding of it.

Some have argued that late in his career, Eliot recanted much of his earlier work as a critic. However, this is disputed. At that time, Eliot stressed the importance of every poet creating his or her own unique personality through his work.

Eliot is considered one of the greatest literary figures of the twentieth century. Famed primarily as a poet, he wrote criticism not solely to examine literature, but also to provide an explanatory basis for his own work.

Two of Eliot's concepts are often cited as major contributions to literary analysis: "objective correlative" and "dissociation of sensibility." In his first important collection of critical essays, The Sacred Wood, Eliot defined the objective correlative as "a set of objects, a situation, a chain of events which shall be the formula of particular emotion" and which have the ability to evoke that emotion in the reader. Although this concept was considered important, Eliot's controversial essay on the lack of an objective correlative in Hamlet led to wide-spread rejection by scholars and critics, and caused Eliot to reassess his approach during the 1930s. "Dissociation of sensibility," as described by Eric Thompson, "is the dislocation of thought from feeling and feeling from thought that occurs when language orbits too far out from a metaphysical centre." For Eliot, the dislocation of sensibility has occured in English literature since the turn of the seventeenth century.

Many of Eliot's other significant critical works stress the importance of tradition, religion, and morality in literature. In the essay "Tradition and the Individual Talent" Eliot argued that creative and critical writing must be able to take its place in the line of literary tradition descending from Homer. After Strange Gods still stands as Eliot's ultimate indictment of the "diabolical" in modern society and a plea for the necessity of both moral and traditional considerations in literature, even though Eliot later retracted many of its ideas.

A fairly accurate assessment of Eliot's critical career was made by F. R. Leavis, who declared: " is a distinguished critic only over an extremely narrow range; his good criticism bears immediately on the problems of the poetic practitioner...." However, the power of Eliot's criticism is demonstrated by the vast influence it has wielded over literary criticism in this century. New Criticism evolved out of Eliot's critical approach, yet equally important are the movements which sought to reverse his critical influence.

Chapter 4

Modernism in T.S. Eliots's The Wasteland

Modernism has been defined as a rejection of traditional 19th-century norms, whereby artists, architects, poets and thinkers either altered or abandoned earlier conventions in an attempt to re-envision a society in flux. In literature this included a progression from objectivist optimism to cynical relativism expressed through fragmented free verse containing complex, and often contradictory, allusions, multiple points of view and other poetic devices that broke from the forms in Victorian and Romantic writing, as can be seen in T.S. Eliot's "The Waste Land"

Modernism in T.S. Eliot's "The Wasteland"

Modernism has been defined as a rejection of traditional 19th-century norms, whereby artists, architects, poets and thinkers either altered or abandoned earlier conventions in an attempt to re-envision a society in flux. In literature this included a progression from objectivist optimism to cynical relativism expressed through fragmented free verse containing complex, and often contradictory, allusions, multiple points of view and other poetic devices that broke from the forms in Victorian and Romantic writing, as can be seen in T.S. Eliot's "The Waste Land" (Levanson).

The varied perspectives or lack of a central, continuous speaker uproots "The Waste Land" from previous forms of poetry; however, it is not simply for the sake of being avant-garde, but to espouse the modernist philosophy, which posits the absence of an Absolute and requires the interpretation of juxtaposed, irreconcilable points of view in order to find meaning. The first stanza illustrates this point. Within the first seven lines, the reader is presented with a "normal" poem that conforms to an ordered rhyme and meter. Suddenly, the German words "Starnbergersee" and "Hofgarten" are introduced, readjusting the reader's own view of the poem, before throwing it completely off-course in line 12: "Bin gar keine...." Just as quickly, though, the lines revert to a previous pattern with the use of "And I...", "And down...", "And when...." "Discontinuity, in other words, is no more firmly established than continuity," writes Michael Levenson (A Genealogy of Modernism).

In his analysis of the initial eighteen lines, it becomes apparent that no clear conclusion may be drawn as to who is speaking, or how many speakers are present. There are several methods of unifying the disjointed speaker, all of which conflict with each other although they may be equally true. Thus faced with this paradox, the reader is privy to one of the modernist themes in the work: individuals are permanently estranged, each bearing a unique identity, yet they are able to connect with each other to create a kind of coherence, however temporary. Of course, Matthew Arnold wrote something very similar in To Marguerite: Continued, but up until Eliot's The Waste Land, this "truth" was never illustrated in the lyrical construction itself.

Eliot also employs fragments in the work, further articulating his modernist ideas. These fragments are sometimes used to blur the lines between speakers, but also serve to blend opposing strands of knowledge. Trying to singularly categorize the usage of fragments is as difficult as finding a unified meaning in the poem and that is the entire point. Yet, in keeping with modernist thought, can there exist an "entire point"? The answer is inevitably fragmented. In lines 307-311, "To Carthage then I came/Burning burning burning burning/O Lord Thou pluckest me out/O Lord Thou pluckest/ burning", the words of St. Augustine from his Confessions and the Buddha's Fire Sermon are crammed together to form a new, incongruous whole. This synthesis hints at some sort of "truth" that may be discovered by joining these ancient bits of wisdom, two differing perspectives. However, if one assumes that something meaningful can be created from "These fragments I have shored against my ruins" in line 430, then an ultimate, final truth will never be reached since there will always be more fragments to append and assimilate. Note that this idea is derived from the content of the text in addition to the actual fragmented form it utilizes.

What separates this, then, from Classical Hegelian philosophy (thesis, antithesis, synthesis)? Again, the "answer" is in fragments. Hegelian philosophy is objective and acts as an end-all, be-all answer to the workings of the universe. However, in keeping with its own ideas, there must be an antithesis to this mode of thought, which came forth in the Romantic and, later, modernist works. In this way, one is presented with the subjective core of modernism that truth will always be relative to the perspective from which it originates, be it Eastern religion, Catholicism, or any combination, the result is still a subjective fragment.

Looking on a more "superficial" level, though again it must be relative, Eliot's poem also describes the modern world, or in his own words, "the immense panorama of futility and anarchy which is contemporary history." Throughout The Waste Land, the reader is affronted with seemingly banal verses. Line 426, "London Bridge is falling down falling down falling down", line 199, "O the moon shone bright on Mrs. Porter" and other quotes ripped straight from popular songs of the time are side by side with allusions to Tristan and Isolde and Kyd's Spanish Tragedy.

That is the essence of modern life. All the trivialities of the era, a period of time still mired in war and pettiness, though it considered itself Enlightened, a hypocritical age, were infused into The Waste Land, a portrait of modern society. Furthermore, advances in anthropology fueled Eliot. Beforehand, myths were thought to be just the quaint byproduct of the cultures they sprang from. However, in the early 20th-century these myths took on a universal nature. They defied rationality, yet defined our humanity. Some have wondered, if Eliot deals with the profane, how can he point out the hypocrisy of the age when he suffers from it? Where does his authority lie? The modernist response is that the authority lies in the subrational or irrational, outside of modern society, which has strayed from its primitive roots, from its original myths and arts and cultures.

Perhaps no true conclusion may be made. The human experience is fragmented and defies logic, and in order to fully convey this, modernist poets such as Eliot had to bend and break conventions, and their own expressions may culminate in something which is not fully expressible within modern society, though modern society was used as an indirect means of getting at this "Inexpressible." A better way of putting it could be that Eliot's The Waste Land was a direct way of getting at something indirect from the modern world, for it required a reinvention of poetics and the very use and meaning of language. Since the modern period is said to extend to this day (it's debated whether it's post-modern or not, since both elements survive), any final say on the matter is difficult. What can be said is that Eliot's poetry, as misinterpreted, misread, and misunderstood as it may be, is a quintessential cornerstone in modernist thought, a fragment in the puzzle, which may yield an emergent whole, though it may not be fully grasped

Chapter 5

T.S. Eliot: Poet and Critic as Historical Theorist

Most people suppose that some people, because they enjoy the luxury of Christian sentiments and the excitement of Christian ritual, swallow or pretend to swallow incredible dogma. For some the process is exactly opposite. Rational assent may arrive late, intellectual conviction may come slowly, but they come inevitably without violence to honesty and nature. To put the sentiments in order is a later, and immensely difficult task: intellectual freedom is earlier and easier than complete spiritual freedom.

Thomas Stearns Eliot

Many writers, philosophers, and artists contribute theories to the field of history without intending to do so. Because most writers and philosophers write about the past at some point or another, and because artists do not create in a vacuum, but in the context of cultural tradition, they often develop ideas about why and how past events occurred as they did and postulate what might take place in the future. For example, historian Karl Lowith's Meaning in History examines the historical theories of Comte, Condorcet, Voltaire, Bossuet, Joachim, and Augustine, thinkers who probably never thought of themselves as historians in the formal sense.

Thomas Stearns Eliot, best known for writing "The Waste Land," which literature scholars still study and acknowledge as the poem of the twentieth century, also wrote literary criticism and cultural philosophies. In confronting the world and its past, present, and future in art and philosophy, Eliot developed an approach to history as complex and mature as any professional historian's. Like Vico and Toynbee, Eliot viewed history in terms of the development of cultures. Grounding himself in the absolute authority of Anglo-Catholic Christianity, Eliot posited religion as the source of all cultures, describing how these cultures develop through the dynamic interactions of unity and diversity, tradition and novelty, and individual perspective and cultural context.

Unlike the Enlightenment historians and their heirs, he did not see progress as an escalating improvement in culture, but as the regeneration of cultural tradition. Like many thinkers of his time, Eliot believed Western culture was a fragmentary mess. He cited the decay of religion — the source of culture — and tradition — the permanence of culture — as the cause of cultural collapse. Though he believed this decay had proceeded too far to be easily reversed, he enjoined thinkers to adopt his theories and draw hope from the understanding they provided. And though Eliot was staunchly conservative in outlook and disposition, his focus on individual perspective made him one of the fathers of post-modem thought.

Born to a well-established Anglo-American family in 1888, Eliot confronted both the early twentieth century's frightening alienation and the collapse of the Western bourgeois synthesis. Western thought had replaced the Christian religion with a combination of capital, progress, and the reification of natural science and positive philosophy. The disaster of world war had proved to Eliot and thinkers like him that the stomping progress of technology and material wealth without a broader meaning or system of values was bankrupt and hopeless.

Since the Renaissance, philosophers had tried to fill the vacuum left by the abandonment of Christianity, but no system they could devise had the authority of traditional religion. Their faith gone and its substitute revealed as an ineffectual charlatan, the Europeans and Americans stumbled about in a shellshocked daze, desperately scrabbling for a foothold of hope and authority and able to find none. Eliot, who detailed this alienation in poems like "The Love Song of J. Alfred Prufrock" and "The Waste Land," himself participated in this search, exploring the philosophy of Henri Bergson, Eros, aestheticism, humanism, idealism, and even Buddhism for doctrines to explain and repair the fragmentation of culture.

Eliot's disposition and intellectual rigor required something more substantial to solve his inner conflicts; the philosophies were, no matter how urgently presented and grasped, wispy artificial constructs, and Eliot feared that Buddhism, though an admirable religion, could strip him of his identity as a Westerner. Five years after writing "The Waste Land," he found the stability he sought, converting to Anglicanism in 1927. As he had grown up in the Unitarian Church, a faith which watered down Christianity to make it amenable to Enlightenment thought, and which Eliot believed encouraged skepticism rather than belief, this conversion constituted a completely new belief system for Eliot. It would shape everything he wrote, from poetry to drama to criticism, from that point onward. It would also provide the foundations of his cultural and historical theories.

From this religious basis, Eliot formulated the most basic tenet of his cultural theory, that religion and culture are essentially "related." <4> In fact, Eliot argued that "no culture has appeared or developed except together with a religion: according to the point of view of the observer, the culture to be the product of the religion, or the religion the product of the culture." They might be thought of as different aspects of the same thing; culture was "the incarnation of the religion of a people." Civilizations which appeared to be secular or humanistic, such as ancient Greece and Rome, were actually religious cultures in decline. Culture could not be preserved, extended, or developed in the absence of religion, nor could religion be preserved and maintained if culture was not.

Eliot reached this connection between religion and culture because he lived in a time in which he saw people, including himself, wandering aimlessly in search of meaning, and because he was finally able to find meaning through Anglicanism. There is much evidence, however, that his conversion was not a conversion of passionate belief, but a conversion of will. Eliot had reached the end of his philosophical rope and so turned reluctantly but determinedly to the last available source of authority and meaning. His friend Virginia Woolf said of his conversion that "a corpse would seem to me more credible than he is." E.M. Forster noted that he was "not a mystic. His work contains several well-turned compliments to religion and Divine Grace, but no trace of religious emotion He has not got it; what he seeks is not revelation, but stability." This said more about the context of Eliot's Christianity and its importance to his cultural theory than it does about his belief itself; Eliot was certainly a sincere Christian who openly acknowledged the intellectualism of his conversion. He believed that, as Christianity did so for him, "any religion, while it lasts, and on its own level, gives an apparent meaning to life, provides the framework for a culture, and protects the mass of humanity from boredom and despair."

Culture, according to Eliot, began in primitive societies as a unified entity, then expanded and specialized, developing a dynamic relationship between its unity and diversity. The aspects of culture, which included religion, politics, science, and art, gradually became distinct from one another; the witch doctor and the king came to have different roles. As they diverged in interests and goals, these societal divisions struggled with one another for dominance, their competition pushing them to flower and prosper. Despite this rivalry, no aspect of culture — urbanity and civility, learning, philosophy, the arts, and so on — could flourish independently of the others. Few definitions of culture included all of the attributes which might be considered, but no one of them alone could confer the wholeness of culture.

Culture, out of necessity, had many other divisions. In one of his most controversial assertions, Eliot insisted that, for a culture to be transferred hereditarily, that culture must preserve its social classes. Culture, to Eliot, was not some exalted holding of the upper classes, but the sum total of the activities of all classes. The upper classes merely preserved the more specialized and conscious domains of culture. Privilege rewarded the efforts of the upper classes, and familial love inspired them to pass this privilege and culture on to their children. Eliot emphasized that he was not interested in the aristocracy as a ruling class so much as the specialized gradation of classes, in which the aristocracy played an important role.

How does the contemporary mind deal with Eliot's seeming endorsement of inequality? Well, to give him the benefit of the doubt, not all people are created equal. Many people have talents and gifts which set them apart from others; others may have deficiencies or handicaps which make them less competent or able than others. Eliot believed that "a democracy in which everybody had an equal responsibility in everything would be oppressive for the conscientious and licentious for the rest." Perhaps this makes sense; the logical conclusion is a merit-based rule, is it not? Well, no, not for Eliot. He toyed with the idea of rule by an elite who rose to prestige and power by their abilities, but rejected it, worried that an elite would not have the social commonality and camaraderie that the classes would; he had not seen an elite system work. An elite system would also serve to disenfranchise the masses from their duties and privileges within society. Eliot did not reserve much sympathy for the unwashed masses, but they are almost as important to his system as the upper classes. The unity of each class would facilitate the passing on of their cultural trusts to their posterity, and it took all of the classes working in tandem for the process to work.

Had Eliot ever experienced the essence of working class life and what it meant to work with his hands for a working class wage? Probably not. He never asserted that members of the upper class are better people than the masses, although his passions and upbringing suggested such chauvinism, but his theories reified the high classes' position in society and allowed for little or no social mobility. He spoke out against the "overeducation" of working people, believing it lowered overall standards of learning and was unnecessary. Only

Marxists would argue hotly against Eliot in favour of a classless society, but Eliot should have been able to appreciate a society in which social mobility was possible, if not easy, and in which the best members of society could rise to positions of leadership. Despite the flawed execution of its ideals, the United States of America had always striven for such a society, and many European countries had followed suit by Eliot's time. Nevertheless, the class system was necessary to the unity and diversity in Eliot's cultural theory.

Eliot also looked for this dynamic in geographic regions within culture and in the religion of the culture. He believed that in a healthy culture, several regions surrounded a dominant central region. People in the central region had a nationalistic allegiance to the culture, while people living in the satellite regions balanced their loyalties between their region and the larger culture. The distinct character of the subculture then contributed a wider perspective and special flavour to the generally blander, less passionate central culture.

The friction between these regions bolstered creativity and kept the entire culture fresh. Imbalance-whether in the form of exaggerated regional conflict, which endangered the culture, or cultural uniformity, which threatened other cultures as the central culture sought new satellites-had to be vigorously avoided. Eliot cited the relationship between the regions of Great Britain-England, as a dominant nation, and Scotland and Wales, as satellites-as an example of regional unity and diversity. Also important was unity and diversity within religion, which, religion being the lynchpin of culture, linked the other two aspects of unified diversity. Although the entirety of a culture should have subscribed to the same religious doctrines, sects and cults should have healthily varied by class and region as well as conviction. This way, the believer could follow his or her conscience regarding religious practice as an individual or as a member of a class or region. Sect and cult thus helped both the gradations of class and distinctions of regions have a voice in society.

To Eliot, the prime mover of culture was the preservation of tradition in a constantly changing world. All of the aspects of culture he enumerated, but especially class, worked to maintain tradition and keep it fresh. Yes, the world changed, and culture expressed itself in new ways as time passed, but in order for these expressions to have structure and context, a body of the best past expressions and ways of life had to endure. Tradition was not a symptom of antiquarian stuffiness, but rather the preservation of something from the past for an appropriately timely use in the present.

This tradition, this canon of continuingly accepted expressions, periodically took in new material, new stimuli which kept it relevant to the present. This evolutionary development was not just a shift in quantity, but also in quality, as the new information changed the culture's perception of the older matter. As Eliot described it: the artist must be aware that the mind of Europe Western culture — the mind of his own country — a mind which he learns in time to be much more important than his own private mind-is a mind which changes, and that this change is a development which abandons nothing en route, which does not superannuate either Shakespeare, or Homer, or the rock drawing of the Magdalenian draughtsmen... the difference between the present and the past is that the conscious present is an awareness of the past in a way and to an extent which the past's awareness of itself cannot show.

In other words, what historians had over the makers of history was hindsight, the ability to understand the context of events and activities as was not possible while they were taking place. Tradition's purpose lay not in futile antiquarianism, but in improving the present, and by extension, the future. If a teaching or tradition had no proper use or relevance to a contemporary culture, the culture threw that teaching out. Studying past cultures gave the present culture a different perspective by which it could become more selfaware through the contrast. At the same time, cultural expression could not simply study the traditional canon, but had to constantly strive to build upon it. If the propagation of culture fell into decay, not only would there be no present culture, but the culture would lose touch with its past and lose all sense of being a culture. A robust culture would apply its generational reflection of mercurially changing standards to the canon. Every new addition to tradition would change the contemporary perspective, giving the society a larger tradition than it had before, a new criterion of appreciation. Each generation had a different interpretation of each work of culture which was appropriate to its time. Eliot's was a progressive theory, not one of hope for steady and inevitable improvement, but one of regenerative utility.

If this view of tradition sounded very relativistic, it also provided a modicum of security, stability, and virtual absolutism. The community as a whole held a common perspective which acted as a grounding, a mortar, for the various individual perspectives within it. This communal prejudice provided a standard of "objectivity" that all within the culture accepted. The preservation of the past and induction of new ideas in tradition served to enlarge this consensus, providing a greater field of objectivity. Eliot felt that language was one of the prime detern-dners and vehicles of expression of a cultural world view; language defined a civilization's perspective. He believed poets made their greatest contribution to their culture by expressing the inexpressible, expanding the language and thus the consciousness of their society.

This communal background stood as the context for the experience of the individual in the world. Personal identity was very important to Eliot's personal concept and to his philosophy, and most of that identity came from the culture in which one had been raised and had learned to think. World view, culture, tradition-the individual learned all through his or her native society, and they composed much of what that person was. Hence Eliot's fear of losing his "Westernness," which kept him from converting to Buddhism. Language, the expression of culture, was another practice Eliot guarded fiercely:

One of the reasons for learning at least one foreign language well is that we acquire a kind of supplementary personality; one of the reasons for not acquiring a new language instead of our own is that most of us do not want to become a different person. Despite the need to preserve identity, the best way for an individual to recognize and understand identity was to explore other cultures and, especially, to cultivate aesthetic experience. Eliot believed the experience of art not only brought people greater joy, but also greater self-understanding:

It is ultimately the function of art, in imposing a credible order upon ordinary reality, and thereby eliciting perception of an order in reality, to bring us to a condition of serenity, stillness, and reconciliation.

Art appreciation served to organize tastes, beliefs, and experiences into a whole, satisfying the human desire for unity and self-realization. It was "a fusion of what was not oneself with oneself," developing and becoming "more oneself by becoming more not oneself." Reflexively, the self-awareness granted by the study of art facilitates the understanding of other aspects of art and culture the individual might encounter.

This concept of the individual in relation to his or her culture and to the rest of the world served as a central point in Eliot's philosophy. Grounded in Anglican belief, Eliot insisted upon the imperfectability of humanity. No one could see with a perfect, holistic, unprejudiced, "God's-eye view." A human being who tried to see with such unstructured sight saw nothing at all. However, though total objectivity was beyond reach, Eliot believed that tremendous empathy, effort, and understanding could make it possible to merge one's horizons with those of an artist or another human being, and thus broaden those horizons.

Eliot also asserted the individual's role in bringing a perspective to a work of art. The standard for interpretation was not the intent of the artist, but rather the reading of the observer, who might be viewing the work from a much later perspective. Moreover, that perspective was not just the worldview of the interpreter's culture, as discussed earlier, but a wholly unique, individual bias. This focus on individual perspective, which approached relativism but had groundings in Eliot's beliefs in religion, local cultures, and traditions, made him one of the primary literary innovators toward post-modern thought. Eliot's willingness to allow innovation within what appeared to be a very conservative scheme stemmed from his belief that a health / culture depended on a balance between the old and the new. If many now interpret him as a stuffy reactionary, he only emphasized tradition so fervently because of the times in which he lived. The rapid change of the nineteenth and twentieth centuries threatened to whisk away Western tradition in a Heraclitian hurricane. Eliot wanted to sound alarms to stop the rapid decay of tradition; temporary reification of that tradition seemed to him the best way to preserve it. Eliot's cultural theory was no absolute theory of history — though he did have a scheme for what had happened and what should happen — but rather a diagnosis of the modern malaise and a plan of action for how to deal with it.

Eliot's Anglicanism was, of course, the root of all of his theories. His Christianity did not sit well with many of his contemporaries, who uncomfortably dismissed it as a throwback to the Dark Ages. In fact, his colleagues often made him feel like an outsider after his conversion. Indeed, as already indicated, Eliot himself found the path to belief a tremendous struggle, but the Christian scheme which would provide the stability he sought would work no other way. The alternatives, particularly secular humanism, provided no solace; its ethics comprised "a s stem of morals which seemed to be founded on nothing but itself. Religion seemed to him the much more viable alternative:

The religious habits of the race are still very strong, in all places, at all times, and for all people. There is no humanistic habit: humanism is, I think, merely the state of mind of a few persons in a few places at a few times. To exist at all, it is dependent upon some other attitude, for it is essentially critical — I would even say parasitical. It has been and can still be, of great value; but it will never provide showers of partridges or abundance of manna for the chosen peoples.

What particularly set Eliot apart from Enlightenment, humanistic, progressive thinkers was his fundamental belief that perfection was reserved for God. Humanity could improve itself, but there would always be an unattainable flawlessness that the race could look to as incentive to improve further. The Platonic absolute could be imagined but not won. If Joachim and the Enlightenment thinkers he influenced predicted a perfected earth, Eliot could not be absolutely optimistic:

We have to remember that the Kingdom of Christ on earth will never be realised; we must remember that whatever reform or revolution we carry out, the result will always be a sordid travesty of what human society should be-though the world is never left wholly without glory.

In the twentieth century, Western civilization was far from Eliot's cultural ideal. After his conversion, Eliot believed that the culture was falling apart not just for its abandonment of tradition, but also for its neglect of Christianity. According to his theory, the past two thousand years of European culture rested on the Christian foundation. Unfortunately, modernism and skepticism had eroded the Christian basis, and what Europe and America had left to them was a negative society which could not succeed either economically or spiritually. To Eliot, the options for endurance were to either establish a new Christian society, or enact a positive pagan society — an idea which curdled Eliot's blood. The new Christian society would not force belief on all those living within it, but would instead operate under rigorous Christian value systems under the custodianship of an elite called the Community of Christians. Eliot noted that, in the situation in which he wrote, modern society was hostile to Christianity, promoting un-Christian aims; therefore, society would have to be re-organized to conform to Christianity. Moreover, in the interests of promoting religion and tradition, a uniform system of education would be executed. A National Church similar to the Church of England would exist in tandem with, but not controlling or under the control of, the state.

Eliot's Christian society may appear to be a megalomaniacal projection of his own beliefs on the entire culture. Still, others have proposed utopias, and they, too, drew from their own beliefs and dreams. For Eliot, nothing else would suffice in what increasingly appeared to him to be a morally bankrupt and spiritually desperate society:

The number of people in possession of any criteria for discriminating between good and evil is very small; the number of the half-alive hungry for any form of spiritual experience, or what offers itself as spiritual experience, high or low, good or bad, is considerable.

Significantly, Eliot put forward his proposal for a Christian society shortly after his England, his chosen homeland, abandoning principle in Eliot's eyes, knuckled under to Adolf Hitler in the crisis of September 1938.

In essence, Thomas Stearns Eliot's theory of history was not concerned with wars or great political events and movements, nor was it a typical Enlightenment theory of progress. These it replaced with the monolithic flow of tradition, a tradition passed from generation to generation with an occasional infusion of novelty to keep it appropriate to the times. This dynamic combination posited a conservative tradition which kept itself fresh through the struggles and growth of its new artists and philosophers. It was Eliot's hope that such a firm tradition would save what he feared was otherwise a doomed culture. In short, his theory was that of a conservatively-minded critic and artist who was intently interested in laying out a future course for Western civilization.

Eliot died in 1965. What would he have thought of the student riots at Columbia University and what they said about the future of authority and tradition? What would he have thought about the youth cultures of the United States and Europe in the 1960s? What would he have thought of the spread of feminism, multiculturalism, and relativism? Of the decline of Christian practice and traditional moral values? All have called for an end to Western tradition. Needless to say, Christianity, abandoned in the West with an increasing sense of lethargy, has played little role in cultural preservation in the past half-century. Doubtless Eliot would pronounce his life's work and efforts a failure and say a prayer for the soul of Western culture. Still, despite the intellectual and moral difficulties contemporary life presents, a richer community demographic now contributes to our culture; more races, religions, and genders speak the peace of their fresh Eliotic perspectives to change culture as we know it and as Eliot knew it. These groups have found their voices both through religious cult (the non-violent Christian efforts of Martin Luther King, Jr. come to mind), as Eliot might have predicted, and through allegiance to ideals which haven't proved nearly so insubstantial as Eliot thought. To Eliot, due to Western hegemony, Western civilization meant, by extension, world civilization. Now many other cultures play a much larger role in defining world civilization. If the postmodern world seems morally bankrupt, human beings are becoming increasingly accountable to one another; if society has not embraced Christianity as a panacea for aimlessness, each individual is learning to follow his or her own path rather than marching on a unified path in a group; distinct perspective no longer indicates aimlessness. Even if the currently subordinate state of tradition might disappoint Eliot, a much more open, inclusive, and diverse human family, a unity in diversity he might have appreciated, will contribute to the tradition of tomorrow.

Chapter 6

T.S. Eliot as Conservative Mentor

T. S. Eliot was indisputably the greatest poet writing in English in the twentieth century. He was also the most revolutionary Anglophone literary critic since Samuel Johnson, and the most influential religious thinker in the Anglican tradition since the Wesleyan movement. His social and political vision is contained in all his writings, and has been absorbed and reabsorbed by generations of English and American readers, upon whom it exerts an almost mystical fascination—even when they are moved, as many are, to reject it. Without Eliot, the philosophy of Toryism would have lost all substance during the last century. And while not explicitly intending it, Eliot set this philosophy on a higher plane—intellectually, spiritually, and stylistically—than has ever been reached by the adherents of the socialist idea. Eliot attempted to shape a philosophy for our times that would be richer and more true to the complexity of human needs than the free-market panaceas that have so often dominated the thinking of conservatives in government. He assigned a central place in his social thinking to high culture. He was a thorough traditionalist in his beliefs but an adventurous modernist in his art, holding artistic modernism and social traditionalism to be different facets of a common enterprise. Modernism in art was, for Eliot, an attempt to salvage and fortify a living artistic tradition in the face of the corruption and decay of popular culture.

Eliot was born in St Louis, Missouri, in 1888, and educated at Harvard, the Sorbonne, and Merton College, Oxford, where he wrote a doctoral thesis on the philosophy of F. H. Bradley, whose Hegelian vision of society exerted a profound influence over him. He came, as did so many educated Americans of his generation, from a profoundly religious and public-spirited background, although his early poems suggest a bleak and despairing agnosticism, which he only gradually and painfully overcame. In 1914 he met Ezra Pound, who encouraged him to settle in England. He married during the following year, which also saw the publication of his first successful poem, "The Love Song of J. Alfred Prufrock." This work, together with the other short poems that were published along with it as Prufrock and Other Observations in 1917, profoundly altered the course of English literature. They were the first truly modernist works in English, although the most visible influences on their imagery and diction were not English but French— specifically, the fin-de-siècle irony of Laforgue, and the symbolism of Rimbaud, Mallarmé, and Verlaine. They were also social poems, concerned to express a prevailing collective mood, even when dressed in the words of a specific protagonist. The wartime generation found themselves in these poems, in a way that they had not found themselves in the pseudo-romantic literature of the Edwardian period. Shortly afterwards Eliot published a book of essays, The Sacred Wood, which was to be as influential as the early poetry. In these essays, Eliot presented his new and exacting theory of the role of criticism, of the necessity for criticism if our literary culture is to survive.

For Eliot, it is no accident that criticism and poetry so often come together in the same intelligence—as in his own case, and the case of Coleridge, whom he singled out as the finest of English critics. The critic, like the poet, is concerned to develop the "sensibility" of his reader— by which term Eliot meant a kind of intelligent observation of the human world. Critics do not abstract or generalize: they look, and record what they see. But in doing so, they also convey a sense of what matters in human experience, distinguishing the false from the genuine emotion. While Eliot was to spell out only gradually and obscurely over many years just what he meant by "sensibility," his elevated conception of the critic's role struck a chord in many of his readers. Furthermore, The Sacred Wood contained essays that were to revolutionize literary taste.

The authoritative tone of these essays gave rise to the impression that the modern world was at last making itself heard in literature—and that its voice was T. S. Eliot's. The Sacred Wood turned the attention of the literary world to the "metaphysical" poets of the sixteenth and seventeenth centuries, and to the Elizabethan dramatists— the lesser predecessors and the heirs of Shakespeare, whose raw language, rich with the sensation of the thing described, provided a telling contrast to the sentimental sweetness that Eliot condemned in his immediate contemporaries. There is also an essay on Dante, discussing a question that was frequently to trouble Eliot—that of the relationship between poetry and belief. To what extent could one appreciate the poetry of the Divine Comedy while rejecting the doctrine that had inspired it?

This question was a real one for Eliot, for several reasons. Eliot was—like his fellow modernists and contemporaries, Ezra Pound and James Joyce—profoundly influenced by Dante, whose limpid verse-form, colloquial style, and solemn philosophy created a vision of the ideal in poetry. At the same time, he rejected the theological vision of the Divine Comedy—rejected it with a deep sense of loss. Yet in his own poetry the voice of Dante would constantly return, offering him turns of phrase, lightning flashes of thought, and—most of all—a vision of the modern world from a point of view outside it, a point of view irradiated by an experience of holiness (albeit an experience that he did not then share). And when Eliot did finally come to share in this vision, he wrote, in the last of the Four Quartets, the most brilliant of all imitations of Dante in English— an imitation which is something far finer than an imitation, in which the religious vision of Dante is transported and translated into the world of modern England. One other essay in The Sacred Wood deserves mention—"Tradition and the Individual Talent," in which Eliot introduces the term which best summarizes his contribution to the political consciousness of the twentieth century: tradition.

In this essay Eliot argues that true originality is possible only within a tradition—and further, that every tradition must be remade by the genuine artist, in the very act of creating something new. A tradition is a living thing, and just as each writer is judged in terms of those who went before, so does the meaning of the tradition change as new works are added to it. It was this literary idea of a living tradition that was gradually to permeate Eliot's thinking, and to form the core of his social and political philosophy. Prufrock and The Sacred Wood already help us to understand the paradox of T. S. Eliot—that our greatest literary modernist should also be our greatest modern conservative. The man who overthrew the nineteenth century in literature and inaugurated the age of free verse, alienation, and experiment was also the man who, in 1928, was to describe himself as "classical in literature, royalist in politics, and Anglo- Catholic in religion." This seeming paradox contains a clue to Eliot's greatness as a social and political thinker. For Eliot recognized that it is precisely in modern conditions— conditions of fragmentation, heresy, and unbelief—that the conservative project acquires its sense. Conservatism is itself a modernism, and in this fact lies the secret of its success. What distinguishes Burke from the French revolutionaries is not his attachment to things past, but rather his desire to live fully in the concrete present, to understand the present in all its imperfections, and to accept the present as the only reality that is offered to us.

Like Burke, Eliot recognized the distinction between a backward-looking nostalgia, which is but another form of modern sentimentality, and a genuine tradition, which grants us the courage and the vision with which to live in the modern world. In 1922 Eliot founded The Criterion, a literary quarterly which he continued to edit until 1939, when he discontinued the journal under the pressure of "depression of spirits" induced by "the present state of public affairs." As the title of the journal suggests, the project was animated by Eliot's sense of the importance of criticism, and of the futility of modernist experiments when not informed by literary judgment and moral seriousness. The journal also contained social philosophy of a conservative persuasion—although Eliot preferred the word "classicism" as a description of its political outlook. The Criterion was the forum in which much of our modernist literature was first published, including the poetry of Pound, Empson, Auden, and Spender. Its first issue contained the work which established Eliot himself as the greatest poet of his generation: The Waste Land.

This poem seemed to its first readers to capture completely the disillusionment and emptiness that followed the hollow victory of the First World War—the conflict in which European civilization had committed suicide, just as Greek civilization had done in the Peloponnesian War. Yet the poem hardly mentioned the war, had none of the vivid imagery of battle that English readers knew from the works of Wilfrid Owen and Siegfried Sassoon, and was choc-a-bloc with references to and quotations from a scholar's library. Its ostensible subject- matter was drawn from works of armchair anthropology—in particular, from Sir James Frazer's The Golden Bough, a work which had also provided the title of The Sacred Wood. The Waste Land was later republished with notes in which Eliot explained some of his references and allusions, such as that contained in the title, which alludes to the Fisher King of the Parsifal legend, and the waste land over which he presides, awaiting the hero who will ask the questions that will destroy winter's bleak enchantment and renew the world. The allegory of modern civilization contained in this reference to the medieval fertility cults, and their literary transformation in Arthurian romance, was not lost on Eliot's readers.

Nor was it the first time that these symbols and legends of medieval romance had been put to such a use—witness Wagner's Parsifal, to which Eliot refers obliquely, by quoting from Verlaine's poem. Nevertheless, there was a peculiar poignancy in the very erudition of the poem, as though the whole of Western culture were being brought to bear on the desert landscape of the modern city in a last effort to encompass it, to internalize it, and to understand its meaning. The use of anthropological conceptions parallels Wagner's use of the Teutonic myths. (In The Waste Land there are more quotations from Wagner than from any other poet.) Eliot is invoking the religious worldview—and in particular the sense that life's renewal depends upon supernatural forces—but as a fact about human consciousness, rather than an item of religious belief. In this way, he was able to avail himself of religious ideas and imagery without committing himself to any religious belief. As he was rapidly discovering, without religious ideas the true condition of the modern world cannot be described. Only by describing modernity from a point of view outside of history can we grasp the extent of our spiritual loss.

After The Waste Land Eliot continued to write poetry inspired by the agonizing dissociation, as he saw it, between the sensibility of our culture and the available experience of the modern world. This phase of his development culminated in a profound Christian statement—the poem Ash Wednesday, in which he abandoned his anthropological manner and announced his conversion to the Anglo-Catholic faith. By now Eliot was ready to take up his own peculiar cross: the cross of membership. No longer playing the part of spiritual and political exile, he threw in his lot with the tradition to which his favourite authors had belonged. He became a British citizen, joined the Anglican Church, and wrote his great verse drama Murder in the Cathedral. In a series of essays, he praised the writings of sixteenth-century Anglican divines and attacked the secular heresies of his time. This phase of Eliot's development at length led to After Strange Gods, a "primer of modern heresy," in which he expressed his conservative antipathy to secular doctrine. It was Eliot's first of several attempts at social philosophy, of which the two most famous are The Idea of a Christian Society and Notes Towards the Definition of Culture. Both these works are marked by a tentativeness and anxiety about the new condition of Europe, which make them far less clear guides to Eliot's vision than the great poem which he wrote at the same time, a poem which has been, for many of my generation, the essential account of our spiritual crisis—and the greatest message of hope that has been given to us. Four Quartets is a profound exploration of spiritual possibilities, in which the poet seeks and finds the vision outside time in which time and history are redeemed. It is a religious work, and at the same time a work of extraordinary lyric power, like the Cimetière marin of Valéry, but vastly more mature in its underlying philosophy. Eliot's life began with a question: the question of modern life and its meaning. His literary work was a long, studious, and sincere attempt to provide an answer.

In the course of this enterprise, Eliot re-shaped the English language, changed the forms of English verse, and produced some of the most memorable utterances in our literature. Although an impressive scholar, with a mastery of languages and literatures that he reveals but does not dwell upon in his writings, Eliot was also a man of the world. He worked first as a teacher, then in a London bank, and then in the publishing house of Faber and Faber, which he made into the foremost publisher of poetry and criticism in its day. His unhappy first marriage did not impede his active participation in the literary life of London, over which he exerted an influence every bit as great as André Breton over the literary life of Paris. His refusal, through all this, to adopt the mantle of the bohemian, to claim the tinsel crown of artist, or to mock the "bourgeois" lifestyle, sets him apart from the continental tradition which he otherwise did so much to promote. He realised that the true task of the artist in the modern world is one not of repudiation but of reconciliation. For Eliot, the artist inherits, in heightened and self-conscious form, the very same anxieties that are the stuff of ordinary experience. The poet who takes his words seriously is the voice of mankind, interceding for those who live around him, and gaining on their behalf the gift of consciousness with which to overcome the wretchedness of secular life. He too is an ordinary bourgeois, and his highest prize is to live unnoticed amidst those who know nothing of his art—as the saint may live unnoticed among those for whom he dies. To find the roots of Eliot's political thinking, we must go back to the modernism that found such striking expression in The Waste Land.

English literature in the early part of the twentieth century was to a great extent captured by pre-modern imagery, by references to a form of life (such as we find in Thomas Hardy) that had vanished forever, and by verse forms which derived from the repertoire of romantic isolation. It had not T.S. Eliot, 1888-1965 undergone that extraordinary education which Baudelaire and his successors had imposed upon the French—in which antiquated forms like the sonnet were wrenched free of their pastoral and religious connotations and fitted out with the language of the modern city, in order to convey the new and hallucinatory sense of an irreparable fault, whereby modern man is divided from all that has preceded him. Eliot's admiration for Baudelaire arose from his desire to write verse that was as true to the experience of the modern city as Baudelaire's had been to the experience of Paris. Eliot also recognized in Baudelaire the new character of the religious impulse under the conditions of modern life: "The important fact about Baudelaire," he wrote, "is that he was essentially a Christian, born out of his due time, and a classicist, born out of his due time." Eliot's indictment of the neo-romantic literature of his day was not merely a literary complaint. He believed that his contemporaries' use of worn-out poetic diction and lilting rhythms betrayed a serious moral weakness: a failure to observe life as it really is, a failure to feel what must be felt towards the experience that is inescapably ours. And this failure is not confined, he believed, to literature, but runs through the whole of modern life.

The search for a new literary idiom is therefore part of a larger search—for the reality of modern experience. Only then can we confront our situation and ask ourselves what should be done about it. Eliot's deep distrust of secular human- ism—and of the socialist and democratic ideas of society which he believed to stem from it—reflected his critique of the neoromantics. The humanist, with his myth of man's goodness, is taking refuge in an easy falsehood. He is living in a world of make- believe, trying to avoid the real emotional cost of seeing things as they are. His vice is the vice of Edwardian and "Georgian" poetry— the vice of sentimentality, which causes us not merely to speak and write in clichés, but to feel in clichés too, lest we should be troubled by the truth of our condition. The task of the artistic modernist, as Eliot later expressed it, borrowing a phrase from Mallarmé, is "to purify the dialect of the tribe": that is, to find the words, rhythms, and artistic forms that would make contact again with our experience— not my experience, or yours, but our experience, the experience that unites us as living here and now. And it is only because he had captured this experience— in particular, in the bleak vision of The Waste Land—that Eliot was able to find a path to its meaning. He summarizes his attitude to the everyday language of modern life and politics in his essay on the Anglican bishop Lancelot Andrewes, and it is worth quoting the passage in full: To persons whose minds are habituated to feed on the vague jargon of our time, when we have a vocabulary for everything and exact ideas about nothing—when a word half-understood, torn from its place in some alien or half-formed science, as of psychology, conceals from both writer and reader the utter meaninglessness of a statement, when all dogma is in doubt except the dogmas of sciences of which we have read in the newspapers, when the language of theology itself, under the influence of an undisciplined mysticism of popular philosophy, tends to become a language of tergiversation—Andrewes may seem pedantic and verbose. It is only when we have saturated ourselves in his prose, followed the movement of his thought, that we find his examination of words terminating in the ecstasy of assent. Andrewes takes a word and derives the world from it.

For Eliot, words had begun to lose their precision—not in spite of science, but because of it; not in spite of the loss of true religious belief, but because of it; not in spite of the proliferation of technical terms, but because of it. Our modern ways of speaking no longer enable us to "take a word and derive the world from it": on the contrary, they veil the world, since they convey no lived response to it. They are mere counters in a game of cliché, designed to fill up the silence, to conceal the void which has come upon us as the old gods have departed from their haunts among us. That is why modern ways of thinking are not, as a rule, orthodoxies, but heresies—a heresy being a truth that has been exaggerated into falsehood, a truth in which we have taken refuge, so to speak, investing in it all our unexamined anxieties and expecting from it answers to questions which we have not troubled ourselves to understand. In the philosophies that prevail in modern life—utilitarianism, pragmatism, behaviorism— we find that "words have a habit of changing their meaning...or else they are made, in a most ruthless and piratical manner, to walk the plank." The same is true, Eliot implies, whenever the humanist heresy takes over: whenever we treat man as God, and so believe that our thoughts and our words need be measured by no other standard but themselves.

Eliot was brought up in a democracy. He inherited that great fund of public spirit which is the gift of American democracy to the modern world, and the cause of so much ignorant hatred of America. But he was not a democrat in his sensibility. Eliot believed that culture could not be entrusted to the democratic process precisely because of the carelessness with words, this habit of unthinking cliché, which would always arise when every person is regarded as having an equal right to express himself. In The Use of Poetry and the Use of Criticism he writes: When the poet finds himself in an age in which there is no intellectual aristocracy, when power is in the hands of a class so democratised that while still a class it represents itself to be the whole nation; when the only alternatives seem to be to talk to a coterie or soliloquize, the difficulties of the poet and the necessity of criticism become greater. Hence, the critic has, for Eliot, an enhanced significance in the modern, democratic world. It is he who must act to restore what the aristocratic ideal of taste would have generated spontaneously—a language in which words are used with their full meaning and in order to show the world as it is. Those nurtured on empty sentiment have no weapons with which to deal with the reality of a God-forsaken world. They fall at once from sentimentality into cynicism, and so lose the power either to experience life or to live with its imperfection. Eliot therefore perceived an enormous danger in the liberal and "scientific" humanism which was offered by the prophets of his day.

This liberalism seemed to him to be the avatar of moral chaos, since it would permit any sentiment to flourish and would deaden all critical judgment with the idea of a democratic right to speak—which becomes, insensibly, a democratic right to feel. Although "human kind cannot bear very much reality"—as he expresses the point, first in Murder in the Cathedral, and then in Four Quartets—the purpose of a culture is to retain that elusive thing called "sensibility": the habit of right feeling. Barbarism ensues not because people have lost their skills and scientific knowledge, nor is it averted by retaining those things; rather, barbarism comes through a loss of culture, since it is only through culture that the important realities can be truly perceived. Eliot's thought here is difficult to state precisely. And it is worth drawing a parallel with a thinker whom he disliked: Friedrich Nietzsche. For Nietzsche, the crisis of modernity had come about because of the loss of the Christian faith. This loss of faith is the inevitable result of science and the growth of knowledge. At the same time, it is not possible for mankind really to live without faith; and for us, who have inherited all the habits and concepts of a Christian culture, that faith must be Christianity.

Take away the faith, and you do not take away a body of doctrine only, nor do you leave a clear, uncluttered landscape in which man at last is visible for what he is. Rather, you take away the power to perceive other and more important truths, truths about our condition which cannot, without the benefit of faith, be properly confronted—such as the truth of our mortality. The solution that Nietzsche impetuously embraced in this quandary was to deny the sovereignty of truth altogether—to say that "there are no truths"—and to build a philosophy of life on the ruins of both science and religion in the name of a purely aesthetic ideal. Eliot saw the absurdity of that response. Yet the paradox remains. The truths that mattered to Eliot are truths of feeling, truths about the weight of human life. Science does not make these truths more easily perceivable: on the contrary, it releases into the human psyche a flock of fantasies—liberalism, humanism, utilitarianism, and the rest—which distract it with the futile hope for a scientific morality. The result is a corruption of the very language of feeling, a decline from sensibility to sentimentality, and a veiling of the human world. The paradox, then, is this: the falsehoods of religious faith enable us to perceive the truths that matter. The truths of science, endowed with an absolute authority, hide the truths that matter, and make human reality imperceivable.

Eliot's solution to the paradox was compelled by the path that he had taken to its discovery—the path of poetry, with the agonizing examples of poets whose precision, perception, and sincerity were the effects of Christian belief. The solution was to embrace the Christian faith—not, as Tertullian did, because of the paradox, but rather in spite of it. This explains Eliot's growing conviction that culture and religion are in the last analysis indissoluble. The disease of sentimentality could be overcome, he believed, only by a high culture in which the work of purification was constantly carried on. This is the task of the critic and the artist, and it is a hard task: And so each venture Is a new beginning, a raid on the inarticulate With shabby equipment always deteriorating In the general mess of imprecision of feeling, Undisciplined squads of emotion.

And what there is to conquer By strength and submission, has already been discovered Once or twice, or several times, by men whom one cannot hope To emulate—but there is no competition— There is only the fight to recover what has been lost And found and lost again and again: and now, under conditions That seem unpropitious.... This work of purification is a dialogue across the generations with those who belong to the tradition: only the few can take part in it, while the mass of mankind stays below, assailed by those "undisciplined squads of emotion." The high culture of the few is, however, a moral necessity for the many, for it permits human reality to show itself, and so to guide our conduct. But why should the mass of mankind, lost as they are in bathos, "distracted from distraction by distraction," be guided by "those who know" (to use Dante's pregnant phrase)? The answer must lie in religion, and in particular in the common language which a traditional religion bestows, both on the high culture of art and on the com- mon culture of a people. Religion is the lifeblood of a culture. It provides the store of symbols, stories and doctrines that enable us to communicate about our destiny. It forms, through the sacred texts and liturgies, the constant point to which the poet and the critic can return—the language alike of ordinary believers and of the poets who must confront the ever-new conditions of life in the aftermath of knowledge, of life in a fallen world.

For Eliot, however, religion in general, and the Christian religion in particular, should not be seen merely in Platonic terms as an attitude towards what is eternal and unchanging. The truth of our condition is that we are historical beings who find whatever consolation and knowledge is vouchsafed to us in time. The consolations of religion come to us in temporal costume, through institutions that are alive with the spirit of history. To rediscover our religion is not to rise free from the temporal order; it is not to deny history and corruption, in order to contemplate the timeless truths. On the contrary, it is to enter more deeply into history, so as to find in the merely transitory the mark and the sign of that which never passes away: it is to discover the "point of intersection of the timeless with time," which is, according to Four Quartets, the occupation of the saint. Thus there emerges the strangest and most compelling of parallels: that between the saint and martyr of Murder in the Cathedral and the meditating poet of Four Quartets.

Just as the first brings, through his martyrdom, the light of eternity into the darkness of the people of Canterbury (represented as a chorus of women), so does the poet "redeem the time," by finding in the stream of time those timeless moments that point beyond time. And the attempt by the poet to rediscover and belong to a tradition that will give sense and meaning to his language is one with the attempt to find a tradition of belief, of behaviour, and of historical allegiance, that will give sense and meaning to the community. The real significance of a religion lies less in the abstract doctrine than in the institutions which cause it to endure. It lies also in the sacraments and ceremonies, in which the eternal becomes present and what might have been coincides with what is.

For Eliot, therefore, conversion was not a matter merely of acknowledging the truth of Christ. It involved a conscious gesture of belonging, whereby he united his poetical labors with the perpetual labour of the Anglican church. For the Anglican church is peculiar in this: that it has never defined itself as "protestant," that it has always sought to accept rather than protest against its inheritance, while embracing the daring belief that the truths of Christianity have been offered in a local form to the people of England. It is a church which takes its historical nature seriously, acknowledging that its duty is less to spread the gospel among mankind than to sanctify a specific community. And in order to fit itself for this role, the Anglican church has, through its divines and liturgists, shaped the English language according to the Christian message, while also bringing that message into the here and now of England. In "Little Gidding," the last of the Four Quartets, the poet finds himself in the village retreat where an Anglican saint had retired to pray with his family.

He conveys what to many is the eternal truth of the Anglican confession, in lines which are among the most famous that have ever been written in English: If you came this way, Taking any route, starting from anywhere, At any time or at any season, It would always be the same: you would have to put off Sense and notion. You are not here to verify, Instruct yourself, or inform curiosity Or carry report. You are here to kneel Where prayer has been valid. And prayer is more Than an order of words, the conscious occupation Of the praying mind, or the sound of the voice praying. And what the dead had no speech for, when living, They can tell you, being dead: the communication Of the dead is tongued with fire beyond the lan guage of the living. Here, the intersection of the timeless moment Is England and nowhere. Never and always. Later, returning to this theme of communication with the dead—our dead—and referring to those brief moments of meaning which are the only sure gift of sensibility, Eliot completes the thought: We are born with the dead: See, they return, and bring us with them. The moment of the rose and the moment of the yew-tree Are of equal duration.

A people without history Is not redeemed from time, for history is a pattern Of timeless moments. So, while the light fails On a winter's afternoon, in a secluded chapel History is now and England. Much has been written about "Little Gidding," the atmosphere of which stays in the mind of every cultivated Englishman who reads it. What is important, however, is less the atmosphere of the poem than the thought which advances through it.

For here Eliot achieves that for which he envies Dante—namely, a poetry of belief, in which belief and words are one, and in which the thought cannot be prized free from the controlled and beautiful language. Moreover, there is one influence throughout which is inescapable—the King James Bible, and the Anglican liturgy that grew alongside it. Without being consciously biblical, and while using only modern and colloquial English, Eliot endows his verse with the authority of liturgy, and with the resonance of faith.

These lines take us back to the core belief of modern conservatism, which Burke expressed in the following terms: Society, he wrote, is indeed a contract; but not a contract among the living only; rather, it is a partnership between the living, the dead, and those yet to be born. And, he argued, only those who listen to the dead are fit custodians of future generations. Eliot's complex theory of tradition gives sense and form to this idea. For he makes clear that the most important thing that future generations can inherit from us is our culture. Culture is the repository of an experience which is at once local and placeless, present and timeless, the experience of a community as sanctified by time. This we can pass on only if we too inherit it. Therefore, we must listen to the voices of the dead, and capture their meaning in those brief, elusive moments when "History is now and England." In a religious community, such moments are a part of everyday life. For us, in the modern world, religion and culture are both to be gained through a work of sacrifice. But it is a sacrifice upon which everything depends.

Hence, by an extraordinary route, the modernist poet becomes the traditionalist priest: and the stylistic achievement of the first is one with the spiritual achievement of the second. To many people, Eliot's theory of culture and tradition is too arduous, imposing an impossible duty upon the educated elite. To others, however, it has been a vital inspiration. For let us ask ourselves just what is required of "one who knows." Should he, in the modern world, devote himself like Sartre or Foucault to undermining the "structures" of bourgeois society, to scoffing at manners and morals, and ruining the institutions upon which he depends for his exalted status? Should he play the part of a modern Socrates, questioning everything and affirming nothing? Should he go along with the mindless culture of play, the post-modernist fantasy world in which all is permitted since neither permission nor interdiction have any sense? To answer yes to any of those questions is in effect to live by negation, to grant nothing to human life beyond the mockery of it. It is to inaugurate and endorse the new world of "transgression," a world which will not reproduce itself, since it will undermine the very motive which causes a society to reproduce.

The conservative response to modernity is to embrace it, but to embrace it critically, in full consciousness that human achievements are rare and precarious, that we have no God-given right to destroy our inheritance, but must always patiently submit to the voice of order and set an example of orderly living. The future of mankind, for the socialist, is simple: pull down the existing order, and allow the future to emerge. But it will not emerge, as we know. These philosophies of the "new world" are lies and delusions, products of a sentimentality which has veiled the facts of human nature. We can do nothing unless we first amend ourselves. The task is to rediscover the world which made us, to see ourselves as part of something greater, which depends upon us for its survival—and which still can live in us, if we can achieve that "condition of complete simplicity/(Costing not less than everything)," to which Eliot directs us. We shall not cease from exploration And the end of all our exploring Will be to arrive where we started And know the place for the first time. Such is the conservative message for our time. It is a message beyond politics, a message of liturgical weight and authority. But it is a message which must be received, if humane and moderate politics is to remain a possibility.

Chapter 7

Lecture on T.S. Eliot's "The Love Song of J. Alfred Prufrock" and The Waste Land

Introduction

This week we are paying close attention to two very short works of poetry, probably the two most famous and influential works of verse in the past one hundred years, not only very fine in themselves but also of major significance in the history of poetic styles, since these are the best examples of the early work of the writer who, more than anyone else, transformed the way poetry in English was written in modern times. It is almost impossible to overestimate T. S. Eliot's effect on our understanding of how we read and write poetry.

Today I would like to address two issues. First, I would like to say something about the context of Eliot's work, because these two poems are deliberately experimental, and they launch something very new, of importance to the understanding not only of poetry but also of our modernist culture (I'll have more to say about that term modernist later on). This contextual review will be necessarily brief and inadequate, but it should help us to understand why these two poem are so different and to read them more fluently. The second purpose of this lecture will be to read together a few sections of The Waste Land so that we can explore how we come to grips with this new style.

I take it that many of you in this room find the poetic style in these poems odd and difficult easily to grasp, especially in comparison to poetry we have read earlier. This verse doesn't seem to make sense readily-just as a lot of modern art seems, at first glance, often incomprehensible. How are we supposed to get any sense of unity or continuity when we have no geographical or argumentative or metaphorical thread to guide our reading, especially when the form of the verse seems to change in bewildering ways for apparently no reason? What I want to do here is to encourage you to discover that this style is not nearly so difficult as it may appear, once we have grasped the point that reading this style requires us to drop some of the conventional expectations we bring to poetry and to let this style do its work in a new way.

To achieve this introduction to a new way of reading poetry, I first have to present some contextual background into the launching of the experimental movement which has come to define so much of modern poetry.

The Imagist Movement

The modern movement in poetry, the transformation of the tradition into something startlingly new, antedates Eliot somewhat. A common and convenient date is 1910, when a small group of practicing poets met in London under the name of their new "movement"-Imagism.

The moving spirit of this group was a young and very brash American, Ezra Pound, a student of European literature and a college teacher who had come to Europe in 1908 after being fired from his job as a college teacher in Indiana for having a girl in his room overnight. Pound, whose energy and flamboyance were notorious (or legendary) immediately set upon a very aggressive campaign demanding reforms in the writing of poetry, and he gathered together a few fellow spirits.

Literary movements, like political, religious, and artistic movements, generally arise as a reaction against the immediate tradition. So if we want to understand the nature of Imagism's demands, we need to consider for a moment what they disliked about the poetry considered at the time acceptable. I am going to use a very misleading term for this tradition, but I want to link our study of Imagism to the poetry we have already studied in this programme. So I'm going to use the label "Wordsworthian Decadence" to characterize the kind of poetry from the immediate tradition which the Imagists despised. With this label I do not mean to impugn Wordsworth, who had died about sixty years earlier (although the Imagists held no particularly high opinion of his style); I refer instead to the tradition inspired largely by his lyric emphasis on the meditative reflections of a solitary speaker often drawing on the imagery of nature.

For the Imagists the Wordsworthian style had become decadent-mushy, rhythmically inert, predictable in its imagery, and emotionally dishonest-it had turned poetry from something vital into something merely decorative. However passionate and innovative Wordsworth's own best poetry had been, by the end of the century the tradition of meditative lyric had lost its vitality, degenerating into subjective posturing often wrapped in the cloudiness of nostalgia or dreams and presented in a flaccid language. Even the best of them, Yeats, Pound characterized as "already a sort of great dim figure with its associations set in the past" (Letter to Harriet Monroe, 30 March 1913).

To illustrate this point, let me consider for a moment the following example from a particularly popular poet then and for many years later (Pound does not use this example and it is not part of his immediate tradition, but it will serve to illustrate some of the characteristics of what his movement objected to under the rubric of what I am calling Wordsworthian decadence):

Sea Magic
My heart faints in me for the distant sea.
The roar of London is the roar of ire
The lion utters in his old desire
For Libya out of dim captivity.
The long bright silver of Cheapside I see,
Her gilded weathercocks on roof and spire
Exulting eastward in the western fire;
All things recall one heart-sick memory:—
Ever the rustle of the advancing foam,

The surges' desolate thunder, and the cry
As of some lone babe in the whispering sky;
Ever I peer into the restless gloom
To where a ship clad dim and loftily
Looms steadfast in the wonder of her home.
Walter de la Mare

What's wrong with this? It seems a relatively pleasant poem, the evocation of a mood we can respond to presented in a style we are immediately familiar with. Well, for a start, the Imagists would insist, the poem is emotional fakery, in the sense that there is nothing sharp, focused, passionate about it. Everything about it is fuzzy and predictable: the imprecise imagery (relying upon a conventional vocabulary designed to evoke an "atmosphere" of significance but with no clarity—"faints," "dim," "heart-sick," "desolate," "lone," "whispering," and so on), the iambic regularity, the predicable rhymes—in short, the overwhelming conventionality. For them, this style is the poetic equivalent of what we call Muzak.

A poem like this is not necessarily easy to write, and it is often (for reasons I'll mention in a moment) quite popular. But it offers no revelation, no surprise, no sense of the sharp particularity of experience. And its effect depends upon our closing down parts of our critical apparatus and surrendering to the conventional associations. For example, consider the lines "The roar of London is the roar of ire/The lion utters in his old desire/For Libya out of dim captivity." What does this mean? It has iambic regularity and a clear rhyme, so we know we're dealing with poetry. But how is my understanding of the emotions being exploring at all illuminated by the comparison of London to the lion? Apart from that, look at the language. Is this English? Does anyone actually talk in phrases like "roar of ire"?

To clarify the point let me give you a more contemporary example. Popular song writing is full of examples of this sort of writing. Many popular artists tap this vein and become rich selling the public this form of shallow emotionalism delivered in a conventional package: Barry Manilow, Englebert Humperdink, Tom Jones, a great deal of Country Music. When we express dissatisfaction with some of these "poets" I think what we most object to is their emotional flaccidity and artistic conventionality. They are gesturing towards an emotion presented in a non-disturbing way, so that we can wallow for a moment without engaging our full imaginations with any serious awareness in anything and certainly without encountering anything surprising or challenging. It's a style that reaches its natural culmination in the Coutt's Hallmark Greeting Card.

There's a name for this sort of style. We call it sentimentality, and it is, in the words of Wallace Stevens, "a failure of feeling." The failure stems from the inability or the refusal to put the emotions one is exploring into a sharp focus in a vital language so that they can register as particular experiences grappled with honestly. Sentiment is, and always has been, very popular—there's more immediate cash to be won from sentiment than from its alternatives (as Walt Disney knows so well). That I would suggest stems from the fact that we all like to bathe in warm treacle now and then, without having to come to terms with anything very challenging. To hear, say, Tammy Wynette singing about Divorce gives me the sense of an emotionally important time without requiring me to reshape my perceptions or understanding of what it really means. All the potential complexities of the experience are soothed away by the predictable words, rhymes, rhythms, and so on.

One might note here, in passing, that it's quite common for a revolutionary artistic movement to arise as a reaction against the decadent sentimentality of the immediate tradition. If the new movement succeeds, it will often revolutionize the style of the art form, only in turn to become a new convention which, in the hands of lesser artists, becomes the new sentimentality. It's worth remembering that Wordsworth sees himself as rejecting the conventional sentimentality of outworn eighteenth century traditions and as introducing new poetic reforms to revitalize English poetry. The Imagists saw themselves with something of the same mission: the Romantic tradition initiated by Wordsworth had lost its energy, its power to move, and had become conventional sentiment (just as Bob Dylan saw himself as bringing to an end an outworn tradition of song writing when he announced "Tin Pan Alley is dead. I killed it").

The Imagist Programme

What did Pound and his fellow imagists have to offer by way of a reform programme? In its main artistic credo, Imagism proselytized a few firm recommendations, as follows:

The first important artistic tenet of Imagism was that the poet must get rid of the omnipresent voice of the poet, the Wordsworthian "I." Whatever poetry was about it must eschew the wallowing in subjective emotionalism, the peeling away of the layers of skin surrounding the poet's psyche. This simply created a sentimental personal emotionalism of the sort exemplified above.

The second tenet, from which the movement derives its name, is that whatever the poet has to communicate, he or she must do so in terms of objective images: clear, objective, precise, concentrated, and fresh symbols which capture, in the way they are presented the emotional qualities under exploration. "The image is itself the speech," proclaimed Pound. Poets should not be telling us how they feel-they should be presenting us with impersonal images which capture the feeling, so that we, as readers, can react to the image without the meddlesome interference of the poetical personality. Poems, in other words, should not be interpreting the experience for us; they should provide the objective means by which we can ourselves, as readers, discover what matters.

Poems thus did not need rational frameworks or conventional logic or meditating poet-narrators to coordinate the meaning. Pound argued that the rationality of speech, both in science and in art, did not come from rational logic but from the combination or juxtaposition of two clear, objective images:

The serious artist is scientific.... That is to say, a good biologist will make a reasonable number of observations of any given phenomenon before he draws a conclusion.... The result of each observation must be precise and no single observation must in itself be taken as determining a general law.... he serious artist is scientific in that he presents the image of his desire, or his hate, of his indifference as precisely as the image of his own desire, hate or indifference. The more precise his record the more lasting and unassailable his work of art.

Imagist poets were very fond of using scientific analogies for what they were doing: Eliot's "platinum catalyst, "non-Euclidean geometry," Fenollos'a "transference of power," Williams's "field of force, and Pound's "sort of inspired mathematics." The habit is, I think, a means above all of emphasizing the importance of the particular and the concrete in contrast to the discursive, so that their poetry could elicit the reader's intuitive response to something specific, unmediated by the personality of the poet.

The most famous statement of this principle came in later years from Eliot himself, who in his essay on Hamlet introduced a key critical terms in modern discussions of art and poetry, the objective correlative:

The only way of expressing emotion in the form of art is by finding an "objective correlative"; in other words, a set of objects, a situation, a chain of events which shall be the formula of that particular emotion; such that when the external facts, which must terminate in sensory experience, are given, the emotion is immediately evoked.

What Eliot means here is that the job of the artist is to find a fictional equivalent to the emotion he wishes to explore, something adequate to the complexity of the feeling which is at issue—the images must be adequate to the emotions, the source of our understanding of them, so that our response arises inevitably out of them, and not from being told directly by the poet what is at stake (Eliot's argument here is that the problems of Hamlet stem, in large part, from Shakespeare's failure to create an appropriate objective correlative for his own work—the emotional quality of the work, he claims, is in excess of the facts presented in it).

This, incidentally, is an principle well worth considering in your own creative writing and critical interpretation: How successfully has the represented fiction (story, character, symbol, and so on) captured the emotionally complexities of the issue at hand? To what extent is the image only a gesture towards something serious? To what extent does the image only illustrate, rather than illuminate, experience

Thus, a poem should not concern itself with a traditional connective (like a firm narrative line or a developing argumentative framework or an interpreting narrator) which interfere with the reader's most important experience, the direct contact with the impersonal image: is not a counter language, but a visual concrete one. It is compromise for a language of intuition which would hand over sensation bodily. It always endeavours to arrest you, and to make you continuously see a physical thing, to prevent you gliding through an abstract process. It chooses fresh epithets and fresh metaphors not so much because they are new, and we are tired of the old, but because the old cease to convey a physical thing and become abstract counters.... Images in verse are not mere decoration, but the very essence of an intuitive language.

The man who wrote the above words, T. E. Hulme, was the closest thing the early Imagists had to a philosophical spirit, and he was, interestingly enough spurred on in his speculations about imagery by the experience of living and working on the Canadian prairies. There he experienced clearly and repeatedly the way in which a very mundane object, like, say, a grain silo, could stand out as a clear single image at a distance and define an emotional complex in a very objective manner.

Thirdly, Imagist practice demanded a break with the old conventions of writing verse, especially with a standard rhythm and rhyme. They declared inappropriate the traditional war horse of English poetry, the iambic pentameter-the medium for virtually all the major poets since Chaucer (Shakespeare, Milton, Dryden, Pope, and so on). Modern verse should emancipate itself from the notion that the language had to fit some preconceived pattern—the pattern should emerge from what was demanded by the language at that particular moment.

Hence, Imagism promoted what came to be called "free verse," liberating the poet from traditional conventions of set rhythms and rhyme and insisting that the formal properties of the poem were to take shape flexibly in the ways best suited to the achievement of the appropriate form of language. Hence, centuries of formalist restrictions were done away with, and a new characteristic of modern poetry emerged—the constantly shifting rhythmic patterns, changing with the particular sections of the work. The Waste Land is one of the finest examples of this, moving from blank verse, to song, to prose, to music hall speech, in short, to whatever the requirements of the particular lines. Gone is the traditional regularity which for so long had defined poetry (and which, for many, still does). Imagists insisted that free verse does not mean that anything goes. No verse is free for the poet who really wants to do a good job Pound claimed. And he grew frustrated at the ways in which, under the banner of Imagism, all sorts of ineffectual experiments justified themselves. What Pound wanted was a new form of poetic discipline.

One can sum up many of these points in one injunction. Modern poetry must address the modern world with modern language and images appropriate to the modern experience, unfettered by the conventions which had grown up over the centuries. This demand was all part of a much wider movement (which Hughes discusses in The Shock of the New) to bring all cultural effort into an age far removed from the pastoral conventions of so much art and poetry. If poetry was to matter-and Pound insisted that poetry must matter—then it must reform itself so that it could communicate intelligently and clearly top a modern urban readership in a modern idiom.

What Pound was seeking he found in an odd place, in Japanese haiku-the very short presentation of images juxtaposed without comment:

In a Station of the Metro
The apparition of these faces in the crowd;
Petals on a wet, black bough.
Alba
As cool as the pale wet leaves

of lily-of-the-valley
She lay beside me in the dawn.

The poems make no argumentative statements, tell no story, make no links to the feelings of the poet. They simply, clearly, and directly present images-and it is up to us to intuit for ourselves what they might "mean" or "say."

Pound himself explained the attraction of this form borrowed from the Japanese tradition: It seemed to offer dry, hard concrete imagery and, without losing any of the essential force of symbolist poetry, avoided direct lyricism. It was the basic unit of the imagiste poem, juxtaposing two images, often in contrast, and containing them within a brief epigrammatic form, omitting all moral and intellectual comment and allowing images to form a "visual chord" in the mind—a third image that unites them—so that a "thing outward and objective transforms itself or darts into a thing inward and subjective."

A favourite sample of the new imagist style (from 1915), a poem highly admired by the Imagists themselves is the following (by Hilda Dolittle or HD, one of the "founders" of the movement):

Oread
Whirl up, sea—
Whirl our pointed pines,
Splash your great pines
On our rocks,
Hurl your green over us,
Cover us with your pools of fir.

Now, these examples illustrate, I think, clearly enough what the Imagists meant by the importance of the imagery, the absence of any dominating Wordsworthian narrative or descriptive "I," and the linguistic variety. Notice, too, especially in comparison with the other poem quoted already, how clean the language is. We have here none of that rhetorical appeal to emotionally resonant but vague adjectives or images.

But these two examples also illustrate a very important problem with this new style—the fact that it seems curiously empty of content. This point is worth dwelling upon. How can a style which takes away the traditional organizing principles of a poem-either the feelings of the narrator or a geographic setting or a coordinating argument or even certain formal elements-and which stresses that the image alone is the crux of the matter, how can such a poem do any more than what these examples appear to do, depict an image or two and then cease? Perhaps they provide intuition, but where is the thought which enables us stay in touch with some coordinating theme or developing meaning? This characteristic was a common point of criticism of the new style ("They've got the bridle and the bit all right/But where's the bloody horse?").

It was the fault of imagism never to let its devotees draw clear conclusions about life and to force the poet to state too much and to deduce rather too little-to lead its disciples too often into a barren aestheticism which was, and is, empty of content.... Poetry merely descriptive of nature as such, however vivid, no longer seems to me enough; there has to be added to it the human judgement, the human evaluation.

The poetry of Pound himself seems to exemplify this problem. Pound's style displays a remarkable command of language, imagery, rhythm, and other formal skills. But too often he appears to have little to say, and his longer poems often come across as merely a collection of images, which do not add up to what he was after, some form of intuitive revelation. Hence he emerges, in some respects, as a consummate poet's poet—someone who (like Spenser, perhaps) opened up to his contemporaries all sorts of important new possibilities with poetic style, without being able in the process to produce a work which might triumphantly justify the movement. He himself was well aware of this problem with his own work.

In fact, it seems clear that Imagism would have been little more than a footnote to the early history of modern culture, but for another American, one who developed his modern poetry style largely on his own, apart from the developing Imagist movement, but whose style, especially with the help of Ezra Pound, created its finest achievements. T. S. Eliot's early poetry provided exactly what Pound saw as the essential ingredients of the modern style. Eliot resolved (for reasons I will mention later) the problems of Imagism I mentioned above and in his early poetry, particularly in The Waste Land, established a transformation of modern poetry that very much redefined how poets write. Eliot's poem, Pound proclaimed, was "the justification of our 'movement,' of our modern experiment."

T.S. Eliot and Ezra Pound

The association between T. S. Eliot and Ezra Pound began around 1912 in England. The two men, whose personalities and family backgrounds were very different, had much in common. They were both from the West or mid-West—Eliot from St. Louis and Pound from Idaho, and both, as young men (Pound was 27 and Eliot 25 at the time their association began) had come to Europe as means of getting more in touch with what they felt unavailable in America. And both ended up staying in Europe for the rest of their lives (with some interruptions).

Pound immediately recognized in "The Love Song of J. Alfred Prufrock" the quality of the new style, and it was largely through Pound's efforts that the poem appeared in print. Their association remained close, and Pound played a huge effort in the production of The Waste Land, acting as an editor and reducing the poem into something significantly shorter than the work Eliot wrote:

It was in 1922 that I placed before him in Paris the manuscript of a sprawling chaotic poem called The Waste Land which left his hands, reduced to about half its size, in the form in which it appears in print. I should like to think hat the manuscript, with the suppressed passages, had disappeared irrevocably; yet, on the other hand, I should wish the blue pencilling to be preserved as irrefutable evidence of Pound's critical genius.

The manuscript with Pound's emendations has survived and was printed after Eliot's death. It is, in my view, the most fascinating example of a critical intelligence working closely on an inspired poetic work, and it should be required reading for all those interested in modern poetry and editing. And it remains, as Eliot hoped it would, an extraordinary testament to Pound's critical genius.

Parenthetically, it is worth noting that Pound was throughout his life an tireless supporter of other poets, helping them with manuscripts, badgering publishers to use their work, seeking out patrons for needy artists, always ready to talk to those interested enough to seek him out. I personally know of this from an academic acquaintance, a graduate student, who visited "Uncle Ezra" in Italy in the mid-1960's after Pound's release from incarceration in the mental home by the US government and who received as cordial a welcome as he could wish. Three of the great masterpieces of early modernist English literature—Joyce's Ulysses, Eliot's Waste Land, and Yeats's The Tower—featured in one way or another the assistance of Ezra Pound. He recognized early on the talent of Robert Frost and many other young poets. There is no doubt that his efforts on behalf of other artists were tireless, unselfish, and often, especially in the case of The Waste Land, decisive.

All of this makes part of Ezra Pound's life particularly sad. And I'd like to take a moment to refer to one of the great literary scandals of the century. In the 1920's, after Pound left England, he finally settled in Rapallo in Italy. There we worked on his major work of poetry, The Cantos, off and on for the rest of his life. During the war he became preoccupied with strange economic theories, especially Social Credit, and with anti-Semitism, both of which prompted him to make some radio broadcasts on behalf of Mussolini's Fascist government.

In 1945, he surrendered to the American Army, and was put in an iron cage out in the heat of the Italian summer sun in Pisa. As a result of that experience he wrote his finest sequence of poems, The Pisan Cantos, for which he was awarded one of the most prestigious literary awards available in America.

This placed the American government in a dilemma. Technically, Pound was a traitor and should be tried and sent off for a long prison term. On the other hand, he was a leading figure of modern American poetry (the recent prize had confirmed this) and had a huge number of supporters, many of whom he had in the past provided valuable help to (including T. S. Eliot). The government resolved its difficulties by declaring Pound unfit for trial and shipping him off to a mental home. Over the years, there were repeated calls for Pound's release-How could America so unfairly incarcerate without trial one of its most important cultural figures of the past fifty years? Eventually, Robert Frost, who by that time was clearly America's leading poet and who had, to his great discredit, refused to come to Pound's assistance, joined in, and President Eisenhower permitted Pound to leave America in 1961. He returned to Rapallo, where he died in 1972.

Comments on Eliot's Style

What was it about the early poems of T. S. Eliot which so immediately caught Pound's attention and transformed the writing of modern English poetry? It is hard to select a single quality, other than to say that Eliot was simply a better poet than his Imagist contemporaries. He has an uncanny genius, characteristic of only the greatest writers, of writing lines which stick in one's mind. But, in addition to that key quality, let me focus on some of the ways in which "The Love Song of J. Alfred Prufrock" and The Waste Land exemplify the reforms of poetic language which the Imagists insisted upon, while at the same time resolving the difficulties the style imposes (which I referred to earlier). I don't mean this to represent a complete discussion of Eliot's style by any means, but it should give some assistance to those who find the style puzzling at first.

The Coordinating Consciousness of the Speaker

The first, and one of the most important contribution Eliot made was a technical one. I mentioned above, in the discussion of sample Imagist poems, the problem of content: How can a collection of images add up to anything more than simply a list of images? What is going to unify a style which assembles a series of haiku-like fragments? Eliot resolved this problem with a technique he learned from the one Victorian poet for whom the Imagists had a high regard, Robert Browning.

The technique is deceptively simple. Eliot makes his poem dramatic utterances, spoken by an invented persona like Prufrock, so that the images, as we encounter them, are all linked, no matter how discrete they may appear, because they are expressions of a single personality. In terms of the language discussed already, the speaking personality operates as an objective correlative, something apart and different from the poet (for Prufrock is clearly not Eliot, and one habit we have to discard immediately in reading this poetry is any tendency, very strong in the Wordsworthian tradition, immediately to identify the speaking voice of the poem, the "I," with the poet writing the piece), towards the clarification of which all the images in the poem contribute. The speaking persona, in other words, is a way of escaping the omnipresence of the poet's personality while at the same time linking the poem to a coordinating consciousness.

Thus, a key technique in reading Eliot is to stop looking for conventional means of coordinating a long poem (a story, a developing description, an argument) and to focus instead on what each apparently discontinuous part of the poem reveals abou the consciousness of the speaking voice, for the definition of the consciousness is the main purpose of the poem. We may, for example, puzzle over what could possibly be the logical connection between, say, the fog, the women who come and go talking of Michelangelo, a crustacean, coffee, Lazarus, Hamlet, and the sea girls. The connection is clear enough, however: they are all expressions of and therefore images illuminating Prufrock himself, glimpses into his emotional state.

And there's a second point to this technique. The discontinuity between the images defining the consciousness of the speaker serves to indicate what for Eliot is a major manifestation of modern life, the loss of the integrated personality. Eliot does this quite deliberately as part of his sense that a fractured world and an inchoate response to it defines what we have become:

The life of a soul does not consist in the contemplation of one consistent world but in the painful task of unifying (to a greater and less extent) jarring and incompatible ones. In The Waste Land the technique, although more complex, is essentially the same. There we have a multiplicity of voices, male and female, young and old, in a variety of languages and styles, and the shifts are unannounced, so that often we do not even know who is speaking, simply that it is someone who sounds different from the voice immediately before. But the unity of the poem emerges from the fact that these all merge into a single personality, something we might call the voice of the modern consciousness. The fact that this modern consciousness cannot settle into a fixed perception of things or even into a consistent language helps to convey a good deal of the sense of the strain of modern living, an important point of the poem.

I think at first reading many students worry unnecessarily about being able clearly to distinguish the different "personalities," sometimes to the extent that the process works to the detriment of their appreciating the key point: the ways in which all these voice are part of the all-inclusive "personality" of the poem. Eliot reminds us of this in the only one of his notes to the poem which is of direct interpretative help to the reader:

Tiresias, although a mere spectator and not indeed a 'character', is yet the most important personage in the poem, uniting all the rest. Just as the one-eyed merchant, seller of currants, melts into the Phoenician Sailor, and the latter is not wholly distinct from Ferdinand Prince of Naples, so all the women are one woman, and the two sexes meet in Tiresias. What Tiresias sees, in fact, is the substance of the poem.

We need, therefore, in reading Eliot's style to attend to how the images serve to illuminate a distinctive personality at once modern, fractured, multilingual, urban, and emotionally uncertain. The personality is by no means unified; in fact, what emerges from both poems as a principal concern is the inability of the modern consciousness either to see unity in the world outside or to bring to a disordered world any sense of inner integrity. What unity the poems possess comes from what is revealed to us about this new conception of the modern self. Part of this sense of the totality of the modern self adding up to a fractured variety emerges, not just from the shifting sense of the images and the speaking voice, but also from the variety in the verse style. It's as if in the modern age, there cannot be a single authoritative way of expressing how one feels (as there was once in the past); there is not enough confidence in the forms of language itself. Just as the traditional community has become the unreal city, a vision of a modern inferno, so the traditional language of the community in the modern personality has become a multiplicity of contrasting styles. Eliot's Irony

A second important feature of Eliot's technique, something which gives his style an urbanity and resonance lacking in much other imagist writing, is his constant use of a certain form of irony, a style known as Romantic irony or, what might be called, the irony of instant deflation.

Romantic irony consists of creating what appears to be a firm assertion or picture of something, only to reveal that what was promised in the original is, in fact, quite different. A good example is something like the following: a stage show presents a beautiful woman who sings a tender, seductive song, celebrating feminine beauty and then, at the end, abruptly the performer rips off her hair to reveal that she is, in fact, a man, and that the audience is a bunch of idiots to have fallen for the illusion.

The irony, in other words, consists of creating something of apparent value and solidity—an affirmation that matters—only to reveal that the value was illusory. This technique is absolutely fundamental to understanding Eliot's poetry. His skill with this technique is responsible, as much as anything, for the sardonic and often pessimistic tone of the poem.

Eliot will use Romantic irony within a single line, where the growing energy of what looks like the start of a confident or at least important statement will be denied by the end of the line. The most famous example of this is the line from "Prufrock": "I have measured out my life in coffee spoons." The first six words lead us to expect, at last, some significant insight into something—the rhetorical build up in the language promises something significant; the prosaic last three words indicate an immediate deflation.

Notice some other examples of this technique:
In a minute there is time for decisions and revisions
which a minute will reverse.
He said, Marie,
Marie, hold on tight. And down we went.
In the mountains, there you feel free.
I read, much of the night, and go south in the winter.
If there were water
And no rock
If there were rock
And also water
And water
A spring
A pool among the rock
If there were the sound of water only
Not the cicada
And dry grass singing
But sound of water over a rock
Where the hermit thrush sings in the pine trees
Drip drop drip drop drop drop drop
But there is no water.

Often, as in the last example above, the rising first part of the ironic structure in these poems is linked to a hypothetical (to an if or a would clause), so that rising hope, as it rises, is conditional and is quickly cancelled by any reflection on the reality. The effect is the constant sense of a consciousness which realizes intelligently enough that something is wrong and that a particular quality is necessary to transform the barrenness of life but which even before the thought is clearly formulated runs out of energy and collapses upon itself.

The ironic technique also, to some degree, governs the structure of the entire "Love Song of J. Alfred Prufrock." The poem starts on a note of energy ("Let us go..."), and for all the rising and falling of the ironic passages seems in places to gather a significant energy. But as soon as we reach "No, I am not Prince Hamlet" whatever energies Prufrock may have generated by his intense dissatisfaction with life dissipate immediately, and we are left with an intelligent, sympathetic, character confronting the realities of his own failure—seeing the emotional sterility of his future but incapable of breaking out, even though at the start of the poem (where the tone is most resolute and imperative) that is what he had set his mind on. He is settling for a life which he knows is empty and meaningless, without music, beauty, movement, except in his dreams.

Eliot's Rhythmic and Tonal Variety: An essential ingredient in Eliot's Romantic irony and in his definition of the consciousness of the speaker is his astonishing command of rhythmic variety. His emancipation from the traditional commitment to a regular verse pattern manifests itself in the juxtaposition of often totally contrasting styles.

This serves a number of important purposes. The first I have already alluded to: the sudden unannounced shift in the rhythm is an important part of the deflationary technique of Eliot's irony, which enables him to moves us through some complex emotional shifts very quickly and effectively:

'Are you alive, or not? Is there nothing in your head?'
But
that Shakespeherian Rag -
It's so elegant
So intelligent
'What shall I do now? What shall I do?'

Here the urgency of an attempt to reach some one else is interrupted by the syncopated rhythms of the popular tune, only to collapse into the prosaic inner self-questioning which we know will lead no where. One might multiply examples like this many times.

A second contribution of Eliot's apparently freewheeling rhythmic and tonal shifts is to reinforce the sense of the loss of a coordinating formal public speech. There are constant echoes in the Waste Land, for example, of all sorts of traditional forms of discourse—Biblical utterance, blank verse, formal lyric grace. But these can never sustain themselves in the face of the radical anxieties and fractured outer world of the modern age. So the apparently formal presentation of the lady in "A Game of Chess," deliberately reminiscent of Shakespeare's magnificent description of Cleopatra cannot sustain emotional stability and breaks into the neurotic conversation of an anxious pair fighting off images of rats eating up the dead.

Thus, an important sense of what we have lost from the past emerges from the constant reminders of past forms of expression up against the modern realities. And this helps to contribute in a decisive way to the definition of the modern consciousness by stressing the lack of a common idiom, any shared and shaping way to interpret experience. We experience, not a common language or a formal set of ways to express our feelings. We are a babble of voices, languages, slangs, desperately seeking significant communication with others and anxiously dreading making such connections.

The world, this style is insisting upon, is in some respects a collection of refugees (and notice the frequency of displaced persons in the poem)—like our cultural past, our languages, and therefore our thoughts exists as fragments. The modern world thus not only features the muddle of collapsing and intermingling and displaced cultures but also brings about a similar situation within the discourse of the self.

Eliot's Use of the Past: Of course, Eliot's use of the past involves a good deal more than simply an evocation of traditional styles. For one immediately noticeable feature of Eliot's style which can cause some difficulties for new readers is his constant use of the past in more explicit ways. Typically Eliot's style will invoke the past directly in one of three ways:

The first is a direct reference to a well known literary or historical or cultural figure (Coriolanus, Hamlet, Michelangelo, Tiresias, and so on). The second is a more or less explicit allusion to the works-often to something immediately reminiscent of a famous passage (like the opening of The Waste Land, which is clearly an allusion to the opening of Chaucer's General Prologue to The Canterbury Tales, or the opening of the Second Section of the same poem, "A Game of Chess," which is equally clearly based on Shakespeare's description of Cleopatra sailing into Alexandria). The third is a direct quote from some famous source. What is one to make of these constant references? How is one to integrate them into one's understanding of the poem? Well, I want to begin by suggesting that one needs to appreciate their importance but (a very important caveat) without giving them an importance incommensurate with their function.

Some readers feel, for example, that this constant and often very esoteric reference to the past makes the poem simply too inaccessible or incomprehensible, and they give up in despair or disgust at what they perceive as willfully elitist and obscurantist: "a piece that passeth all understanding," "the agonized outcry of a sensitive romanticism drowning in a sea of jazz"; "to all but anthropologists so much waste paper". Such a response was by no means uncommon in the first critical reviews of the work. a pompous parade of erudition, a lengthy extension of the deadlier disillusion, a kaleidoscopic movement in which the bright coloured pieces fail to atone for the absence of an integrated design.... mingling of wilful obscurity and weak vaudeville.

This response to the poem is understandable—the style does rely upon a cultural background that can be easily interpreted as unnecessarily academic and elitist (a charge that is commonly leveled against a good deal of Modernist culture), and the feature does indeed repel many readers. I have considerable sympathy with the view, especially since, as you may have gathered by now, I am suspicious of any artistic style which self-consciously and deliberately isolates itself from a wide general readership.

Pound somewhere observes, by way of justification for this technique, that one doesn't stop writing just because the common people don't know Latin. Well, maybe not. But if your poetry demands a knowledge of Latin and of a great many rather obscure classical references, then you should not exp ct many of the folk to care very much for or to benefit from you efforts. Put more simply, a writer who turns his back on the general readers should not be surprised if they turn their backs on him.

On the other hand, before making a decision one way or

the other, perhaps we should explore a little more into how these references function, because it may well be that having a firm grasp on all these references is less important than it may at first appear. Yes, the style is unnecessarily erudite and allusive, but we don't have to throw it all away because of that. So let me try to ease the difficulty in a moment.

It is not uncommon for some readers to feel that in order to appreciate Eliot's style one has to have as full a command of the tradition he is using as he does. This impression is strongly reinforced by the notes Eliot adds to the poem. There is wide agreement that these notes are unfortunate, because they really reinforce the impression I have been describing, which can seriously interfere with a direct experience of the sort Imagism wished to make central to the reading of poetry.

On this point I do not wish to be misunderstood. Obviously, if one can recognize and respond significantly to the reference Eliot is making, then the poem becomes all the richer. However, it is also clear that understanding all those often very esoteric references is not a necessary condition for responding intelligently to the poem. For if one concentrates on what the language is actually doing, then one can usually derive a clear sense of what is going on, an interpretative response adequate to formulating a coherent approach to the poem. Take, for example, the very opening, the famous lines about April being the cruellest month. This imagery functions to summon up a particular (and startling) image of spring as a fearful time, something hostile to life because it rouses us from our winter torpor. Eliot is doing here something very common in modernist writing generally, and especially in his early poems: reversing the traditional associations with a conventional poetic image. Just as the opening lines of "Prufrock" provide, in that image of a city anaesthetized, a startlingly new and severe image of early evening (often celebrated in poetry as a time of quiet and calm reflection), so the opening of The Waste Land wrenches apart our conventional poetic associations with an invocation of spring. All that is clear enough from a reading of the words without any knowledge of Chaucer's lines. If we do recognize Chaucer's original under that text (and many of us will), then the passage becomes all the richer for us, because we see an important point Eliot is making in drawing our attention to The Canterbury Tales, the extent to which the healthy union of erotic and religious sensibilities which Chaucer's great work celebrates has been lost in the modern age.

Many of the references to the past works in a similar way. They force us, as readers, if we recognize them (or some of them) constantly to juxtapose the sensibilities expressive of the modern consciousness of the speaker with the very different visions of the past, when people brought to the complexities of life things we seem to have lost: courage, erotic confidence, a love of nature, a sense of the divine. There was a time, these references constantly say, when human beings were capable of spiritually intense experience, when people were willing to suffer, to celebrate, to express themselves heroically. References to, for example, Cleopatra, Hamlet, Coriolanus, Augustine, Queen Elizabeth, Tristan and Isolde, like the reminders of the great artists of the past-Shakespeare, Michelangelo, Chaucer, and so on serve to create and sustain an ironic sense of loss.

This element brings out one of the essential features of what has come to be called Modernist art-the attempt to sort out some adequate relationship to the past, an issue that is a foremost concern among writers, painter, poets, sculptors, and philosophers. Where does one go after Nietzsche? What faith can one place in a tradition which led to the Great War of 1914-1918? Is there something worth salvaging, or should we junk the entire tradition? In one way or another, most artists for the first half of the twentieth century wrestled with this question in a way that had not happened before.

Eliot's early poetic style, especially in The Waste Land, really brings out the sense of the collapse of the past, a pile of fragments shored up against ruins, and he deliberately invokes the past to insist upon this point. What once had meaning no longer does. These ancient visions of a life so much more passionately full and coherent than the present age are gone. They remain only as isolated bits, reminders of the inadequacy of our own times: eros has become a tired mechanical ritual, the beautiful aspects of nature have filled up with cigarette butts and garbage or turned threatening, faith has become empty, the centres of the ancient civilization are being destroyed in the universal technological chaos of war, and the world is filling up with refugees (an important element in the characters of the poem).

One thing you might like to consider in exploring these reference to the past is the presence in them of any patterns, especially those which coincide with the patterns established in the imagery. One feature that immediately strikes me is how many of these past reference are to famous lovers, t ose passionately committed to somene else and ready to sacrifice a great deal for a powerfully achieved faith and trust in eros: Antony and Cleopatra, Tristan and Isolde, Elizabeth and Leicester, Ferdinand, Dante. I'm tempted to see in this pattern and the insistence on the aridity of the Waste Land some important source of the malaise of the modern world. This seems to me a much more promising approach than to rush off to read that modest volume From Ritual to Romance, a familiarity with which (in my experience) does little to assist with a close understanding of Eliot's poem.

The point I'm trying to insist upon here, to get back to the Imagist manifesto with which we started, is that the best way to read The Waste Land and "Prufrock" is simply to read the text, slowly and repeatedly, without getting too worried about all the external apparatus you think you need to bring to the poem. Let Eliot's images, rhythms, ironies—all of which are so extraordinary—do their work unmediated. You will, I think, fairly soon come to realise the uniquely great quality of this style.

If we read the poem in this way, however, we have to confess, I think, that it is not always easy or even possible to make coherent connections between the images and someone coordinating meaning. That is, many of the images clearly point beyond themselves and create pressure on us to make connections with something that might help to create an overarching meaning. But again and again we are unable to do this is a satisfactory manner. A common experience of reading this poem is a sharpened desire to make sense of it together with a sense of defeat-if there is a total coherence to be found, it eludes us.

This particular feature of the poem is yet another common characteristic of much modernist art-nowhere more eloquent and disturbing than in the writer we are going to encounter in two weeks, Franz Kafka. One does not have to be an expert in a great deal of modernist painting to recognize that the e, too, the technique of the symbol or the image directing us so ewhere that we can never attain is a common stylistic ingredie t.This, in fact, becomes a commonplace of modernism.

It's as if in the modern world we are surrounded by re inders and promises of meaning but, unlike earlier artists, we have no means of coordinating these into an integrated world picture (in the way that, say, Dante or Hildegard could) or into an integrated sense of the self

Postscript: Since I began by putting these two poems in something of a historical context, I would like to conclude with a few remarks on a few details of the effect of these poem and of the later career of T. S. Eliot himself. These remarks will necessarily be somewhat cursory, but they may help to arouse interest in an important and intriguing part of the history of modern English literature.

I have already made passing reference to some of the hostile comments made in the press about The Waste Land, and I can remember from my childhood BBC radio reports on funding to the arts in which hostile critics quoted a chunk of "Prufrock" ("I grow old... I grow old.../I shall wear the bottom of my trousers rolled") as examples of the idiocy of governmental support for the arts.

However, the effect of The Waste Land on young poets was immediate and decisive:

"To us... The Waste Land very definitely made a pronouncement. It pronounced doom"

Then out of the blue the Dial brought out the Waste Land and all our hilarity ended. It wiped out our world as if an atom bomb had been dropped upon it and our brave sallies into the unknown were turn to dust. To me especially it struck like a sardonic bullet. I felt at once that it had set me back twenty years, and I'm sure it did. Critically Eliot returned us to the classroom just at the moment when I felt that we were on the point of an escape to matters much closer to the essence of the new art form itself-rooted in the locality which should give it fruit. I knew that in certain ways I was defeated.

The style that Eliot launched transformed the writing of poetry. It also contributed to shifting the centre of gravity for English poetry from England to North America, largely because so many young Englishmen died in the war (including, for example, Rosenberg, Owen, Brooke, and countless others). And the reforms the Imagists insisted upon and the style of poetry they favoured became and have remained one of the mainstreams of modern English poetry. That is not to say that all elements of Eliot's style immediately became the standard. Not all poets agreed with Eliot's extensive concentration upon the use of the European past, which to some, like the American William Carlos Williams indicated "men content with the connotations of their masters".

Eliot himself took many of the elements of his style and applied to the critical understanding of poetry, becoming one of the major and most influential literary critics of the century. There is no time here to explore his enormous contribution our transformed understanding of poetry, although we might note in passing that the renewed interest in the lyrics of John Donne, in the poetry of Dante, the New Critical approach to literature, in the reassessment of Milton, in Renaissance drama, all these and other significant trends in the study of English literature were decisively influenced by T. S. Eliot.

Eliot himself seems to have been somewhat surprised by the success of The Waste Land—especially the praise from those who celebrated it as a modernist epic of sorts. And he steadfastly refused (with occasional exceptions) to offer his own commentary upon it.

Various critics have done me the honour to interpret the poem in terms of criticism of the contemporary world, have considered it, indeed, as an important bit of social criticism. To me it was only the relief of a personal and wholly insignificant grouse against life. It is just a piece of rhythmical grumbling.

This comment seems rather disingenuous. Eliot was indeed going through a particularly difficult time in his marriage, and it may well be that the pain the poem expresses has strong roots in his emotional pain about his relationship with is wife (at her insistence some lines were removed from the poem: "And we shall play a game of chess;/The ivory men make company between us/Pressing lidless eyes and waiting for a knock upon the door"; Eliot restored the lines in 1960, after his wife's death).

Shortly after completing The Waste Land, Eliot sought refuge from the distress of his perceptions of modern life by converting to Christianity, adopting the High Anglican faith, and by becoming an outspoken defender of certain elements of the tradition. He became a leading figure in the attempts to revive verse drama (producing his best known play Murder in the Cathedral and a modern adaptation of Aeschylus's Eumenides—The Family Reunion). He established himself as the leading literary and cultural critic of the time, and it is fair to claim that no American has ever wielded such power over the official cultural establishment in England as T. S. Eliot.

The major emphasis of T. S. Eliot's poetry changed correspondingly. The centre of attention moves from the sense of the apocalypse, which so many people saw in the early poems, to redemption, to a revitalization of faith. Once this happened, critics went back to The Waste Land and discovered that the seeds of this change are, indeed, there. Other interpreters of the early poems contest that claim.

Few writers have played a more decisive role in my own education than T. S. Eliot. He shaped the approach to poetry of most of those who taught me, and I cut my teeth as a critic by reading his essays, still among the finest works of concise and decisive evaluation one can read. When he died in 1965, there was a spontaneous outpouring of tributes in London, where I was then living, and I attended a special reading of his work which the theatrical community instantly organized.

As to the long-term influence of his early style on the writing of poetry, there is disagreement. That it had an enormous influence, few critics will d spute. What one might like to debate is the value of that inıluence. I have already mentioned the deliberately "elitist" tendency of Eliot (and Pound's) views of poetry. The extraordinary quality of Eliot's early poems, one might argue, encouraged a style that helped to remove modern "high" poetry further and further from the reach of the average reader. I'm not prepared to defend this accusation at the moment, except perhaps to observe that, if that is the case, it is part of the widespread tendency in many areas of modernist art to promote styles guaranteed to minimize readership, simply because the language becomes too obscure, private, and inaccessible.

That this tendency is an important feature of much modern poetry, fiction, and art, few will deny. And the effect is a denial of what many an Enlightenment writer or artist (including Wordsworth) saw as a major responsibility: to address the widest possible audience. Thus, however eloquent and sophisticated the style Imagism (and Eliot) encouraged, it tended to drive further a wedge between "serious" art and the public consciousness. Or, alternatively put, it removed art further and further from the realm of public discourse, thus marginalizing art from the most immediate questions confronting the citizen.

I have no time to go into this complex question here. But it may be worth noting that there is potentially a fertile connection between avant garde styles in art and poetry and oppressive regimes, simply because the more remote an artistic style is from public discourse, the less impact it is going to have. And it is relatively easy for a politically tyranny to foster such art, as opposed to promoting the forms of art most congenial to the Enlightenment temper-a widely accessible medium addressing questions of urgent public concern. There may be thus a certain irony in seeing The Waste Land as the triumph of the Imagists' modernist aesthetic. Yes, it did indeed demonstrate that poetry could address wide social issues and confront the immediate issues of contemporary culture. On the other hand, the price was high, for the style would seem severely to limit the readership for this new style and thus the public importance of serious poetry. More than one critic has observed that Eliot, in setting himself so strongly against the immediate Romantic tradition of his time, may have exacerbated some of the inner problem of Romanticism, so as to enormously weaken the accessibility of poetry:

The subjective personal content of the Romantic poem has become private, esoteric, at times an almost impenetrable secret; the Romantic interest in image and symbol has become an obsession: poems have been written in what can only be called code; Romantic 'sensibility' is now expressed in its purest possible form, free from all the distortions of conventional communication: the vestigial rhetoric the Romantics allowed themselves has finally been dispensed with-not even the laws of grammar and syntax need now apply.... Poetry seems not to be developing, but disintegrating. (P. Stone)

Apart from that, of course, there is the still controversial question about the nature of the relationship between a self-consciously "elitist" and esoteric style and various forms of tyranny, a question constantly brought to the forefront by new facts about the connections between many of the leading figures in modernist art and, for example, anti-Semitism and Fascism. This raises the complex (perhaps impossible) question about the extent to which a refusal to endorse any instinctively creative urge from within as the direct subject for poetry, the insistence on the externality of the object, may limit the creative possibilities of the poem—a lack of contact with aspects of human nature which require more consideration before being dismissed.

Chapter 8

Text

The Burial of the Dead

April is the cruelest month, breeding
Lilacs out of the dead land, mixing
Memory and desire, stirring
Dull roots with spring rain.
Winter kept us warm, covering
Earth in forgetful snow, feeding
A little life with dried tubers.
Summer surprised us, coming over the Starnbergersee
With a shower of rain; we stopped in the colonnade,
And went on in sunlight, into the Hofgarten,
And drank coffee, and talked for an hour.
Bin gar keine Russin, stamm' aus Litauen, echt deutsch.
And when we were children, staying at the arch-duke's,
My cousin's, he took me out on a sled,
And I was frightened. He said, Marie,
Marie, hold on tight. And down we went.
In the mountains, there you feel free.
I read, much of the night, and go south in the winter.
What are the roots that clutch, what branches grow
Out of this stony rubbish?Son of man,
You cannot say, or guess, for you know only
A heap of broken images, where the sun beats,
And the dead tree gives no shelter, the cricket no relief,
And the dry stone no sound of water. Only
There is shadow under this red rock,
(Come in under the shadow of this red rock),

And I will show you something different from either
Your shadow at morning striding behind you
Or your shadow at evening rising to meet you;
I will show you fear in a handful of dust. 30
Frisch weht der Wind 31
Der Heimat zu
Mein Irisch Kind
Wo weilest du?
'You gave me hyacinths first a year ago;
'They called me the hyacinth girl.'
-Yet when we came back, late, from the hyacinth garden,
Your arms full, and your hair wet, I could not
Speak, and my eyes failed, I was neither
Living nor dead, and I knew nothing,
Looking into the heart of light, the silence.
Oed' und leer das Meer. 42
Madame Sosostris, famous clairvoyante,43
Had a bad cold, nevertheless
Is known to be the wisest woman in Europe,
With a wicked pack of cards. Here, said she, 46
Is your card, the drowned Phoenician Sailor,
(Those are pearls that were his eyes. Look!)
Here is Belladonna, The Lady of the Rocks,
The lady of situations.
Here is the man with three staves, and here the Wheel,
And here is the one-eyed merchant, and this card,
Which is blank, is something he carries on his back,
Which I am forbidden to see. I do not find
The Hanged Man. Fear death by water. 55
I see crowds of people, walking round in a ring.
Thank you. If you see dear Mrs. Equitone,
Tell her I bring the horoscope myself:
One must be so careful these days.
Unreal City, 60
Under the brown fog of a winter dawn,
A crowd flowed over London Bridge, so many,
I had not thought death had undone so many. 63
Sighs, short and infrequent, were exhaled, 64

And each man fixed his eyes before his feet.
Flowed up the hill and down King William Street,
To where Saint Mary Woolnoth kept the hours
With a dead sound on the final stroke of nine. 68
There I saw one I knew, and stopped him, crying: 'Stetson!
'You who were with me in the ships at Mylae!
'That corpse you planted last year in your garden,
'Has it begun to sprout? Will it bloom this year?
'Or has the sudden frost disturbed its bed?
'O keep the Dog far hence, that's friend to men, 74
'Or with his nails he'll dig it up again!
'You! Hypocrite lecteur! - mon semblable, - mon frère!'
Title Page

A Game of Chess

The Chair she sat in, like a burnished throne, 77
Glowed on the marble, where the glass
Held up by standards wrought with fruited vines
From which a golden Cupidon peeped out
(Another hid his eyes behind his wing)
Doubled the flames of sevenbranched candelabra
Reflecting light upon the table as
The glitter of her jewels rose to meet it,
From satin cases poured in rich profusion.
In vials of ivory and coloured glass
Unstoppered, lurked her strange synthetic perfumes,
Unguent, powdered, or liquid - troubled, confused
And drowned the sense in odours; stirred by the air
That freshened from the window, these ascended
In fattening the prolonged candle-flames,
Flung their smoke into the laquearia, 92
Stirring the pattern on the coffered ceiling.
Huge sea-wood fed with copper
Burned green and orange, framed by the coloured stone,
In which sad light a carvèd dolphin swam.
Above the antique mantel was displayed
As though a window gave upon the sylvan scene 98
The change of Philomel, by the barbarous king 99

So rudely forced; yet there the nightingale 100
Filled all the desert with inviolable voice
And still she cried, and still the world pursues,
'Jug Jug' to dirty ears. And other withered stumps of time
Were told upon the walls; staring forms
Leaned out, leaning, hushing the room enclosed.
Footsteps shuffled on the stair.
Under the firelight, under the brush, her hair
Spread out in fiery points
Glowed into words, then would be savagely still.
'My nerves are bad to-night. Yes, bad. Stay with me.
'Speak to me. Why do you never speak. Speak.
'What are you thinking of? What thinking? What?
'I never know what you are thinking. Think.'
I think we are in rats' alley 115
Where the dead men lost their bones.
'What it that noise?'
The wind under the door. 118
'What is that noise now? What is the wind doing?'
Nothing again nothing.
'Do
'You know nothing? Do you see nothing?
Do you remember
'Nothing?'
I remember
Those are pearls that were his eyes.
'Are you alive, or not? Is there nothing in your head?' 126
But
O O O O that Shakespeherian Rag - 128
It's so elegant
So intelligent
'What shall I do now? What shall I do?'
'I shall rush out as I am, and walk the street
'With my hair down, so. What shall we do tomorrow?
'What shall we ever do?'
The hot water at ten.
And if it rains, a closed car at four.
And we shall play a game of chess, 138

Pressing lidless eyes and waiting for a
knock upon the door.
When Lil's husband got demobbed, I said -
I didn't mince my words, I said to her myself,
HURRY UP PLEASE IT'S TIME
Now Albert's coming back, make yourself a bit smart.
He'll want to know what you done with that
money he gave you
To get herself some teeth. He did, I was there.
You have them all out, Lil, and get a nice set,
He said, I swear, I can't bear to look at you.
And no more can't I, I said, and think of poor Albert,
He's been in the army for four years, he wants a good time,
And if you don't give it him, there's others will, I said.
Oh is there, she said. Something o' that, I said.
Then I'll know who to thank, she said, and
give me a straight look.
HURRY UP PLEASE IT'S TIME
If you don't like it you can get on with it, I said.
Others can pick and choose if you can't.
But if Albert makes off, it won't be for a lack of telling.
You ought to be ashamed, I said, to look so antique.
(And her only thirty-one.)
I can't help it, she said, pulling a long face,
It's them pills I took, to bring it off, she said.
(She's had five already, and nearly died of young George.)
The chemist said it would be all right, but
I've never been the same.
You are a proper fool, I said.
Well, if Albert won't leave you alone, there it is, I said,
What you get married for if you don't want children?
HURRY UP PLEASE IT'S TIME
Well, that Sunday Albert was home,
they had a hot gammon,
And they asked me in to dinner, to get
the beauty of it hot -
HURRY UP PLEASE IT'S TIME
HURRY UP PLEASE IT'S TIME

Goonight Bill. Goonight Lou. Goonight May. Goonight.
Ta ta. Goonight. Goonight.
Good night, ladies, good night, sweet ladies,
good night, good night. 172

The Fire Sermon

The river's tent is broken; the last fingers of leaf
Clutch and sink into the wet bank. The wind
Crosses the brown land, unheard.
The nymphs are departed.
Sweet Thames, run softly, till I end my song. 176
The river bears no empty bottles, sandwich papers,
Silk handkerchiefs, cardboard boxes, cigarette ends
Or other testimony of summer nights.
The nymphs are departed.
And their friends, the loitering heirs of City directors
Departed, have left no addresses.
By the waters of Leman I sat down and wept...
Sweet Thames, run softly till I end my song,
Sweet Thames, run softly, for I speak not loud or long.
But at my back in a cold blast I hear
The rattle of the bones, and chuckle
spread from ear to ear.
A rat crept softly through the vegetation
Dragging its slimy belly on the bank
While I was fishing in the dull canal
On a winter evening round behind the gashouse
Musing upon the king my brother's wreck
And on the king my father's death before him. 192
White bodies naked on the low damp ground
And bones cast in a little low dry garret,
Rattled by the rat's foot only, year to year.
But at my back from time to time I hear 196
The sound of horns and motors, which shall bring 197
Sweeney to Mrs. Porter in the spring.
O the moon shone bright on Mrs. Porter 199
And on her daughter
They wash their feet in soda water

Et O ces voix d'enfants, chantant dans la coupole! 202
Twit twit twit
Jug jug jug jug jug jug
So rudely forc'd.
Tereu
Unreal City
Under the brown fog of a winter noon
Mr. Eugenides, the Smyrna merchant
Unshaven, with a pocket full of currants
C.i.f. London: documents at sight, 210
Asked me in demotic French
To luncheon at the Cannon Street Hotel
Followed by a weekend at the Metropole.
At the violet hour, when the eyes and back
Turn upward from the desk, when
the human engine waits
Like a taxi throbbing waiting,
I Tiresias, though blind, throbbing between two lives, 218
Old man with wrinkled female breasts, can see
At the violet hour, the evening hour that strives
Homeward, and brings the sailor home from sea, 221
The typist home at teatime, clears her breakfast, lights
Her stove, and lays out food in tins.
Out of the window perilously spread
Her drying combinations touched by the sun's last rays,
On the divan are piled (at night her bed)
Stockings, slippers, camisoles, and stays.
I Tiresias, old man with wrinkled dugs
Perceived the scene, and foretold the rest -
I too awaited the expected guest.
He, the young man carbuncular, arrives,
A small house agent's clerk, with one bold stare,
One of the low on whom assurance sits
As a silk hat on a Bradford millionaire.
The time is now propitious, as he guesses,
The meal is ended, she is bored and tired,
Endeavours to engage her in caresses
Which are still unreproved, if undesired.

Flushed and decided, he assaults at once;
Exploring hands encounter no defence;
His vanity requires no response,
And makes a welcome of indifference.
(And I Tiresias have foresuffered all
Enacted on this same divan or bed;
I who have sat by Thebes below the wall
And walked among the lowest of the dead.)
Bestows one final patronising kiss,
And gropes his way, finding the stairs unlit...
She turns and looks a moment in the glass,
Hardly aware of her departed lover;
Her brain allows one half-formed thought to pass:
'Well now that's done: and I'm glad it's over.'
When lovely woman stoops to folly and 253
Paces about her room again, alone,
She smoothes her hair with automatic hand,
And puts a record on the gramophone.
'This music crept by me upon the waters' 257
And along the Strand, up Queen Victoria Street.
O City city, I can sometimes hear
Beside a public bar in Lower Thames Street,
The pleasant whining of a mandoline
And a clatter and a chatter from within
Where fishmen lounge at noon: where the walls
Of Magnus Martyr hold 264
Inexplicable splendour of Ionian white and gold.
The river sweats 266
Oil and tar
The barges drift
With the turning tide
Red sails
Wide
To leeward, swing on the heavy spar.
The barges wash
Drifting logs
Down Greenwich reach
Past the Isle of Dogs.

Weialala leia
Wallala leialala
Elizabeth and Leicester 279
Beating oars
The stern was formed
A gilded shell
Red and gold
The brisk swell
Rippled both shores
Southwest wind
Carried down stream
The peal of bells
White towers
Weialala leia
Wallala leialala
'Trams and dusty trees.
Highbury bore me. Richmond and Kew 293
Undid me. By Richmond I raised my knees
Supine on the floor of a narrow canoe.'
'My feet are at Moorgate and my heart
Under my feet. After the event
He wept. He promised "a new start."
I made no comment. What should I resent?'
'On Margate Sands. 301
I can connect
Nothing with nothing.
The broken fingernails of dirty hands.
My people humble people who expect
Nothing.'
la la
To Carthage then I came 307
Burning burning burning burning 308
O Lord Thou pluckest me out 309
O Lord Thou pluckest
burning

Death by Water

Phlebas the Phoenician, a fortnight dead,

Forgot the cry of gulls, and the deep sea swell
And the profit and loss.
A current under sea
Picked his bones in whispers. As he rose and fell
He passes the stages of his age and youth
Entering the whirlpool.
Gentile or Jew
O you who turn the wheel and look windward,
Consider Phlebas, who was once
handsome and tall as you.

What the Thunder Said

After the torchlight red on sweaty faces
After the frosty silence in the gardens
After the agony in stony places
The shouting and the crying
Prison and palace and reverberation
Of thunder of spring over distant mountains
He who was living is now dead
We who were living are now dying
With a little patience
Here is no water but only rock
Rock and no water and the sandy road
The road winding above among the mountains
Which are mountains of rock without water
If there were water we should stop and drink
Amongst the rock one cannot stop or think
Sweat is dry and feet are in the sand
If there were only water amongst the rock
Dead mountain mouth of carious teeth that cannot spit
Here one can neither stand not lie nor sit
There is not even silence in the mountains
But dry sterile thunder without rain
There is not even solitude in the mountains
But red sullen faces sneer and snarl
From doors of mudcracked houses
If there were water
And no rock

If there were rock
And also water
And water
A spring
A pool among the rock
If there were the sound of water only
Not the cicada
And dry grass singing
But sound of water over a rock
Where the hermit-thrush sings in the pine trees
Drip drop drip drop drop drop drop 357
But there is no water
Who is the third who walks always beside you?
When I count, there are only you and I together 360
But when I look ahead up the white road
There is always another one walking beside you
Gliding wrapt in a brown mantle, hooded
I do not know whether a man or a woman
- But who is that on the other side of you?
What is that sound high in the air 366
Murmur of maternal lamentation
Who are those hooded hordes swarming
Over endless plains, stumbling in cracked earth
Ringed by the flat horizon only
What is the city over the mountains
Cracks and reforms and bursts in the violet air
Falling towers
Jerusalem Athens Alexandria
Vienna London
Unreal
A woman drew her long black hair out tight
And fiddled whisper music on those strings
And bats with baby faces in the violet light
Whistled, and beat their wings
And crawled head downward down a blackened wall
And upside down in air were towers
Tolling reminiscent bells, that kept the hours
And voices singing out of empty cisterns

and exhausted wells.
In this decayed hole among the mountains
In the faint moonlight, the grass is singing
Over the tumbled graves, about the chapel
There is the empty chapel, only the wind's home.
It has no windows, and the door swings,
Dry bones can harm no one.
Only a cock stood on the rooftree
Co co rico co co rico 392
In a flash of lightning. Then a damp gust
Bringing rain
Ganga was sunken, and the limp leaves
Waited for rain, while the black clouds
Gathered far distant, over Himavant.
The jungle crouched, humped in silence.
Then spoke the thunder
DA
Datta: what have we given? 401
My friend, blood shaking my heart
The awful daring of a moment's surrender
Which an age of prudence can never retract
By this, and this only, we have existed
Which is not to be found in our obituaries
Or in memories draped by the beneficent spider 407
Or under seals broken by the lean solicitor
In our empty rooms
DA
Dayadhvam: I have heard the key
Turn in the door once and turn once only 411
We think of the key, each in his prison
thinking of the key, each confirms a prison
Only at nightfall, aethereal rumours
Revive for a moment a broken Coriolanus
DA
Damyata: The boat responded
Gaily, to the hand expert with sail and oar
The sea was calm, your heart would have responded
Gaily, when invited, beating obedient

To controlling hands
I sat upon the shore
Fishing, with the arid plain behind me 424
Shall I at least set my lands in order?
London Bridge is falling down falling down falling down
Poi s'ascose nel foco che gli affina 427
Quando fiam uti chelidon - O swallow swallow 428
Le Prince d'Aquitaine à la tour abolie 429
These fragments I have shored against my ruins
Why then Ile fit you. Hieronymo's mad againe. 431
Datta. Dayadhvam. Damyata. 401
Shantih shantih shantih 433

Chapter 9

Summary of the Text

The Waste Land Section I: "The Burial of the Dead"

Summary

The first section of The Waste Land takes its title from a line in the Anglican burial service. It is made up of four vignettes, each seemingly from the perspective of a different speaker. The first is an autobiographical snippet from the childhood of an aristocratic woman, in which she recalls sledding and claims that she is German, not Russian (this would be important if the woman is meant to be a member of the recently defeated Austrian imperial family). The woman mixes a meditation on the seasons with remarks on the barren state of her current existence ("I read, much of the night, and go south in the winter"). The second section is a prophetic, apocalyptic invitation to journey into a desert waste, where the speaker will show the reader "something different from either/Your shadow at morning striding behind you/Or your shadow at evening rising to meet you;/He will show you fear in a handful of dust" (Evelyn Waugh took the title for one of his best-known novels from these lines). The almost threatening prophetic tone is mixed with childhood reminiscences about a "hyacinth girl" and a nihilistic epiphany the speaker has after an encounter with her. These recollections are filtered through quotations from Wagner's operatic version of Tristan und Isolde, an Arthurian tale of adultery and loss. The third episode in this section describes an imaginative tarot reading, in which some of the cards Eliot includes in the reading are not part of an actual tarot deck. The final episode of the section is the most surreal. The speaker walks through a London populated by ghosts of the dead. He confronts a figure with whom he once fought in a battle that seems to conflate the clashes of World War 1 with the Punic Wars between Rome and Carthage (both futile and excessively destructive wars). The speaker asks the ghostly figure, Stetson, about the fate of a corpse planted in his garden. The episode concludes with a famous line from the preface to Baudelaire's Fleurs du Mal (an important collection of Symbolist poetry), accusing the reader of sharing in the poet's sins.

Form

Like "Prufrock," this section of The Waste Land can be seen as a modified dramatic monologue. The four speakers in this section are frantic in their need to speak, to find an audience, but they find themselves surrounded by dead people and thwarted by outside circumstances, like wars. Because the sections are so short and the situations so confusing, the effect is not one of an overwhelming impression of a single character; instead, the reader is left with the feeling of being trapped in a crowd, unable to find a familiar face.

Also like "Prufrock," The Waste Land employs only partial rhyme schemes and short bursts of structure. These are meant to reference—but also rework— the literary past, achieving simultaneously a stabilizing and a defamiliarizing effect. The world of The Waste Land has some parallels to an earlier time, but it cannot be approached in the same way. The inclusion of fragments in languages other than English further complicates matters. The reader is not expected to be able to translate these immediately; rather, they are reminders of the cosmopolitan nature of twentieth-century Europe and of mankind's fate after the Tower of Babel: We will never be able to perfectly comprehend one another.

Commentary

Not only is The Waste Land Eliot's greatest work, but it may be—along with Joyce's Ulysses—the greatest work of all modernist literature. Most of the poem was written in 1921, and it first appeared in print in 1922. As the poem's dedication indicates, Eliot received a great deal of guidance from Ezra Pound, who encouraged him to cut large sections of the planned work and to break up the rhyme scheme. Recent scholarship suggests that Eliot's wife, Vivien, also had a significant role in the poem's final form. A long work divided into five sections, The Waste Land takes on the degraded mess that Eliot considered modern culture to constitute, particularly after the first World War had ravaged Europe. A sign of the pessimism with which Eliot approaches his subject is the poem's epigraph, taken from the Satyricon, in which the Sibyl (a woman with prophetic powers who ages but never dies) looks at the future and proclaims that she only wants to die.

The Sibyl's predicament mirrors what Eliot sees as his own: He lives in a culture that has decayed and withered but will not expire, and he is forced to live with reminders of its former glory. Thus, the underlying plot of The Waste Land, inasmuch as it can be said to have one, revolves around Eliot's reading of two extraordinarily influential contemporary cultural/anthropological texts, Jessie Weston's From Ritual to Romance and Sir James Frazier's The Golden Bough.

Both of these works focus on the persistence of ancient fertility rituals in modern thought and religion; of particular interest to both authors is the story of the Fisher King, who has been wounded in the genitals and whose lack of potency is the cause of his country becoming a desiccated "waste land." Heal the Fisher King, the legend says, and the land will regain its fertility. According to Weston and Frazier, healing the Fisher King has been the subject of mythic tales from ancient Egypt to Arthurian England. Eliot picks up on the figure of the Fisher King legend's wasteland as an appropriate description of the state of modern society. The important difference, of course, is that in Eliot's world there is no way to heal the Fisher King; perhaps there is no Fisher King at all. The legend's imperfect integration into a modern meditation highlights the lack of a unifying narrative (like religion or mythology) in the modern world.

Eliot's poem, like the anthropological texts that inspired

it, draws on a vast range of sources. Eliot provided copious footnotes with the publication of The Waste Land in book form; these are an excellent source for tracking down the origins of a reference. Many of the references are from the Bible: at the time of the poem's writing Eliot was just beginning to develop an interest in Christianity that would reach its apex in the Four Quartets. The overall range of allusions in The Waste Land, though, suggests no overarching paradigm but rather a grab bag of broken fragments that must somehow be pieced together to form a coherent whole. While Eliot employs a deliberately difficult style and seems often to find the most obscure reference possible, he means to do more than just frustrate his reader and display his own intelligence: He intends to provide a mimetic account of life in the confusing world of the twentieth century.

The Waste Land opens with a reference to Chaucer's Canterbury Tales. In this case, though, April is not the happy month of pilgrimages and storytelling. It is instead the time when the land should be regenerating after a long winter. Regeneration, though, is painful, for it brings back reminders of a more fertile and happier past. In the modern world, winter, the time of forgetfulness and numbness, is indeed preferable. Marie's childhood recollections are also painful: the simple world of cousins, sledding, and coffee in the park has been replaced by a complex set of emotional and political consequences resulting from the war. The topic of memory, particularly when it involves remembering the dead, is of critical importance in The Waste Land. Memory creates a confrontation of the past with the present, a juxtaposition that points out just how badly things have decayed. Marie reads for most of the night: ostracized by politics, she is unable to do much else. To read is also to remember a better past, which could produce a coherent literary culture.

The second episode contains a troubled religious proposition. The speaker describes a true wasteland of "stony rubbish"; in it, he says, man can recognize only " heap of broken images." Yet the scene seems to offer salvation: shade and a vision of something new and different. The vision consists only of nothingness—a handful of dust—which is so profound as to be frightening; yet truth also resides here: No longer a religious phenomenon achieved through Christ, truth is represented by a mere void. The speaker remembers a female figure from his past, with whom he has apparently had some sort of romantic involvement. In contrast to the present setting in the desert, his memories are lush, full of water and blooming flowers. The vibrancy of the earlier scene, though, leads the speaker to a revelation of the nothingness he now offers to show the reader. Again memory serves to contrast the past with the present, but here it also serves to explode the idea of coherence in either place.

In the episode from the past, the "nothingness" is more clearly a sexual failure, a moment of impotence. Despite the overall fecundity and joy of the moment, no reconciliation, and, therefore, no action, is possible. This in turn leads directly to the desert waste of the present. In the final line of the episode attention turns from the desert to the sea. Here, the sea is not a locus for the fear of nothingness, and neither is it the locus for a philosophical interpretation of nothingness; rather, it is the site of true, essential nothingness itself. The line comes from a section of Tristan und Isolde where Tristan waits for Isolde to come heal him. She is supposedly coming by ship but fails to arrive. The ocean is truly empty, devoid of the possibility of healing or revelation.

The third episode explores Eliot's fascination with transformation. The tarot reader Madame Sosostris conducts the most outrageous form of "reading" possible, transforming a series of vague symbols into predictions, many of which will come true in succeeding sections of the poem. Eliot transforms the traditional tarot pack to serve his purposes. The drowned sailor makes reference to the ultimate work of magic and transformation in English literature, Shakespeare's The Tempest ("Those are pearls that were his eyes" is a quote from one of Ariel's songs). Transformation in The Tempest, though, is the result of the highest art of humankind. Here, transformation is associated with fraud, vulgarity, and cheap mysticism. That Madame Sosostris will prove to be right in her predictions of death and transformation is a direct commentary on the failed religious mysticism and prophecy of the preceding desert section. The final episode of the first section allows Eliot finally to establish the true wasteland of the poem, the modern city. Eliot's London references Baudelaire's Paris ("Unreal City"), Dickens's London ("the brown fog of a winter dawn") and Dante's hell ("the flowing crowd of the dead"). The city is desolate and depopulated, inhabited only by ghosts from the past. Stetson, the apparition the speaker recognizes, is a fallen war comrade. The speaker pesters him with a series of ghoulish questions about a corpse buried in his garden: again, with the garden, we return to the theme of regeneration and fertility. This encounter can be read as a quest for a meaning behind the tremendous slaughter of the first World War; however, it can also be read as an exercise in ultimate futility: as we see in Stetson's failure to respond to the speaker's inquiries, the dead offer few answers. The great respective weights of history, tradition, and the poet's dead predecessors combine to create an oppressive burden.

The Waste Land Section II: "A Game of Chess"

Summary

This section takes its title from two plays by the early 17th-century playwright Thomas Middleton, in one of which the moves in a game of chess denote stages in a seduction. This section focuses on two opposing scenes, one of high society and one of the lower classes. The first half of the section portrays a wealthy, highly groomed woman surrounded by exquisite furnishings. As she waits for a lover, her neurotic thoughts become frantic, meaningless cries. Her day culminates with plans for an excursion and a game of chess. The second part of this section shifts to a London barroom, where two women discuss a third woman.

Between the bartender's repeated calls of "HURRY UP PLEASE IT'S TIME" (the bar is closing for the night) one of the women recounts a conversation with their friend Lil, whose husband has just been discharged from the army. She has chided Lil over her failure to get herself some false teeth, telling her that her husband will seek out the company of other women if she doesn't improve her appearance. Lil claims that the cause of her ravaged looks is the medication she took to induce an abortion; having nearly died giving birth to her fifth child, she had refused to have another, but her husband "won't leave her alone." The women leave the bar to a chorus of "good night" reminiscent of Ophelia's farewell speech in Hamlet.

Form

The first part of the section is largely in unrhymed iambic pentameter lines, or blank verse. As the section proceeds, the lines become increasingly irregular in length and meter, giving the feeling of disintegration, of things falling apart. As the woman of the first half begins to give voice to her paranoid thoughts, things do fall apart, at least formally: We read lines of dialogue, then a snippet from a nonsense song. The last four lines of the first half rhyme, although they are irregular in meter, suggesting at least a partial return to stability.

The second half of the section is a dialogue interrupted by the barman's refrain. Rather than following an organized structure of rhyme and meter, this section constitutes a loose series of phrases connected by "I said" and "she said." This is perhaps the most poetically experimental section of the entire poem. Eliot is writing in a lower-class vernacular here that resists poetic treatment. This section refutes the prevalent claim that iambic pentameter mirrors normal English speech patterns: Line length and stresses are consistently irregular. Yet the section sounds like poetry: the repeated use of "I said" and the grounding provided by the barman's chorus allow the woman's speech to flow elegantly, despite her rough phrasing and the coarse content of her story.

Commentary

The two women of this section of the poem represent the two sides of modern sexuality: while one side of this sexuality is a dry, barren interchange inseparable from neurosis and self-destruction, the other side of this sexuality is a rampant fecundity associated with a lack of culture and rapid aging. The first woman is associated by allusion with Cleopatra, Dido, and even Keats's Lamia, by virtue of the lushness of language surrounding her (although Eliot would never have acknowledged Keats as an influence). She is a frustrated, overly emotional but not terribly intellectual figure, oddly sinister, surrounded by "strange synthetic perfumes" and smoking candles. She can be seen as a counterpart to the title character of Eliot's earlier "Love Song of J. Alfred Prufrock," with whom she shares both a physical setting and a profound sense of isolation. Her association with Dido and Cleopatra, two women who committed suicide out of frustrated love, suggests her fundamental irrationality.

Unlike the two queens of myth, however, this woman will never become a cultural touchstone. Her despair is pathetic, rather than moving, as she demands that her lover stay with her and tell her his thoughts. The lover, who seems to be associated with the narrator of this part of the poem, can think only of drowning (again, in a reference to The Tempest) and rats among dead men's bones. The woman is explicitly compared to Philomela, a character out of Ovid's Metamorphoses who is raped by her brother-in-law the king, who then cuts her tongue out to keep her quiet.

She manages to tell her sister, who helps her avenge herself by murdering the king's son and feeding him to the king. The sisters are then changed into birds, Philomela into a nightingale. This comparison suggests something essentially disappointing about the woman, that she is unable to communicate her interior self to the world. The woman and her surroundings, although aesthetically pleasing, are ultimately sterile and meaningless, as suggested by the nonsense song that she sings (which manages to debase even Shakespeare). The second scene in this section further diminishes the possibility that sex can bring regeneration—either cultural or personal. This section is remarkably free of the cultural allusions that dominate the rest of the poem; instead, it relies on vernacular speech to make its point. Notice that Eliot is using a British vernacular: By this point he had moved to England permanently and had become a confirmed Anglophile. Although Eliot is able to produce startlingly beautiful poetry from the rough speech of the women in the bar, he nevertheless presents their conversation as further reason for pessimism. Their friend Lil has done everything the right way—married, supported her soldier husband, borne children—yet she is being punished by her body. Interestingly, this section ends with a line echoing Ophelia's suicide speech in Hamlet; this links Lil to the woman in the first section of the poem, who has also been compared to famous female suicides. The comparison between the two is not meant to suggest equality between them or to propose that the first woman's exaggerated sense of high culture is in any way equivalent to the second woman's lack of it; rather, Eliot means to suggest that neither woman's form of sexuality is regenerative.

The Waste Land Section III: "The Fire Sermon"

Summary

The title of this, the longest section of The Waste Land, is taken from a sermon given by Buddha in which he encourages his followers to give up earthly passion (symbolized by fire) and seek freedom from earthly things. A turn away from the earthly does indeed take place in this section, as a series of increasingly debased sexual encounters concludes with a river song and a religious incantation. The section opens with a desolate riverside scene: Rats and garbage urround the speaker, who is fishing and "musing on the king my brother's wreck." The river-song begins in this section, with the refrain from Spenser's Prothalamion: "Sweet Thames, run softly till I end my song." A snippet from a vulgar soldier's ballad follows, then a reference back to Philomela (see the previous section). The speaker is then propositioned by Mr. Eugenides, the one-eyed merchant of Madame Sosostris's tarot pack. Eugenides invites the speaker to go with him to a hotel known as a meeting place for homosexual trysts.

The speaker then proclaims himself to be Tiresias, a figure

from classical mythology who has both male and female features ("Old man with wrinkled female breasts") and is blind but can "see" into the future. Tiresias/the speaker observes a young typist, at home for tea, who awaits her lover, a dull and slightly arrogant clerk. The woman allows the clerk to have his way with her, and he leaves victorious. Tiresias, who has "foresuffered all," watches the whole thing. After her lover's departure, the typist thinks only that she's glad the encounter is done and over.

A brief interlude begins the river-song in earnest. First, a fisherman's bar is described, then a beautiful church interior, then the Thames itself. These are among the few moments of tranquility in the poem, and they seem to represent some sort of simpler alternative. The Thames-daughters, borrowed from Spenser's poem, chime in with a nonsense chorus ("Weialala leia/Wallala leialala"). The scene shifts again, to Queen Elizabeth I in an amorous encounter with the Earl of Leicester. The queen seems unmoved by her lover's declarations, and she thinks only of her "people humble people who expect/ Nothing." The section then comes to an abrupt end with a few lines from St. Augustine's Confessions and a vague reference to the Buddha's Fire Sermon ("burning").

Form

This section of The Waste Land is notable for its inclusion of popular poetic forms, particularly musical ones. The more plot-driven sections are in Eliot's usual assortment of various line lengths, rhymed at random. "The Fire Sermon," however, also includes bits of many musical pieces, including Spenser's wedding song (which becomes the song of the Thames-daughters), a soldier's ballad, a nightingale's chirps, a song from Oliver Goldsmith's The Vicar of Wakefield, and a mandolin tune (which has no words but is echoed in "a clatter and a chatter from within").

The use of such "low" forms cuts both ways here: In one sense, it provides a critical commentary on the episodes described, the cheap sexual encounters shaped by popular culture (the gramophone, the men's hotel).

But Eliot also uses these bits and pieces to create high art, and some of the fragments he uses (the lines from Spenser in particular) are themselves taken from more exalted forms. In the case of the Prothalamion, in fact, Eliot is placing himself within a tradition stretching back to ancient Greece (classically, "prothalamion" is a generic term for a poem-like song written for a wedding).

Again this provides an ironic contrast to the debased goings-on but also provides another form of connection and commentary. Another such reference, generating both ironic distance and proximate parallels, is the inclusion of Elizabeth I: The liaison between Elizabeth and Leicester is traditionally romanticized, and, thus, the reference seems to clash with the otherwise sordid nature of this section. However, Eliot depicts Elizabeth—and Spenser, for that matter—as a mere fragment, stripped of noble connotations and made to represent just one more piece of cultural rubbish. Again, this is not meant to be a democratizing move but a nihilistic one: Romance is dead.

Commentary

The opening two stanzas of this section describe the ultimate "Waste Land" as Eliot sees it. The wasteland is cold, dry, and barren, covered in garbage. Unlike the desert, which at least burns with heat, this place is static, save for a few scurrying rats. Even the river, normally a symbol of renewal, has been reduced to a "dull canal." The ugliness stands in implicit contrast to the "Sweet Thames" of Spenser's time. The most significant image in these lines, though, is the rat. Like the crabs in Prufrock, rats are scavengers, taking what they can from the refuse of higher-order creatures. The rat could be said to provide a model for Eliot's poetic process: Like the rat, Eliot takes what he can from earlier, grander generations and uses the bits and pieces to sustain life. Somehow this is preferable to the more coherent but vulgar existence of the contemporary world, here represented by the sound of horns and motors in the distance, intimating a sexual liaison.

The actual sexual encounters that take place in this section of the poem are infinitely unfruitful. Eugenides proposes a homosexual tryst, which by its very nature thwarts fertility. The impossibility of regeneration by such means is symbolized by the currants in his pocket—the desiccated, deadened version of what were once plump, fertile fruits. The typist and her lover are equally barren in their way, even though reproduction is at least theoretically possible for the two. Living in so impoverished a manner that she does not even own a bed, the typist is certainly not interested in a family. Elizabeth and Leicester are perhaps the most interesting of the three couples, however.

For political reasons, Elizabeth was required to represent herself as constantly available for marriage (to royalty from countries with whom England may have wanted an alliance); out of this need came the myth of the "Virgin Queen." This can be read as the opposite of the Fisher King legend: To protect the vitality of the land, Elizabeth had to compromise her own sexuality; whereas in the Fisher King story, the renewal of the land comes with the renewal of the Fisher King's sexual potency. Her tryst with Leicester, therefore, is a consummation that is simultaneously denied, an event that never happened. The twisted logic underlying Elizabeth's public sexuality, or lack thereof, mirrors and distorts the Fisher King plot and further questions the possibility for renewal, especially through sexuality, in the modern world.

Tiresias, thus, becomes an important model for modern existence. Neither man nor woman, and blind yet able to see with ultimate clarity, he is an individual who does not hope or act. He has, like Prufrock, "seen it all," but, unlike Prufrock, he sees no possibility for action. Whereas Prufrock is paralyzed by his neuroses, Tiresias is held motionless by ennui and pragmatism.

He is not quite able to escape earthly things, though, for he is forced to sit and watch the sordid deeds of mortals; like the Sibyl in the poem's epigraph, he would like to die but cannot. The brief interlude following the typist's tryst may offer an alternative to escape, by describing a warm, everyday scene of work and companionship; however, the interlude is brief, and Eliot once again tosses us into a world of sex and strife. Tiresias disappears, to be replaced by St. Augustine at the end of the section. Eliot claims in his footnote to have deliberately conflated Augustine and the Buddha, as the representatives of Eastern and Western asceticism. Both seem, in the lines Eliot quotes, to be unable to transcend the world on their own: Augustine must call on God to "pluck him out," while Buddha can only repeat the word "burning," unable to break free of its monotonous fascination. The poem's next section, which will relate the story of a death without resurrection, exposes the absurdity of these two figures' faith in external higher powers. That this section ends with only the single word "burning," isolated on the page, reveals the futility of all of man's struggles

The Waste Land Section IV: "Death by Water"

Summary

The shortest section of the poem, "Death by Water" describes a man, Phlebas the Phoenician, who has died, apparently by drowning. In death he has forgotten his worldly cares as the creatures of the sea have picked his body apart. The narrator asks his reader to consider Phlebas and recall his or her own mortality.

Form

While this section appears on the page as a ten-line stanza, in reading, it compresses into eight: four pairs of rhyming couplets Both visually and audibly, this is one of the most formally organized sections of the poem. It is meant to recall other highly organized forms that often have philosophical or religious import, like aphorisms and parables. The alliteration and the deliberately archaic language ("o you," "a fortnight dead") also contribute to the serious, didactic feel of this section.

Commentary

The major point of this short section is to rebut ideas of renewal and regeneration. Phlebas just dies; that's it. Like Stetson's corpse in the first section, Phlebas's body yields nothing more than products of decay. However, the section's meaning is far from flat; indeed, its ironic layering is twofold. First, this section fulfills one of the prophecies of Madame Sosostris in the poem's first section: "Fear death by water," she says, after pulling the card of the Drowned Sailor. Second, this section, in its language and form, mimics other literary forms (parables, biblical stories, etc.) that are normally rich in meaning. These two features suggest that something of great significance lies here. In reality, though, the only lesson that Phlebas offers is that the physical reality of death and decay triumphs over all. Phlebas is not resurrected or transfigured. Eliot further emphasizes Phlebas's dried-up antiquity and irrelevance by placing this section in the distant past (by making Phlebas a Phoenician).

Chapter 10

Study Questions

Q. Discuss the images used in The Waste Land

Or

Q. Do you think T. S. Eliot's writing style is very esoteric, having very hidden meanings in every single word?

In T. S. Eliot's The Waste Land one may
perceive many images from the
writing style he uses. In lines 386 - 399 he writes:
In this decayed hole among the mountains
In the faint moonlight, the grass is singing
Over the tumbled graves, about the chapel
There is the empty chapel, only the wind's home.
It has no windows, and the door swings,
Dry bones can harm no one.
Only a cock stood on the rooftree
Co co rico co co rico
In a flash of lightning. Then a damp gust
Bringing rain
Ganga was sunken, and the limp leaves
Waited for rain, while the black clouds
Gathered far distant, over Himavant.
The jungle crouched, humped in silence.

In these lines he seems to tell of a graveyard near a chapel in an upcoming storm. Different images can be seen from the decayed hole in the moonlight, the empty chapel without windows, and the rooster's crows as the lightning and black clouds arrive.

In line 386, "In this decayed hole among the mountains," probably refers to an empty grave that brings images of death and the end of life, or possibly the beginning of a new life to mind. The grave is lit by moonlight, possibly referring to the white light many people see when they have near-death experiences. You get a creepy feeling when the wind blows and makes the "grass sing" in line 387. In these first three lines it talks of tumbled graves, possibly disturbed by nature, which could tell of troubled lives, or a troubled second life. The empty chapel without windows is nearby, as you perceive from lines 389 and 390:

There is the empty chapel, only the wind's home.
It has no windows, and the door swings

It's image makes you shiver. It could possibly represent itself, in the sense that many people die there, as in baptism, as well as dying, where this place may be the starting point for a second, never-ending life. The chapel has no windows, maybe so that the people inside would not loose focus from the sermon. The chapel could represent death as well, since you go in and cannot look back out.

The rooster in lines 392 and 393 may symbolize the beginning of another day, or another life. Roosters crow in the early morning to wake people up and to alert that a new day has begun. However, the rooster's crow, "Co co rico co co rico," in line 393 may just be here to foreshadow the upcoming weather. It has been said that certain animals can sense bad weather, and as the rooster crows, dark clouds and lightning arrive, which may show that death is near.

This part of the poem seems to display rebirth. Many images, from the grave to the lightning, describe death as well as birth, possiblyCforeshadowing birth and rebirth. T. S. Eliot's writing style is very esoteric, having very hidden meanings in every single word.

Q. Do you think that "All is Not Well in The Waste Land"

Or

Q. Discuss that the poem The Waste Land does not offer a cause or an explanation

Eliot's "The Waste Land" doesn't make sense. No matter how many symbols and allusions are explained by critics or Eliot himself, no matter how many fertility gods and Eastern philosophies are dragged into it, the poem does not make sense. But then, it doesn't need to in order to be good or to have a purpose. All it needs is to have meaning, and something need not make sense to mean something. The meaning "The Waste Land" holds for me is of something wrong - something so twisted and "rotten," as to be intrinsically wrong. For me, this wrongness winds itself in and out of the passages and images of the poem and doesn't seem to have any hope of being righted until the end - in the last few lines.

In every time, in every place in "The Waste Land," something is wrong. The world of the poem is one where April, the season when growing things return after winter, is "the cruellest month, breeding/Lilacs out of the dead land," the "son of man" knows only "a heap of broken images," and there is "fear in a handful of dust." Each symbol and each allusion contains a grotesque element - one that was already there or one incorporated by Eliot. Lines 72-73 are such a nice, normal way to speak about a garden ("'Has it begun to sprout? Will it bloom this year?/'Or has the sudden frost disturbed its bed?'"), except that the thing which has been planted is a corpse, and it's in danger of being dug up by a Dog.

T'ie different ways of looking at life are all tainted. Someone says, "'I shall rush out as I am, and walk the street/ 'With my hair down, so. What shall we do tomorrow?/'What shall we ever do'?'" The talkative woman gossips of the problems in another woman's marriage and of her abortion, ending with the last words of Ophelia, spoken in her madness. Tiresias, the blind prophet, foretells the scene of a woman who endures the caresses of her lover, and, glad when they are over and he is gone, forgets about the incident entirely. She merely "puts a record on the gramophone." The descriptions are often shocking and ugly, especially in the midst of a beautiful scene. "The river sweats/Oil and tar/The barges drift/With the turning tide/Red sails/Wide/To leeward, swing on the heavy spar." In a place of mountains, "there is not even solitude.../But red sullen faces sneer and snarl/From doors of mudcracked houses." Other things point to the wrongness that pervades the poem. The mountains are all rock, and there is no water

("If there were water/And no rock/If there were rock/And also water"). And what if there were? "But there is no water." The poem does not answer its own questic ı, maybe because the presence of water would make things ˌight. The end of "The Waste Land" seems to hold some comfort, some hope that the wrongness in the world need not be perpetuated. "Shall I at least set my lands in order?/...Datta. Dayadhvam. Damyata./ Shantih shantih shantih." The poem does not offer a cause or an explanation - a reason why, - nor does it have any real solution, but it seems to me that each situation presented in Eliot's "The Waste Land" is another way of showing how all is not as it should be and never has been, although there is a possibility that it could be.

Q. "The memory itself becomes a waste".Discuss

Or

Q. How does Eliot show that no life can ever be brought to a dead land in The Waste Land

As The Waste Land begins, Eliot enters into the barren land, which the audience journeys across with the author through the course of the poem. "The roots that clutch" immediately evoke a feeling of desperation. Roots in the rocky soil Eliot describes are a base from which to grow; just as roots in plants gain nourishment from soil, these roots "clutch" infertile ground, desperately seeking something to gain from nothing. The question "what branches grow" suggests skepticism as to life's ability to survive in "stony rubbish," the waste that offers no forgiveness.

"You know only a heap of broken images" alludes to memory. Memory can be a composite of many smaller memories, creating discontinuity. "Broken images" are similar to the entire poem, which has a tendency to jump between snippets of different lives and desolate imagery of a desert waste. Eliot creates a memory lacking value for its indistinctness. Because only "broken images" exist, the memory itself becomes a waste. Just as life cannot grow in a barren land, people cannot be whole without coherent memories to identify with. The incomplete memory also suggests aging: as a person grows closer to death, all of the images accumulated throughout life gradually fade and break apart. Some things are forgotten, and others begin to meld together. The audience is reminded again of the absence of life with "the dead tree gives no shelter." The "dead tree" can no longer offer protection as it once might have. There is no comfort in death, especially if after death there is no rebirth, or new life. "The dry stone no sound of water" provides still more images of a forsaken land. "No sound of water" is particularly important. The lack of water ensures the lifelessness. Life cannot exist without water; however, water can also destroy life.

Eliot suggests that water cannot only provide life, but it can take it. Drowning is mentioned more than once in The Waste Land. This particular selection seems to require water for life. Later images of drowning, as in 4. Death by Water, are not necessarily suggesting the kind of lifelessness present in the desert imagery. Dying by water, a life-giving force, perhaps offers the rebirth Eliot seeks throughout this poem. "I will show you something different from either/Your shadow at morning striding behind you/Or your shadow at evening rising to meet you."

These lines point east, facing the rising sun. This alludes to Eastern philosophy, which Eliot explores extensively later in the poem. The importance of facing the rising sun goes beyond religion; it is a more pleasant image than the waste, it provides hope and looks positively at the future. However, Eliot wishes to convey emotions different from hope. Eliot offers "fear in a handful of dust," extinguishing any hope the previous lines may have evoked. The dust of the desert soil is infertile; no life can grow from such dry soil. There is finality in this line: no life can ever be brought to a dead land.

Q. Do you think the borrowed motifs in The Waste Land are shown to have themselves been borrowed by a succession of Cultures.

Or

Q. Do you think Eliot's poem eludes a literary grasp.

The Waste Land is, to begin with, a poem that includes an interpretation as part of the poem, and it is therefore a poem that makes a problem of its meaning precisely by virtue of its apparent (and apparently inadequate) effort to explain itself. We cannot understand the poem without knowing what it meant to its author, but we must also assume that what the poem meant to its author will not be its meaning. The notes to The Waste Land are, by the logic of Eliot's philosophical critique of interpretation, simply another riddle—and not a separate one to be solved. They are, we might say, the poem's way of treating itself as a reflex, a "something not intended as a sign," a gesture whose full significance it is impossible, by virtue of the nature of gestures, for the gesturer to explain."

And the structure of the poem—a text followed by an explanation—is a reproduction of a pattern that, as the notes themselves emphasize, is repeated in miniature many times inside the poem itself, where cultural expressions are transformed, by the mechanics of allusion, into cultural gestures. For each time a literary phrase or a cultural motif is transposed into a new context—and the borrowed motifs in The Waste Land are shown to have themselves been borrowed by a succession of cultures—it is reinterpreted, its previous meaning becoming incorporated by distortion into a new meaning suitable to a new use.

So that the work of Frazer and Weston is relevant both because it presents the history of religion as a series of appropriations and reinscriptions of cultural motifs, and because it is itself an unreliable reinterpretation of the phenomena it attempts to describe. The poem is, in other words, not about spiritual dryness so much as it is about the ways in which spiritual dryness has been perceived. And the relation of the notes to the poem proper seems further emblematic of the relation of the work as a whole to the cultural tradition it is a commentary on. The Waste Land is presented as a contemporary reading of the Western tradition, which (unlike the "ideal order" of "Tradition and the Individual Talent") is treated as a sequence of gestures whose original meaning is unknown, but which every new text that is added to it makes a bad guess at.

The author of the notes seems to class himself with the

cultural anthropologists whose work he cites. He reads the poem as a coherent expression of the spiritual condition of the social group in which it was produced. But the author of th poem, we might say, does not enjoy this luxury of detachme t. He seems, in fact, determined to confound, even at the cos of his own sense of coherence, the kind of interpretive kn wingness displayed by the author of the notes.

The author of the poem classes himself with the diseased characters of his own work—the clairvoyants with a cold, the woman whose nerves are bad, the king whose insanity may or may not be feigned. He cannot distinguish what he intends to reveal about himself from what he cannot help revealing: he would like to believe that his poem is expressive of some general reality, but he fears that it is only the symptom of a private disorder. For when he looks to the culture around him, everything appears only as a reflection of his own breakdown: characters and objects metamorphose up and down the evolutionary scale; races and religions lose their purity ("Bin gar keine Russin, stamm' aus Litauen, echt deutsch"); an adulterated "To His Coy Mistress" describes the tryst between Sweeney and Mrs. Porter, and a fragmented Tempest frames the liaison of the typist and the young man carbuncular; "London bridge is falling down."

The poem itself, as a literary object, seems an imitation of this vision of degeneration: nothing in it can be said to point to the poet, since none of its stylistic features is continuous, and it has no phrases or images that cannot be suspected of—where they are not in fact identified as—belonging to someone else. The Waste Land appears to be a poem designed to make trouble for the conceptual mechanics not just of ordinary reading (for what poem does not try to disrupt those mechanics?) but of literary reading. For insofar as reading a piece of writing as literature is understood to mean reading it for its style, Eliot's poem eludes a literary grasp.

Q. Discuss the underlying myths in The Waste Land

Or

Q. Do you think "the poem's focus is on negation as a philosophically meditated position."

The underlying myths that Eliot uses to provide a framework for "The Waste Land" are those of the Fisher King and the Grail Quest. Both of these myths come to Christian civilization through the ancient Gaelic tradition. Neither is found in the Bible, but both were important enough to Europeans that there was a need to incorporate them into the new European mythology, and so the stories became centered on the story of the death and resurrection of Jesus. Other examples of these myths can be found in Eschenbach's Parsifal, in de Troyes' Quest of the Grail, and in the various stories of the grail quest surrounding King Arthur and his knights. It is described in works of anthropology, as well, two of which Eliot recommends to readers: Jessie L. Weston's From Ritual to Romance and Sir James Frazier's Golden Bough.

In the Fisher King stories, a journeyer comes to a barren land and discovers a wounded king whose wound has caused the land to become sterile. In some cases, the wounding of the king was sexual in nature. Because these ancient peoples believed that the king and the land were united as one and that they reflected on each other, it was necessary to heal the king in order to heal the land. The journeyer then needs to undertake a quest (which fits the archetypal hero's journey pattern) to heal the wounded king and, through him, the land. In the Grail legends, which are frequently intertwined with the Fisher King legends, a questor searches throughout the land for the Holy Grail, undergoing tests of purity, his character, and his dedication to the quest on the way.

The nature of the Grail differs from one account to another: It is sometimes thought of as a cup which caught the blood of Christ when he was pierced by a spear while hanging on the cross (which may be derived from the Celtic legends describing the Grail as a cauldron of rebirth which allowed resurrection to warriors killed in battle but did not allow them to speak of the experience of rebirth — a pattern into which the story of Lazarus roughly falls), and it is sometimes thought to be a stone (in Eschenbach's Parsifal, the Grail is described as a gem struck from the crown of Lucifer when he was ejected from Heaven).

Perhaps the most important way that Eliot uses these underlying myths in "The Waste Land" to comment on the modern world is to describe modern cultural emptiness within the context of ancient myths of a heroic quest that gives meaning and relevance to life. By doing so, Eliot points out the simple fact of this cultural emptiness and its accompanying spiritual dryness and gives hints throughout the poem of where an individual can search for remedies to it.

"These fragments I have shored against my ruins," writes Eliot in line 431. The entire poem can be seen as a collection of "fragments" which provide hints in various ways, especially through the many and diverse literary references that Eliot uses to suggest works that the reader can examine to see how others have attempted their own heroic quests for meaningful existence. Eliot uses the fragmentary descriptions of cultural emptiness and many juxtapositions with descriptions of past cultural richness to point to what he calls the "disassociation of sensibilities" — the unhinging of the connection of heart and mind in, for instance, modern science.

The Waste Land: A New Understanding: The Waste Land, Eliot's first long philosophical poem, can now be read simply as it was written, as a poem of radical doubt and negation, urging that every human desire be stilled except the desire for self-surrender, for restraint, and for peace. Compared with the longing expressed in later poems for the "eyes" and the "birth," the "coming" and "the Lady" (in "The Hollow Men," the Ariel poems, and "Ash-Wednesday"), the hope held out in The Waste Land is a negative one. Following Hugh Kenner's recommendation, we should lay to rest the persistent error of reading The Waste Land as a poem in which five motifs predominate: the nightmare journey, the Chapel, the Quester, the Grail Legend, and the Fisher King.

The motifs are indeed introduced, as Eliot's preliminary note to his text informs us, but if (as this note says) "the plan and a good deal of the incidental symbolism of the poem were suggested by Miss Jessie L. Weston's book on the Grail legend," the plan can only have been to question, and even to propose a life without hope for, a quest, or Chapel, or Grail in the modern waste land. The themes of interior prison and nightmare city—or the "urban apocalypse" elucidated by Kenner and Eleanor Cook—make much better sense when seen as furnishing the centripetal "plan" and "symbolism," especially when one follows Cook's discussion of the disintegration of all European cities after the First World War and the poem's culminating vision of a new Carthaginian collapse, imagined from the vantage point of India's holy men. A passage canceled in the manuscript momentarily suggested that the ideal city, forever unrealizable on earth, might be found (as Plato thought) "in another world," but the reference was purely sardonic.

Nowhere in the poem can one find convincing allusions to any existence in another world, much less to St. Augustine's vision of interpenetration between the City of God and the City of Man in this world. How, then, can one take seriously attempts to find in the poem any such quest for eternal life as the Grail legend would have to provide if it were a continuous motif—even a sardonic one?

It seems that only since Eliot's death is it possible to read his life forward—understanding The Waste Land as it was written, without being deflected by our knowledge of the writer's later years. Before Eliot's death the tendency was to read the poem proleptically—as if reflecting the poems f the later period. This is how Cleanth Brooks, writing the first fully elucidative essay on The Waste Land, read it, stressing the Grail legends, the longing for new life, rather than the purely negative aspects of the theme. Thus Brooks interpreted the Sibyl's appeal for death at the beginning of the poem as exactly parallel to the Magus's appetite for death in the Ariel poems (the Magus's, of course, filled with the pain of knowing that Christ had subjected himself to weak mortality and not knowing yet the Resurrection).

To make the Sibyl and the Magus parallel was to read Eliot's development backward—perhaps an irresistible temptation when the pattern in his life was so little known and when (as then in 1939) Brooks was acquainted with the man at work on Four Quartets, who had recently produced the celebrated Murder in the Cathedral. It was also irresistible, in a culture still nominally Christian, to hope that The Waste Land was about a world in which God was not dead. But the poem was not about such a world.

Within ten years after finishing The Waste Land, Eliot recognized that the poem had made him into the leader of a new "way." His own words of 1931, however, require us to read the poem as having pushed this roadway through to its end—for him. It was no Grail quest. Those who followed him into it, and stayed on it, he said in "Thoughts After Lambeth," "are now pious pilgrims, cheerfully plodding the road from nowhere to nowhere." There could be no more decisive reference to the negative way he had followed till 1922, and also to the impasse where it ended.

A good reading of The Waste Land must begin, then, with recognition that while it expressed Eliot's own "way" at the time, it was not intended to lay down a way for others to follow. He did not expect that his prisonhouse would have corridors connecting with everyone else's. "I dislike the word 'generation' he said in "Thoughts After Lambeth"), which has been a talisman for the last ten years; when I wrote a poem called The Waste Land some of the more approving critics said that I had expressed the 'disillusionment of a generation,' which is nonsense. I may have expressed for them their own illusion of being disillusioned, but that did not form part of my intention." Dismay at finding his personal, interior journey (which he later called "rhythmic grumbling") converted into a superhighway seems to have been one of the main impulses toward his discovery of a new way after 1922.

If we listen attentively to the negations of The Waste Land, they tell us much about the poem that was missed when it was read from the affirmative point of view brought to it by its early defenders and admirers. Ironically, it was only its detractors—among them Eliot's friend Conrad Aiken—who acknowledged its deliberate vacuity and incoherence and the life-questioning theme of this first venture into "philosophical" poetry on Eliot's part. Aiken considered its incoherence a virtue because its subject was incoherence, but this was cool comfort either to himself or to Eliot, who was outraged by Aiken's opinion that the poem was "melancholy." It was far from being a sad poem—like the nineteenth-century poems that Eliot had criticized precisely because of their wan melancholias, based as he said on their excesses of desire over the possibilities that life can afford. Neither Aiken, who found the poem disappointing, nor I. A. Richards, who was exhilarated by its rejection of all "belief, " spotted the poem's focus on negation as a philosophically meditated position.

Q. What is the current relevance of The Waste Land

Or

Q. What are the three practices that Eliot suggests as cures for the ills plaguing the waste land.

Eliot's poem, The Waste Land, is at least as relevant to life today as it was in 1922, when it was first published. All of the themes stated at the beginning of the Norton Anthology's introduction to the poem ("spiritual dryness," a lack of "regenerating belief" to give meaning to life, and deat without resurrection) are with us to an even greater degree than they were at the time the poem was first published. The attit des toward sexuality that are implicitly condemned throughout he work have not changed in any way that Eliot would be likely to see as an improvement, either.

"The Waste Land" does not merely present an anthropological description of a culture, however, and the solution proposed by Eliot seems as relevant today as it must have been in 1922. Like Blake, Eliot constructs a personal mythology, but Eliot draws on a larger number of sources than Blake does: various religions from both the east and the west, works of literature from around the world, and works of philosophy and anthropology. Eliot refers to the fragmentary references throughout the poem at the end of the poem by saying, "These fragments I have shored against my ruins" — that is, Eliot has taken fragmentary references and pieced them together in an attempt to come to grips with the modern situation in which he finds himself. (line 431) The references from the poem are nearly always references to the past, when a cultural heritage was common to an entire people, the themes described in the Norton Anthology's introduction were nonexistent (or were problematic to a much lesser degree than in the modern era), and when sexuality found its expression in a context Eliot would have seen as appropriate — a mature relationship between men and women that expresses both love and physical passion.

Perhaps more important than the building of this personal mythology, however, is the solution Eliot explicitly offers in "What the Thunder Said." Eliot weaves in a Hindu story in which gods, devils, and humans each ask their common father, Prajapati, for advice. Prajapati replies to each with the single syllable da, which is interpreted as Datta, Dayadhvam, and Damyata — Hindu words meaning "to give alms," "to sympathize with others," and "to practice self-control." Eliot suggests these three practices as cures for the ills plaguing the waste land. Each of these practices also addresses the problems that the introduction in the Norton Anthology explains as major themes of the poem and leads to an emotion that Eliot closes the poem with: "the peace that passeth understanding."

Q. Do you think that there is truth through complexity in The Waste Land

Or

Q. Do you think symbols represent dramatized instances of the theme in The Waste Land

The basic method used in The Waste Land may be described as the application of the principle of complexity. T S Eliot uses a parallel structure on the surface to develop an ironic contrast, and then uses surface contrasts in a parallel form. To the reader, this gives the effect of chaotic experience ordered into a new whole, though the realistic surface of experience is faithfully retained. The fortune-telling of "The Burial of the Dead" will illustrate the general method very satisfactorily. On the surface of the poem the poet reproduces the patter of the charlatan, Madame Sosostris, and there is the surface irony: the contrast between the original use of the Tarot cards and the use made by Madame Sosostris. But each of the details (justified realistically in the palaver of the fortune-teller) assumes a new meaning in the general context of the poem.

There is then, in addition to the surface irony, something of a Sophoclean irony too, and the "fortune-telling," which is taken ironically by a twentieth-century audience, becomes true as the poem develops—true in a sense in which Madame Sosostris herself does not think it true. The surface irony is thus reversed and becomes an irony on a deeper level. The items of her speech have only one reference in terms of the context of her speech: the "man with three staves," the "one-eyed merchant," the "crowds of people, walking round in a ring," etc. But transferred to other contexts they become loaded with special meanings. To sum up, all the central symbols of the poem head up here; but here, in the only section in which they are explicitly bound together, the binding is slight and accidental. The deeper lines of association only emerge in terms of the total context as the poem develops—and this is, of course, exactly the effect which the poet intends.

The poem would undoubtedly be "clearer" if every symbol had a single, unequivocal meaning; but the poem would be thinner, and less honest. For the poet has not been content to develop a didactic allegory in which the symbols are two-dimensional items adding up directly to the sum of the general scheme. They represent dramatized instances of the theme, embodying in their own nature the fundamental paradox of the theme.

We shall better understand why the form of the poem is right and inevitable if we compare Eliot's theme to Dante's and to Spenser's. Eliot's theme is not the statement of a faith held and agreed upon (Dante's Divine Comedy) nor is it the projection of a "new" system of beliefs (Spenser's Faerie Queene). Eliot's theme is the rehabilitation of a system of beliefs, known but now discredited. Dante did not have to "prove" his statement; he could assume it and move within it about a poet's business. Eliot does not care, like Spenser, to force the didacticism. He prefers to stick to the poet's business. But, unlike Dante, he cannot assume acceptance of the statement. A direct approach is calculated to elicit powerful "stock responses" which will prevent the poem's being read at all. Consequently, the only method is to work by indirection.

The Christian material is at the centre, but the poet never deals with it directly. The theme of resurrection is made on the surface in terms of the fertility rites; the words which the thunder speaks are Sanscrit words.

We have been speaking as if the poet were a strategist trying to win acceptance from a hostile audience. But of course this is true only in a sense. The poet himself is audience as well as speaker; we state the problem more exactly if we state it in terms of the poet's integrity rather than in terms of his strategy. He is so much a man of his own age that he can indicate his attitude toward the Christian tradition without falsity only in terms of the difficulties of a rehabilitation; and he is so much a poet and so little a propagandist that he can be sincere only as he presents his theme concretely and dramatically.

To put the matter in still other terms: the Christian terminology is for the poet a mass of clichés. However "true" he may feel the terms to be, he is still sensitive to the fact that they operate superficially as clichés, and his method of necessity must be a process of bringing them to life again. The method adopted in The Waste Land is thus violent and radical, but thoroughly necessary. For the renewing and vitalizing of symbols which have been crusted over with a distorting familiarity demands the type of organization which we have already commented on in discussing particular passages: the statement of surface similarities which are ironically revealed to be dissimilarities, and the association of apparently obvious dissimilarities which culminates in a later realization that the dissimilarities are only superficial—that the chains of likeness are in reality fundamental. In this way the statement of beliefs emerges through confusion and cynicism—not in spite of them.

Q. How can you define a hero with reference to Eliot's The Wasteland

Or

Q. The Wasteland is the barrenness of mind and soul.Comment

The Wasteland, based on the texts, is a varied and diverse

environment of barrenness and death. In my life, and in society today, the Wasteland is not much different; the barrenness is one of mind and soul, and we have the same lack of knowledge about death now that these authors did when recording their thoughts on paper. A hero is needed in this harsh environment, to guide the multitude, or merely set the example for all others to follow. Though few characters meet the qualifications of a true hero, many come close in several aspects of their lives. The wastelands in which they must survive involve bleak environmental conditions, truth, and destiny: difficult, though not insurmountable, conditions of life.

In my life, the barrenness that most is the inability to grasp with abstract thoughts the concrete, yet ever-changing, life around me. This would be a failure of the mind, which, in turn, would lead to failure of the body. As The Scarlet Letter shows, the mind has such a powerful influence over the body that it can physically mold it to match the present level of consciousness and self-image: "his form grew emaciated; his voice, though still rich and sweet, had a certain melancholy prophecy of decay in it". This decaying of his bodily form is due to another of society's wastelands, that of secrecy and lies. Although shame is the focus of The Scarlet Letter and is a major contributor to the fate of its characters, shame is not the wasteland of the book or society. For Hester, shame is perpetual, yet she lives on and prospers with the shame. It is the lies that are most grievous to the characters (Dimmesdale and Chillingworth), what undermines them, body and soul.

Another focus of society's Wasteland today is, in fact, a lack of focus. In other words, the ambiguity that surrounds certain situations is intolerable, and lack of understanding leads to frustration and the need to gain more knowledge, to fully grasp the situation. In my life I have also seen this occur; I always (or, more accurately, often) feel the need to understand a situation from every angle, each point of view. Social situations are no exception (who likes whom? Oh yes, she likes him but he...you get the picture). This does not merely apply to human interaction, however; natural circumstances, such as relationships between organisms, are no exception to the rule. Symbiosis, parasites, and all others are of interest to me; what benefits does each get? Is one of the organisms harmed? How do they respond to this interaction, positively or negatively? If all of this becomes a blur, we lose sight of why we are here, what our purpose in life is, and also what we are doing at present. These blurs in our existence can stem from senses, as in T.S. Eliot's "Waste Land," "troubled, confused and drowned the sense in odors," and, among other things, from our perception of fear and death: "I will show you fear in a handful of dust...Unreal city, under the brown fog of a winter dawn,/A crowd flowed over London Bridge, so many,/I had not thought death had undone so many". By describing his Wasteland as this blur of fear, fog, dust, and death, T.S. Eliot illustrates his wonder with the mysteries of life, and as the greatest mystery of all is death itself, Eliot refers to it constantly and spontaneously. In "The Love Song of J. Alfred Prufrock," Eliot even begins his love-less poem with th deathly image of a "patient etherised upon a table". This concentration on death in much of his poetry is also evid nt throughout Saul Bellow's Henderson the Rain King: "Evident y I happen to have a great death potential". Death is not truly feared by either of the characters in these writings, yet their constant absorption in the subject shows how little they know about it, and their desire to gain a tighter grasp on the concept. This emptiness called death is an unwanted blankness in most people's lives, and for those who worry or obsess over it, death becomes the ultimate wasteland of vacancy.

A huge wasteland in our society today is that of the "formulated phase" which Eliot writes about in his "The Love Song of J. Alfred Prufrock": the infamous stereotype. They are everywhere; in advertisements on every channel, spoken by my father, in almost every joke known to man, and especially, in school. From the lunchroom to the classroom, stereotypes are the predominant form of both jokery and prejudice. This can take the form of labeling (which, I say rather unhappily, my grandparents still do, nationality-wise, not negatively, to a certain extent), or, more vividly put, "When I am pinned and wriggling on the wall". As collectors like to organize their archives of insects, putting wild, chaotic nature in order, so do humans like to organize their compatriots. This superficial society also leads Prufrock to ask insignificant questions about his own life, his own appearance: "Shall I part my hair behind? Do I dare to eat a peach?" He is pushed to do this by society's constant, unfair scrutiny within itself, mano a mano, slowly and surely undermining the confidence of all those except the flawless, the ideal.

And what is the Ideal? To many, possessing the American Dream is where it's at-nice house, big yard, dog, two kids, beautiful spouse, cool car...it goes on and on. But what if the dream is a false one? Willy Loman trains and guides his mind and efforts towards this goal for his entire life. All he wants is the model life, a life of a carefree, well-off salesman. Due to either his unlucky situation, or perhaps to a pre-existent mental block on success (or at least how to go about getting there), Willy fails in his pursuit. When he discovers his misjudgement of how far the dream can take someone, and how short of a distance he himself has come, he is crushed under the weight of his fallen ideal, lapsing into moments of questionable sanity: "I have such thoughts, I have such strange thoughts". His wasteland becomes one of failure to achieve this "perfect" model of happiness, one embraced by society and unattainable by him. By spending his entire life working towards this one goal, Willy has deprived himself of true satisfaction in life's pleasures. He needs instead to be "well liked," which is his form of happiness in life.

For a person working towards the American dream, he surrounds himself in physically depressing surroundings, all "windows and bricks," devoid of "air and sunlight". To Willy, "an air of the dream clings to the place, a dream rising out of reality", and gives the impression, at least in his own mind, that he "mae the grade". The greatest failure Willy undergoes, however, is the termination of his own life. By ending his own life, he proves his inability to survive in the wasteland of suburbia, making tangible his role as an antihero.

Acting as the opposite of Willy Loman is Gene Henderson, the man trying to shed his wasteland, in search of the American

Dream. Unlike Willy, Henderson begins life already owning the materials of the dream, as a millionaire by inheritance, and throughout his life tries harder and harder to strip himself of material possessions. This is the ultimate reason behind his trip to Africa, and the cause for his frustration surrounding the decked-out expedition his friend Charlie has arranged; "'Charlie, this wasn't the way we fought the war. Hell, we're a couple of old soldiers. What is this?' It wounded me to travel in Africa this way". All of the extra equipment serves only to complicate Henderson's situation, and the material complications (as well as mental ones, those of society) are what he is trying to shed in his journey of "becoming."

Simple is what he likes: "It was all simplified and splendid". He needs this simplicity of body in order to gain his desired state of mind. While many people would feel fulfilled upon attaining the American Dream and all its tangible ingredients, Henderson cannot: he began life feeling this fulfillment, and now the material products of that dream have become tiresome to him, sometimes to the point of sorrow: "the crimson begonias, and the dark green and the radiant green and the spice that pierces and the sweet gold and the dead transformed, the brushing of the flowers on my undersurface are just misery to me".

Inserting the "dead" so casually into the midst of the beautiful, cheering flowers illustrates how similarly he sees all material objects, dead beings included. Henderson's wasteland is one of tangibility, filled with the material, devoid of the thoughts he desires to grasp. The wasteland of today's society is a wasteland of the incomplete, where we are all trained to move on to the newest, the best, even before we are finished with what we are doing at the present time. A prime example of this rushed society is the Internet, where impatience flourishes. All who utilize its services constantly inquire, "what's next? what's next?" and surfing the web proves to be an endless cycle of "I want..., I want..."

To be a hero in this world is a sign of honour, bravery, and accomplishment; it is the highest rank of a human within this society. But what if that society were not a mixture of both good and evil? What if that society transformed into a complete and endless wasteland, barren to both the eye and the mind? Then the hero would not be the savior of all; he would be the only one to survive. This person's equipment would be everyone's envy, and attainable by all if they were only to free their minds from the bonds of prejudice, fear, and time. By having mental freedom, all other necessary characteristics would be liberated to do their good work, protecting our hero from the harsh conditions of his barren environment.

To begin with, the hero must have two basic characteristics: intelligence and health. All other traits can be learned over time, providing good influences and positive m ral forces. Intelligence is needed for several reasons, the first being the abilit to discern the real from the deceptive parts of society. The ability to see through society's ploys is not useful solely in the profession of a hero, as E.B. White illustrates in "The Door": "'Here you have the maximum of openness in a small room'". This marketing trickery merely means, "here you have a small, empty cubicle," although White's version sounds endlessly more enticing. For the salesman of this new apartment, deceitful words may mean the difference between "sale pending" and "open house next weekend," yet intelligent buyers will see through this trick every time. Understanding society's deceptions goes hand in hand with the knowledge of society's truths, which is exceedingly the more significant of the two.

As Dimmesdale discovers too late in his life, revealing the truth is the only way to free oneself from past deceit. Upon revealing his true self to the crowd, he finally attains the relief he desires: "in the crisis of acutest pain, he had won a victory". Another literary figure corrupted by false identity is Jay Gatsby, who purposefully shrouds himself in a cloak of lies as soon as he has the chance, namely, when he meets Dan Cody. Resulting from this endless policy of building lies upon deceit, and deceit upon falseness, Gatsby becomes only a shell of a man, with none of his true feelings or needs visible to the outside world. This prevents him from having true success in life (and certainly does not qualify him for the position of "hero of the wasteland"). When Nick, his neigbbour and friend, discovers how false Gatsby's life truly is, a realization dawns upon him: "A sudden emptiness seemed to flow now from the windows and the great doors, endowing with complete isolation the figure of the host who stood on the porch, his hand up in a formal gesture of farewell"

This false self that James Gatz creates has indeed "isolated" him from the world, including the person to whom he has given "five years of unwavering devotion," his beloved Daisy. A hero must have self-reliance, which Gatsby certainly shows, but isolating his true self entirely from the world serves only to demolish his dreams, not bolster them.

The second basic trait necessary for success as a hero is good health, both physically and mentally. Good physical health is where Henderson excels; he is, "strong, healthy, rude and aggressive," and these traits allow him to continue in search of the missing key to his mental health, how to shed the bonds of society and the American Dream. Poor mental health, on the other hand, is where the failure of Willy Loman originates: "I'm-I can't seem to-keep my mind to it". Without complete mental health with which to guide oneself through life, losing sight of hopes and dreams is inevitable. To remedy his frustration at his own lack of accomplishments, Willy uses the lives of his sons to give him happiness. Upon commencement of this mode of living, Willy fails in yet another qualification of a hero: living one's life happily and not depending on others to provide fulfillment. For if the "others" that are depended upon fail in their pursuits, the person living vicariously now has to shoulder the weight of two failed existences.

Just as Willy is dependent on his children for life support, Bartelby is dependent on the narrator and his good will to remain stationary and survive. Unlike Gatsby and Dimmesdale, Bartelby is one of the most honest people ever to live. He doesn't express himself with profuse verbiage; instead, he "prefers" to keep his statements short and to the point. This honesty gains the trust of others: "I had singular confidence in his honesty", and yet it simultaneously raises suspicions. This is only natural, as the man seemed barely a member of the human species: "Had there been anything ordinarily human about him, doubtless I should have violently dismissed him from the premises". His seemingly inhuman aspect of perpetually showing no emotion gives him what the narrator dubs a "cadaverously gentlemanly nonchalance", or "deathly serenity."

This lack of emotion allows Bartelby to see every situation unprejudiced, and respond with unprecedented honesty. Because of this unique ability, Bartelby is the closest character to a hero encountered in this year's literature. He survives in his wasteland of change by remaining "stationary" in the wasteland of frustration with complete and total calm, and in the wasteland of falseness by "preferring" and being honest. The downside to his lack of emotion is the isolation he comes to have: no one can touch him, it seems-he is beyond the reach of other mortals. This alienation comes to a point where the narrator feels that Bartelby "seemed alone, absolutely alone in the universe". His complete solitude is his one failing, as a hero must be connected with the people around him; this is the only thing distinguishing a god from a hero- some connection with other human beings. And so, Bartelby cannot survive the trials of social and location change and perishes as a result of his forced migration.

The second character close to heroism is one who shuns society, despising its restrictions and seemingly endless limitations. Huckleberry Finn has endless physical freedom, yet a seemingly short supply of mental or moral freedom. The society in which he lives is one filled with innumerable social confinements, and Huck adds even more of his own items to this list of discomforts, "living in a house and sleeping in a bed pulled on me pretty tight mostly". Huck's feelings of utter confinement lead to his escape onto his raft, gliding down the Mississippi with unparalleled pleasure: "you feel mighty free and comfortable on a raft". The moral dilemmas he encounters on this journey arise from the slavery practices of the day and from his upbringing. He was taught throughout his childhood that Africans were far inferior to whites naturally, and that they should be treated that way. He does treat Jim in an inferior manner at times, and racist comments abound in the novel: "well, if ever I struck anything like it, I'm a nigger. It was enough to make a body ashamed of the human race". The extent of the racism in this society (evidently its wasteland) was so deep as to permeate even the minds of those being discriminated against: "Jim he couldn't see no sense in the most of it, but he allowed we was white folks and knowed better than him; so he was satisfied".

Despite all of the moral struggles and challenges Huck has to deal with, he does make several morally sound decisions which show that the boy's true character is wholesome. The most memorable of these occurs as he decides to save Jim, and by doing this gives up his passage into heaven: "all right, then, I'll go to hell". This statement is as relieving (for the decision) as it is troubling (for the inference that to free a slave is a sin). If it weren't for all of his moral conflicts, Huck would be an excellent example of a hero, even at his young age. But due to his environmental and social influences, his conscience has been "deformed" (Culture Shock) and the conflicting feelings that arise cause him to make his effort to escape from society. He is as close as he can come to a true hero, and if he existed in today's less prejudiced society, he may indeed have been renowned as one.

Each of the characters presented thus far has not fully succeeded in his society, and would therefore not seem to be a hero, but an antihero. Each human character encountered in this year's literature has not reached perfection as a hero in his society, because, in the words of Dr. Perry Davis, "as humans, we are not perfect." This is somewhat disheartening for us of the species Homo sapiens, yet it also keeps life diverse and interesting. Among the real reasons each hero did not succeed were moral faults, faults in honesty, and allowing society to gain undue influence over him or his mind. Certainly there could exist a person with all of the characteristics of a hero, but none of these particular characters achieve true heroism. The figure nearest to the ideal hero is not a human at all, in fact, but is the river in T.S. Eliot's "The Dry Salvages."

Also dubbed the "strong brown god", the river achieves near-heroism much more easily than a human would, for it is exempt from many of the same influences and faults to which we are subject. Nonetheless, this "river...within us" is the one character proven steady and able to survive the test of time and thrive in the wasteland of society. First of all, the almost unending life of the river has eliminated the need for energy to be wasted on any unnecessary thoughts of death or future; yet, it is also exposed to an indefinitely lengthier past to ponder. None of this hinders the river's determination to live (to as great an extent as a river lives); it is "sullen, untamed, and intractable".

This inability to be dragged from life (in-tractable) provides the determination, while it is "patient to some degree" in order to survive the abuses of its existence. All of the river's actions are natural; therefore, we deem them to be the correct ones to make. By making all the "right actions," the river has no regrets as to its past behaviour, and therefore has no reason to attempt to gain happiness through others. Instead, it proclaims, "fare forward, travelers! not escapng from the past", and continues, "you shall not think 'the past is finished' or 'the future is before us'". This not only supports the doctrine of no regrets, it vividly illustrates the need to concentrate on the present, what is occurrring at this moment. Thus no time will be wasted; no worries about last week or next week or even death will pass through the mind of this river/god.

Unfortunately, by illustrating the river as the near-hero, many of the 'human' qualities a hero should have are lost. These include good morals, intelligence, and honesty. The first of these a river really has no capacity to judge (because it lacks the second), and the third does not apply; rivers can be deceptive. These three are the only missing major characteristics needed to be a hero, as all others, are part of the many-faceted profile of the river.

Whether this society's hero is the imperfect human form or the near-perfect non-human, someone will always be able to overcome the challenges of his or her world. Maintaining an open mind, clear conscience, and healthy body and soul are the basic needs of a hero, while traits like reason and patience come with age and experience. The question of society today is not "what is our wasteland?" but "who is our hero?" Individuals often speak of a certain movie star or tv actor as "their hero," but how true is this? Is he overcoming the demands of society, or merely glorifying them? That is what each of us needs to decide for himself; who our hero is and what he can help us to overcome. Once we accomplish this, our idols will become valid ones, and we can all learn to overcome our wastelands and not only survive, but thrive, in today's society.

Q. How does The Waste Land parallel with Other Myths

Or

Q. Discuss the influence of other authors on Eliot in the use of myths

The Waste Land summarizes the Grail legend, not precisely in the usual order, but retaining the principal incidents and adapting them to a modern setting. Eliot's indebtedness both to Sir James Frazer and to Jessie L. Weston's From Ritual to Romance (in which book he failed to cut pages 138-39 and 142-43 of his copy) is acknowledged in his notes. Jessie L. Weston's thesis is that the Grail legend was the surviving record of an initiation ritual. Later writers have reaffirmed the psychological validity of the link between such ritual, phallic religion, and the spiritual content of the Greek Mysteries. Identification of the Grail story with the common myth of the hero assailing a devil-dragon underground or in the depths of the sea completes the unifying idea behind The Waste Land. The Grail legend corresponds to the great hero epics, it dramatizes initiation into maturity, and it bespeaks a quest for sexual, cultural, and spiritual healing. Through all these attributed functions, it influenced Eliot's symbolism.

Parallels with yet other myths and with literary treatments of the "quest" theme reinforce Eliot's pattern of death and rebirth. Though The Tempest, one of Eliot's minor sources, scarcely depicts an initiation "mystery," Colin Still, in a book of which Eliot has since written favorably, had already advanced the theory in 1921 that it implies such a subject." And Tiresias is not simply the Grail knight and the Fisher King but Ferdinand and Prospero, as well as Tristan and Mark, Siegfried and Wotan. In his feminine role he is not simply the Grail-maiden and the wise Kundry but the sibyl, Dido, Miranda, Brünnhilde. Each of these represents one of the three main characters in the Grail legend and in the mystery cults—the wounded god, the sage woman (transformed in some versions of the Grail legend into a beautiful maiden), and the resurrected god, successful quester, or initiate. Counterparts to them figure elsewhere; Eliot must have been conscious that the "Ancient Mariner" and "Childe Roland" had analogues to his own symbolism.

In adopting fertility symbolism, Eliot was probably influenced by Stravinsky's ballet Le Sacre du printemps. The summer before writing The Waste Land he saw the London production, and on reviewing it in September he criticized the disparity between Massine's choreography and the music. He might almost have been sketching his own plans for a work applying a primitive idea to contemporary life: In art there should be interpenetration and metamorphosis. Even the Golden Bough can be read in two ways: as a collection of entertaining myths, or as a revelation of that vanished mind of which our mind is a continuation. In everything in the Sacre du Printemps, except in the music, one missed the sense of the present. Whether Stravinsky's music be permanent or ephemeral I do not know; but it did seem to transform the rhythm of the steppes into the scream of the motor horn, the rattle of machinery, the grind of wheels, the beating of iron and steel, the roar of the underground railway, and the other barbaric cries of modern life; and to transform these despairing noises into music.

Q. Discuss the fertility myth in The Waste Land

Or

Q. How can you say that the world today offers too much of the physical with reference to The Waste Land

Eliot's waste land suffers from a dearth of love and faith. It is impossible to demarcate precisely at every point between the physical and the spiritual symbolism of the poem; as in "Gerontion" the speaker associates the failure of love with his spiritual dejection. It is clear enough, however, that the contemporary waste land is not, like that of the romances, a realm of sexless sterility. The argument emerges that in a world that makes too much of the physical and too little of the spiritual relations between the sexes, Tiresias, for whom love and sex must form a unity, has been ruined by his inability to unify them. The action of the poem, as Tiresias recounts it, turns thus on two crucial incidents: the garden scene in Part I and the approach to the Chapel Perilous in Part V.

The one is the traditional initiation in the presence of the Grail; the other is the mystical initiation, as described by Jessie L. Weston, into spiritual knowledge. The first, if successful, would constitute rebirth through love and sex; the second, rebirth without either. Since both fail, the quest fails, and the poem ends with a formula for purgatorial suffering, through which Tiresias may achieve the second alternative after patience and self-denial—perhaps after physical death. The counsel to give, sympathize, and control befits one whom direct ways to beatitude cannot release from suffering.

Q. Compare and contrast The Waste Land and Pablo Picasso's "Guernica"

Or

Q. Analyse the impact of war in The Waste Land and Pablo Picasso's "Guernica"

The similarities are striking. This is probably due, in no small part, to the inspiration for both works. Picasso and Eliot shared a common inspiration for their masterpieces the atrocities of war. Guernica was a response by Picasso to the German Luftwaffe's bombing of the Basque town of Guernica during the Spanish Civil War. During this 1937 attack hundreds of civilians were killed.

T.S. Eliot's The Waste Land is similar to Guernica in this way. It was written as a commentary on the state of the world after WWII. Printed in 1922 it depicts more vividly the changes of the world after the war, rather than a specific moment during the war, as Picasso does.

Aside from the conditions, which lead to the creation of these works, they share a number of other common threads. Symbolism aside these works are very similar on the surface. Both are a collection of seemingly disjointed images, which when put together by the reader or observer serve up a strong social message. That messages being that the wars and conflicts of the times have twisted the world. This is reinforced by the contorted and misshapen images in both works.

There are a number of these images in the works. Many of Picasso's are fairly evident the burning man in the right corner for example or the severed head on the bottom. These show the devastation of the world, as we know it. Eliot has recurring images not unlike these in The Waste Land. Eliot continually refers to the unnatural lack of water in the wasteland or the meaningless broken sex in the society of his day. However neither of these artists would be as highly considered, as they are, if these were the only images in their works. Indeed, it is the ambiguity of these images that makes them so great. Picasso overlaid in Guernica the images of Harlequins. The largest is hidden behind the surface imagery and is crying a diamond tear for the victims of the bombing.

Another is the interesting set of images if found if the observer flips the painting over. Here in the left half of the painting there are two images, one of a puppet and an observer kneeling to view the show.

This is interesting because Picasso loved puppetry and before the turn of the century he helped produce shows in Barcelona. So Picasso is empathizing with the victims and commenting on the absurdity of the bombing.

Subtly is also a forte of T.S. Eliot. An example is the Hyacinth girl who becomes a recurring image in the poem. This is a girl who loses her virginity in the Hyacinth garden and instead of being happy she views it as a negative. It shows the way sex has a twisted significance in the waste land. Eliot also makes a play on his society when he talks about the fiery hared girl in "A Game Of Chess". The woman in this scene has on her wall a painting that refers to the scene of a rape. It is the rape of Philomel by her sister's husband Tereus, when all was said and done they were turned into birds by the gods and these birds become recurring images in the poem. The painting points out the irony in society everything they value is really bad.

Another allusion common to both Guernica and The Waste Land is that to Wagner's Opera Parsifal. The broken sword in Guernica is a reference to the breaking of Parsifal's sword during a battle while questing for the grail. Eliot uses Parsifal, more specifically the choir of children from Parsifal, in contrast to the drunken singing of soldiers. In both cases it highlights the death of purity in the world.

Death, which is the greatest of the images, in these works is used for many reasons. For Eliot it is the death of spirituality and social morals. Picasso worries more about the death of reason and compassion in the world. Guernica has hidden images that demonstrate this point. The most prominent being the bull goring the horse of propaganda, this relates to the goring of the horse during a bullfight.

This act also has strong sexual overtones. Death, in Eliot's work was used more as a tool. Eliot tried to get across the idea that the symbolic death of society could be overcome by looking to the past. This is why he makes a number of references to Christ, Osiris, and Sybil. Each of these figures escaped death, which is what we must strive for in our wasteland. To leave it behind we must over come the restraints of our society.

Q. How can youn say that the Cantos and The Waste Land are an aesthetic Form in Modern Poetry

OR

Q. Discuss dislocated the temporality of language far more radically the Cantos and The Waste Land

In the Cantos and The Waste Land, it is clear that a radical transformation was taking place in aesthetic structure; but this transformation has been touched on only peripherally by modern critics. R.P. Blackmur comes closest to the central problem while analyzing what he calls Pound's "anecdotal" method. The special form of the Cantos, Blackmur explains, "is that of the anecdote begun in one place, taken up in one or more other places, and finished, if at all, in still another. This deliberate disconnectedness, this art of a thing continually alluding to itself, continually breaking off short, is the method by which the Cantos tie themselves together. So soon as the reader's mind is concerted with the material of the poem, Mr. Pound deliberately disconcerts it, either by introducing fresh and disjunct material or by reverting to old and, apparently, equally disjunct material."

Blackmur's remarks apply equally well to The Waste Land, where syntactical sequence is given up for a structure depending on the perception of relationships between disconnected word-groups. To be properly understood, these word-groups must be juxtaposed with one another and perceived simultaneously. Only when this is done can they be adequately grasped; for, while they follow one another in time, their meaning does not depend on this temporal relationship. The one difficulty of these poems, which no amount of textual exegesis can wholly overcome, is the internal conflict between the time-logic of language and the space-logic implicit in the modern conception of the nature of poetry.

Aesthetic form in modern poetry, then, is based on a space-logic that demands a complete reorientation in the reader's attitude toward language. Since the primary reference of any word-group is to something inside the poem itself, language in modern poetry is really reflexive. The meaning-relationship is completed only by the simultaneous perception in space of word-groups that have no comprehensible relation to each other when read consecutively in time. Instead of the instinctive and immediate reference of words and word-groups to the objects or events they symbolize and the construction of meaning from the sequence of these references, modern poetry asks its readers to suspend the process of individual reference temporarily until the entire pattern of internal references can be apprehended as a unity.

It would not be difficult to trace this conception of poetic form back to Mallarmé's ambition to create a language of "absence" rather than of presence—a language in which words negated their objects instead of designating them; nor should one overlook the evident formal analogies between The Waste Land and the Cantos and Mallarmé's Un Coup de dés. Mallarmé, indeed, dislocated the temporality of language far more radically than either Eliot or Pound has ever done; and his experience with Un Coup de dés showed that this ambition of modern poetry has a necessary limit.

If pursued with Mallarmé's relentlessness, it culminates in the self-negation of language and the creation of a hybrid pictographic "poem" that can only be considered a fascinating historical curiosity. Nonetheless, this conception of aesthetic form, which may be formulated as the principle of reflexive reference, has left its traces on all of modem poetry. And the principle of reflexive reference is the link connecting the aesthetic development of modern poetry with similar experiments in the modern novel.

Q. Discuss Eliot's treatment of women in his poetry

Or

Q. Do you think that Eliot shows women to be contributors to his downcast view of society

The women in Eliot's poems are often used as a device to show the antithesis of the protagonist, who represents Eliot himself. The emphasis placed on the theme of a deteriorating society is enforced through the women in Eliot's poems being ignorant of the demise occurring around them. At other times Eliot uses women as inanimate tools, where they are mentioned but have no impact on the narrator's view. However, women are involved more than men in Eliot's poems and so he may in fact see women as a device to show that what may appear to be a complete unknown to you may in fact be more similar than first realised. Eliot shows women to be contributors to his downcast view of society.

In 'The Love Song of J. Alfred Prufrock' the protagonist's sense of inadequacy is heightened as "the women come and go/Talking of Michelangelo". Prufrock tries in vain to find a partner who he can connect with, but women's high expectations of men can leave them to feel derisory. This view is reinforced by Prufrock's description of other "lonely men in shirt-sleeves, leaning out of windows"; Eliot depicts a society where women are shown as the cause for men's unhappiness. This creates a very negative view of women, who often are the antagonist to Eliot's vision of a better society. 'Portrait of a Lady' shows women as ignorant and small-minded, even in the presence of a protagonist who so desperately wishes for a meaningful relationship with them. The lady's speech follows a regular and conventional rhyme scheme with her voice "like the insistent out-of-tune/Of a broken violin". Here women are depicted as too shallow to s are the narrator's pessimistic view of society and instead f llow social convention by continually "serving tea to fr ends". In part III of 'Preludes' Eliot gives a very sordid description of a lonely women, whose feet have yellow soles" along with her "soiled hands".

In 'Rhapsody on a Windy Night' the moon is referred to as female, with her "feeble eye" and "a washed-out smallpox" that cracks her face. This appears to be more of a direct slur on women rather than impartial use of imagery. Eliot frequently compares women to the squalid aspects of life that are the focus of so many of his poems.

Eliot's descriptions of women are also often to depict them as lifeless and insignificant. In '...Prufrock' the protagonist increases his sense of isolation with the women characters by commenting how their "arms... lie along a table, or wrap about a shawl". To Prufrock, the women there are not conducting actions themselves but rather are objects. The women characters in Eliot's poems are isolated from the men, as Prufrock shows by his lack of communication with women. They "come and go/Talking of Michelangelo" amongst themselves. When Prufrock attempts to communicate with one they cannot understand one another, as shown through her reply of "That is not what I meant at all".

Eliot imparts the blame on the women themselves. Prufrock's misery is enhanced when he hears "mermaids singing, each to each", but Prufrock does not believe "they will sing to me". This could be a declaration of Prufrock's frustration at being isolated from women, who are intentionally withdrawn from men who do not meet their high standards set by Michelangelo. Eliot therefore segregates women into a similar category as to objects, as they are so different to men they cannot be referred to as the same. In 'Gerontion' the protagonist displays a similar, although more demeaning, attitude towards women. He refers to the woman who looks after him merely as "the woman". He gives a very belittling description of what she does; she "keeps the kitchen" and "sneezes at evening". Women's lack of importance in Eliot's poems shows them as mere details in a wider web of problems apparent in his view of society; their lack of importance perhaps shows Eliot's underlying lack of respect for women.

The fact that Eliot writes so much about women in his poems could conversely show that he actually sees women's role as pivotal in the depiction of society. 'Portrait of a Lady' centres on the narrator's interaction with a female character. Despite describing the events as false and staged with "an atmosphere of Juliet's tomb", the narrator later questions his disparaging attitude to the lady by asking whether "these ideas are right or wrong". Eliot here may be showing that isolation from others, in this case isolation from women, is caused more by someone's own attitudes rather than the feelings of another. The lady is given a derogatory view in 'Part I' of the poem, where she seems to be the antithesis of the narrator. In the next part of the poem, however, she shows that she is quite similar to him and understands how his mind works.

The lady says how "youth... smiles at situations which it cannot see", highlighting the arrogance of the narrator due to his youth. The characters who do not interact with women in Eliot's poems, such as Prufrock and Gerontion, are isolated individuals who make no active attempt to battle their loneliness. Eliot uses women as a symbol of what will appear to be a total contrast of yourself if you live in isolation, rather than using women as an example of 'an other'. In conclusion, the numerous negative references to women in Eliot's poems may be seen as critical as they are used as a device to show the harm that isolation can cause. Women can be used as a symbol of 'the other' to lonely men as although characters like

Prufrock can find a small sense of solace through other "lonely men, leaning out of windows", their interactions with women would be limited. This could also be seen as creating a negative view of women, as there are no real female characters in Eliot's poems but rather characters used solely as devices to highlight the loneliness apparent in the characters. The use of women only as a symbol of the danger of isolation in fact increases the isolation of the protagonists in Eliot's poems, and may therefore result in a negative view of women being portrayed.

Q. What kind of male and female relationship is prevalent inT.S. Eliot's The Wasteland ?

Or

Q. How can you say that the relationship between male and female is devoid of love ?

Uncusessfull male, female relationships are prevelant thourghout T.S. Eliot's poem "The Waist Land." Eliot reies on literary contrasts to illustrate the specific values of meaningful, effectual Ceremonies are prevalent throughout T.S. Eliot's poem The Waste Land. Eliot relies on literary contrasts to illustrate the specific values of meaningful, effectual rituals of primitive society in contrast to the meaningless, broken, sham rituals of the modern day. These contrasts serve to show how ceremonies can become broken when they are missing vital components, or they are overloaded with too many. Even the way language is used in the poem furthers the point of ceremonies, both broken and not.

The imagery of a primal ceremony is evident in the passage found in section V of The Waste. The last line of He who was living is now dead shows the passing of the primal ceremony; the connection to it that was once viable is now dead. The language used to describe the event is very rich and vivid: red, sweaty, stony. These words evoke an event that is without the cares of modern life- it is primal and hot. A couple of lines later Eliot talks of red sullen faces sneer and snarl/From doors of mudcracked houses. These lines too seem to contain language that has a primal quality to it. From the primal roots of ceremony Eliot shows us the contrast of broken ceremonies. Some of these ceremonies are broken because they are lacking vital components. A major ceremony in The Waste Land is that of sex. The ceremony of sex is broken, however, because it is missing components of love and consent. An example of this appears in section II, lines 99-100, The change of Philomel, by the barbarous king/So rudely forced; this is referring to the rape of Philomel by King Tereus of Thrace. The forcing of sex on an unwilling partner breaks the entire ceremony of sex. Rape is not the only way a broken sex ceremony can take place. The broken ceremony can also occur when there is a lack of love, as shown in lines 222-256.

This passage describes a scene between the typist and the young man carbuncular. What passes between these two individuals is a sex ceremony that is devoid of love and emotion (except for, perhaps, the emotion of lust on the part of the young man). The typist is indifferent to the whole event and the young man's vanity requires no response. For a ceremony to be effective, the participants have to have some degree of faith in what they are doing. They must believe that the ceremony will result in something worthwhile. The participants in this broken ceremony had no faith in what they were doing; they were just going through the motions. This is made obvious when the secretary says 'Well now that's done: and I'm glad it's over.'. Another way that broken ceremonies (broken due to lack of components) are presented in the poem, are ceremonies of nature.

It seems as though the waste land is always waiting for the ceremony of rain, the bringing of water, to the dry land. For most of the poem the water never arrives because there is always something missing. In lines 331 and 332 Eliot says, Here is no water but only rock/Rock and no water. In line 342 there is, dry sterile thunder without rain. The lack of water in ceremonies of nature that require it, lead to a broken ceremony.. Even at the beginning of the poem Eliot tells us that we, know only/A heap of broken images, where the sun beats,/And the dead tree gives no shelter, the cricket no relief,/ And the dry stone no sound of water.. Clearly this is wrong, and this lack of water is a main theme, and a main broken ceremony in The Waste Land. Conversely, ceremonies can also be broken when there are too many components in the ceremony, a something extra that serves to break them. In The Waste Land this is demonstrated by the presence of a third person in a ceremony that should contain only two. In lines 139-166, Eliot presents a scene with one too many. A husband and a wife are about to be reunited after Albert's four year absence. What should be a happy reunion ceremony is broken by the intrusion of a third person- Lil's friend.

She belittles Lil and then threatens her by saying, And if you don't give it a good time to him, there's others will, I said./ Oh is there, she said. Something o'that, I said./Then I'll know who to thank, she said, and gave me a straight look.. For a true bond occur in a relationship there must be a true connection between two people. If one of the people in the relationship is cheating on the other, this is another example of a third person breaking a two person ceremony. In lines 360-366, Eliot writes, Who is the third who walks always beside you? When I count, there are only you and I together But when I look ahead up the white road There is always another one walking beside you Gliding wrapt in a brown mantle, hooded I do now know whether a man or a woman -But who is that on the other side of you This passage shows a relationship between two people. One of them sees a third party.

It is unknown if this is actually another person (as in the case of unfaithfulness) or if it is a secret wrapt in a brown mantle, hooded that is manifesting itself as an intruder on the walking couple. Whatever it is, it is breaking the ceremony of the relationship and obviously bothers the speaker who mentions the other walking beside you three times in just seven lines. Language is very important in the genre of poetry and Eliot makes good use of it to show components of ceremonies. The way the language is used in the poem creates broken parts everywhere in the poem. Eliot's use of anaphora is reminiscent of the chant that often accompanies religious ceremonies.

The repeating in lines 121-122 (Do you know nothing? Do you see nothing? Do you remember nothing?) is like a catechism in form. Lines 322-324 (After the...After the...After the...) also further the ritualistic, ceremonious feeling of the poem. The analectic style that Eliot employs gives the poem a disjointed, broken feeling, almost as if the whole poem is a ceremony, and all of the analects are little cracks in what is ultimately broken. The fragmented use of allusions, combined with the foreign languages and different speakers, help establish the unwhole feeling of the poem. Eliot shows the dry, cracked waste land, but in the ending of the poem he gives us hope with the ritualistic chant of, Shantih shantih shantih which translates as The Peace which passeth underezding. Ceremonies are prevalent throughout T.S. Eliot's poem The Waste Land. The contrast between rituals that contain too little and rituals that contain too much show just how broken the waste land is. The actual literary tools that Eliot uses helps give the poem an apparent broken feel.

Q. Critically Analyse T.S. Eliot's The Waste Land

Or

Q. Is it right to say that The Waste Land is an allusive and complex poem

Thomas Stearns Eliot, author of The Waste Land, has been called the most influential poet of the twentieth century. He was born in St. Louis, Missouri, but became a British subject in 1927. For this reason, his works may be studied in British or American literature courses.

In 1906 he attended Harvard, where he was influenced by student groups who were interested in Elizabethan and Jacobean literature, the humanism of Irving Babbitt, and Indian mystical philosophy. He received additional education at the Sorbonne and at Oxford. In 1914 he moved to London and took a position at Lloyd's Bank. He held this job until 1925, when he joined the publishing firm of Faber and Gwyer. The firm became Faber and Faber in 1929, and Eliot was appointed a director. In 1948 he won the Nobel Prize for literature.

The Waste Land first appeared in October, 1922, in the Criterion, a periodical founded and edited by Eliot. In November of the same year it was published in the Dial, an American publication. At a later date it was published as a book with notes added, and it has also appeared in numerous anthologies.

The Waste Land is an allusive and complex poem. As such, it is subject to a variety of interpretations, and no two critics agree completely on its meaning. It may be interpreted on three levels: the person, the society, and the human race. The personal interpretation seeks to reveal Eliot's feelings and intentions in writing the poem. At the society level, a critic looks for the meaning of the poem in relation to the society for which it was written. Finally, the human level extends the societal level to include all human societies - past, present, and future (Thompson 144).

Since the human level is an extension of the societal level, the basic themes are the same for both. The main theme is "modern life as a waste land." Eliot supports the theme by showing what was wrong with society in the early twentieth century. These shortcomings include lack of faith, lack of communication, fear of both life and death, corruption of the life-water symbol, and corruption of sex.

There are two kinds of people in the modern waste land, according to Eliot. These are seen in the crowd that flows over London Bridge. He states, "I had not thought death had undone so many." This is a reference to Dante's description of the people in Limbo. They were the dead who were neither bad nor good, just secularized. This is one category of people in the waste land (Williamson 133). The other is given by another reference to Dante: "Sighs, short and infrequent, were exhaled." This is descriptive of people in the first level of hell, those who were born before Christ. They have no knowledge of salvation and cannot be saved (according to Dante.) The reference shows that there are also people in the twentieth c ntury who have no faith (Brooks 13).

Eliot illustrates the lack of faith at several points. In lines 301-302, one of the Thames daughters states, "I can connect/ Nothing with nothing." Because she has no faith, there are no connections and no meaning in her life (Wheelwright 97). There are several references in the poem to "hooded hordes walking in a ring." Madame Sosostris sees them, and the protagonist meets them as he journeys to the Perilous Chapel. The hooded hordes are hooded because they cannot see the hooded figure, the "third that always walks beside you," who represents Christ (Brooks 26). They are walking in a ring, with no sense of purpose or direction, because they have no faith (Williamson 149).

Another indication of the people's lack of faith is the story of the merchant. Traditionally, the merchants carried the secrets of the vegetation cult - the mythology which forms the basis of the poem - to all the countries they visited. However, the merchant Eliot describes does not do this. Instead of inviting the protagonist to a meeting that will introduce him to life-giving secrets, the merchant asks him to a weekend of homosexual debauchery that can only bring death (Brooks 21). In addition, Madame Sosostris is prohibited from seeing what the merchant carries on his back. She, likes the others in her world, cannot know about the secrets of life (Wheelwright 97). The world has lost its faith.

The people in the waste land also have problems with communication. This is first illustrated in the Hyacinth girl scene. She indicates that she is unable to speak, and therefore cannot communicate with the protagonist (Unger, Moments 120). Similarly, the lady of situations says "Speak to me. Why do you never speak? Speak." She feels the need to communicate but does not know how (Traversi 35). The response to the command "Dayadhvam" (sympathize) also shows that the people cannot communicate. They are all sitting in their prisons, thinking of the keys that will release them, yet never getting out. Their pride and selfishness keep them from understanding each other (Matthiessen 108). Finally, the encounter between the typist and the young man reinforces the problem of selfishness. Neither the typist nor her visitor is interested in the other. They just want to please themselves. Because of this focus on self, there is no communication between them

The opening lines of the poem describe the feelings of the protagonist as spring arrives. Instead of being joyful, he is disturbed. The new beginnings around him make him afraid, because he does not want a new beginning in his own life. He is afraid to live life (Brooks 12). However, he is also afraid of death. The statement "I will show you fear in a handful of dust" refers to fear of death, or fear of becoming just a handful of dust (Traversi 26). Another example of fear of life is in the planting of the corpse described in lines 69-75. The protagonist asks if the corpse has sprouted. He seems to be afraid of what might happen if it does (Williamson 134). However, the horror of rats' alley illustrates the fear of death again. Although the inhabitants of the waste land do not want to fully live, they are too afraid to die.

A traditional symbol of life is water, since human life is believed to have come from the water through the evolution of fish. Many religions, including the vegetation cults, held water as sacred and life-giving. Unfortunately, the people in the waste land have lost this ancient belief, according to Eliot. They have corrupted the life symbol and made it into something to be feared instead of revered. For example, the Phoenician sailor dies by drowning. Water certainly does not represent life to him! The clairvoyant Madame Sosostris advises the protagonist, "Fear death by water." Since he does not have faith (as illustrated above), water means death to him. He cannot live in it (Williamson 125). He also states "By the waters of Leman I sat down and wept...".

Leman means "lust." The protagonist indicates here that the prevalence of unbridled lust has disturbed him. Water has been corrupted - it now represents the death that results from the lack of self control. It no longer stands for life (Williamson 139). Another instance of this is Eliot's quote from an Australian song, "O the moon shone bright on Mrs. Porter/ and on her daughter/They wash their feet in soda water". In the legends of the Fisher King a footwashing ceremony preceded the restoration of the king. These lines tell us that ordinary water can no longer be used in footwashing - its symbolism has been lost (Brooks 20).

An important theme is corruption of sex — Eliot stresses this by giving many examples. The first is found in the description of the lady of situations. A "sylvan scene" is displayed above her mantel. The scene depicts "the change of Philomel," who was raped by King Tereus, husband of her sister Procne. Eliot states in line 102, "And still she cried, and still the world pursues." The change of Philomela took place many centuries ago, yet it is still happening today (Williamson 142). A second illustration of corrupted sex is in the pub scene. Albert "wants a good time" and he doesn't care who he hurts to get it. He is not concerned about the possibility of his wife dying in childbirth. Her friend, who is speaking, doesn't care either. The feelings of the society are that lust should be satisfied no matter what the consequences may be (Brooks 17-18). This theme is seen once more in the meeting of the typist and the young man. The typist is "bored and tired." The young man is "flushed and decided." Eliot states, "His vanity requires no response,/and makes a welcome of indifference." He isn't interested in exciting or pleasing her; he is only interested in his own satisfaction. "Love" in modern society is not really love - it is merely the fulfillment of instinctive desires. It is practical, boring, and meaningless (Matthiessen 61).

These three scenes are fairly lengthy, but Eliot also shows the corruption of love in short references. For example, lines 196-198 state "But at my back from time to time I hear/The sound of horns and motors, which shall bring/Sweeney to Mrs. Porter in the spring." The first line is a reference to Marvell's "To His Coy Mistress." The other two lines refers to Day's "Parliament of Bees" — "A noise of horns and hunting, which shall bring/Actaeon to Diana in the spring." The references appear in Eliot's notes. The contrasts of "hunting" with "motors" as well as "Actaeon and Diana" with "Sweeney and Mrs. Porter" illustrate the significant changes in the pursuit of love. Love was once treasured, but it is now reduced to sex for pleasure and not much else. In addition, Eliot contrasts the love of Elizabeth and Leicester with lovers of the present day (represented by the Thames daughters). The love of the past was enduring and real, while the love of the modern world is transitory and phony (Brooks 23).

Eliot is very discouraged about the society he has described as a waste land, but he does offer hope and a means of recovery. In Part V "What the Thunder Said," the three interpretations of DA - Datta, Dayadhvam (sympathize) and

Damayata are the keys to new life for the waste land. They are the antithesis of modern problems. If people learn to give, sex will gain new meaning as an expression of emotion and it will no longer be corrupted. If they sympathize with each other, they will be able to communicate their true feelings and listen to those of others. Finally, if they develop self-control, their faith will return and they will no longer fear life or death.

Most critics have confined themselves to the societal/ human interpretation of Eliot's work, since Eliot had warned them away from trying to determine his true purpose in writing his poetry. However, one theory has been put forward concerning his personal background and the meaning of the poem. When Eliot was studying in Paris he had a close friend, Jean Verdenal, who was killed at Gallipolli during World War I. Eliot was never quite sure how he died, but "death by water" is a possible explanation since the battle occurred offshore. Eliot dedicated his first volume of poems, Prufrock and Other Observations, to this friend. Information gathered from his first wife and from his personal papers indicates that he loved Jean Verdenal very much. The theory that has been set forth is that he wrote The Waste Land to express and to partially alleviate his grief, as Tennyson did with In Memoriam.

The world may never be certain exactly what Eliot had in mind when he wrote his most famous poem. However, we can determine the meaning of the poem to the "Lost Generation" and to all generations, as expressed in the themes I have described.

Chapter 11

Critical Essays

Modernism in the Poetry of T.S. Eliot and Christopher Okigbo

Christopher Okigbo's poetry has often been compared to that of T. S. Eliot, partly because Okigbo uses Eliot's signature linguistic devices such as exploiting metaphor to create a dense y symbolic dimension to his poetry. In addition, he also ap ears at times to be consciously invoking comparisons w th Eliot through such means as similarity of titles, as in he correspondence between his own Four Canzones and Eliot's our Quartets. Also like Eliot, Okigbo's poetry forces a critical ssessment that moves beyond the content of the works themselves to enlarge the discussion about broader topics such as the meaning of poetry and the purpose of the poet in modern society.

Christopher Okigbo's poetry reveals a man who was not merely aware of the work of Eliot, but who effectively drew upon him as a model for bringing to African poetry a modernist perspective. This may be due in part because he saw in Eliot's bifurcated identity as an American who is best known as a British poet an accurate reflection of his own sense of himself as an outsider; an African poet infusing his work with the sensibilities of Anglo modernism. Finally, both Okigbo and Eliot have each suffered the slings of criticism that their poetry, for all its technical virtuosity, too often gives in to pessimism and thus deprives the reader of the joy that is assumed to be a vital component for all great verse.

Of course, the most striking contrast between these two

poets is that Eliot's name is known by even those unfamiliar with his work, while Okigbo remains a relatively obscure fi ure outside African and poetry circles. T.S. Eliot is deserving o his esteemed position in 20th century literature as one of th greatest poets of the century. Even those who don't place hi atop the heap recognise his tremendous importance in revolut onising poetry. Eliot was one of the most successful experimente s of poetry of all time, forever challenging the method by wh ch readers should address all aspects of a poem. Eliot's greates accomplishment, perhaps, is that he forced subsequent poe s to intellectualise the traditional emotional and aesthetic elemen s of poetry.Eliot's ability to appeal to readers on various levels at once clearly influenced Christopher Okigbo.

Just as Eliot's poetry intellectualises the emotional void of a modern western world confronted by social and technological upheavals of the turn of the century, Okigbo sets out to address in an intellectual manner the emotional upheaval of colonialism upon African natives. Exploration of ritual can be found within the poets of both men as they use symbolist techniques such as allusion to force an understanding of how traditional guides contemporary thought and future destiny.

Eliot engages in ancient myth to underscore contemporary themes; Okigbo differentiates himself from previous African poets by introducing colonialist ideas in order to provide a thematic framework that reflects the amalgamation of native and European cultures and values to create the sense of confusion of identity that marks African peoples.

The urge to piece together the fractured and fragmented identity for both Eliot and Okigbo contains a certain undeniable element of the search for spiritual satisfaction. At the heart of this concern for both is the image of the wasteland and the annihilation of tradition and universal truths that have been exposed as ill-equipped to handle the psychic needs of modern society. The sense of underlying pessimism that distresses certain critics can therefore be viewed from the alternative perspective as necessary modernist conceit of no longer having the will to accept the falsity of disproved beliefs and shaky theoretical constructs of morality. In essence, the best poetry of both Eliot and Okigbo can easily be interpreted as the reaction to an acknowledgement of the disconnect engendered by the wasteland and the subsequent purification ritual aimed toward a kind of spiritual reconnect.

Comparing the poetry of Christopher Okigbo to that T.S. Eliot is significant in part due to thematic and linguistic similarities, but also because it is impossible to ignore the abundance of direct and conscious evocation of Eliot by Okigbo. In "Tradition and the Individual Talent", T.S. Eliot urged the poets of the 20th century compose with a sense of history and "a feeling that the whole of the literature of Europe from Homer and within it the whole of the literature of his own country has a simultaneous existence". Okigbo succeeds in this, but appears to have traded Homer for Eliot as his guidepost. That is not to say that Okigbo copies or plagiarises Eliot. Okigbo's invocation of specific elements of Eliot's poems is perhaps a bit more obvious than Eliot's usage of ancient precursors in his own poetry, but this can clearly be interpreted as an attempt by Okigbo to introduce into African literature a precursor he finds to be as significant as Eliot finds Homer. Eliot's knowledge of literary history cannot be argued and he engages the mythic qualities of that literature to revolutionary levels that effectively succeeded in changing the very nature of poetry. Okigbo's answer to that can be criticised for lacking the wealth of knowledge that Eliot possesses, or it can be extolled for his intellectual choice to replace the arcane allusive quality that dominates Eliot's poetry with the more relevant insight into the historical and social fabric of colonial Africa.

Eliot's poems are often striking for the manner in which ancient myths are utilised to comment on contemporary human condition. Okigbo meets this challenge by forcing African tradition to confront the foreign intrusion of colonisers. Once again, the question of reconnecting a splintered identity is introduced and in many poems from both men the result is language that is equally fragmented, containing multiple elements that inform Eliot's idea of a simultaneous existence created by the entire history of the world and not just the poet's own inner psychological architecture. Identity and society are viewed as not only labyrinths, but labyrinthine processes that are intended to infuse the very act of writing poetry. The critique that a streak of pessimism permeates the work of both conveniently ignores the fact that the physical act of writing poetry is itself a denial of any nihilist convictions. Further underscoring the illegitimacy of this critique is the obvious intellectual effort required to produce poetry of this caliber. If there is a feeling of pessimism that can be said to course throughout the poetry of Eliot and Okigbo, then it may be said to inform the possibility for spiritual reawakening in a world facing the devastation of ancient traditions as those traditions are reworked into a modern perspective.

T. S. Eliot demonstrates a complex relationship exists between the language and the spiritual deliberation. In his Four Quartets poem "Burnt Norton," Eliot confronts the restrictions and restraints inherent in language in its attempt to adequately lend meaning to spiritual perceptions. The opening stanza of "Burnt Norton" dives right into a thematic commonality that exists between Eliot and Okigbo, that of the connection between the past and the future. Stanza two serves to illuminate another solid modernist technique shared by the two poets, that of experimentations in voice and tone.

Eliot's use of vibrant adjectival imagery stands in stark contrast to the abstractions that are delineated in the first stanza. The movement is from starkly archaic to a more fluid contemporary quality; it is a terse an example of language evolving. That evolution of how words are used to describe abstract ideas gives rise to the greater thematic concerns of time and how it affects tradition and the clash of cultures. The cyclical nature of societal progression is intimately intertwined with the inference that language evolves over time as well. Eliot exhibits this relationship by juxtaposing the fragmentation that exists between the sacred and the secular. In "Burnt Norton" this fragmentation arises as an obstacle to understanding and reach forward to a greater spiritual awareness when he writes that language "will not stay in place/ Will not say still". The commotion caused by language often being ill-equipped to deal with the abstractions of contemporary life arises again when Eliot asserts that writing is always a process of beginning anew each time the pen is set to paper. Eliot's poetry in the first of the two quartets engages the modernist issue and presage the postmodernist concerns of interpretation. In these specific poems, Eliot addresses the issue of how language often serves to create problems in the communication of ideas directly related to knowledge and spiritual matters. There is a concurrence of ideas at work that underscores the unspoken belief that transcendence can onl be achieved through a dualistic process in which light and shad w co-exist to form a synthesis.

Eliot consistently makes indication to the evolution of words and meaning, implicitly associating that this dualistic relationship may hold the key to arriving at a deeper understanding of how cultural fragmentation works to construct a synthesis. Any synthesis of ideas based on language is subject to certain limits of ambiguity, but this is all the more so if one accepts that language if very often an obstacle toward understanding even the intent of the wording, much less the meaning beneath the language.

The critique that Eliot allows pessimism to enter into his poetry may be viewed from the perspective of really being nothing darker than cynical scepticism, and that is illustrated here in the form of hesitation in "Burnt Norton" such as when he writes "What might have been is an abstraction/Remaining a perpetual possibility". This weary wariness of possibility negated can be interpreted as a statement on the dangers inherent in the ambiguity of language itself, as well as how language is utilised to communicate what may be viewed as incommunicable. The poem raises serious questions about the elusive nature of the truthfulness of anything that one may ever experience in life, as demonstrated in the poem's sequence describing the actions that take place in the garden.

Within the poems contained in the first two quartets are many allusions to myth that serve Eliot's intention to punctuate the realism of the events described with a meaning more heightened in experiential substance. This is accomplished, however, through what appears to be simple linguistic devices such as descriptive imagery heavy on the usage of adjectival description.

The predicament facing the synthesis of the fragmentation that exists because of the ambiguous nature of language and the ephemeral quality of spirituality that makes it so very difficult to define rests on the horn of the inescapable dilemma that meaning cannot be divorced from medium. In other words, language is an absolute necessity in order to both understand and then relate the higher meanings that exist in the philosophical spheres that dominate the greatest poetry. In "Burnt Norton" Eliot writes that "Only by the form, the pattern,/Can words or music reach/The stillness as a Chinese jar". These lines propose that context is inseparable from the process of fully understanding and appreciating the significance of language, but context is almost always complicated by the introduction of interpretation.

An example of this occurs in Okigbo's "The Passage," during the section that retells the story of the bird finding itself in a foreign land and urging itself to stand astride just one leg because it does not fully understand the traditions of the new culture. The incident reflects the contextual significance of understanding language, as well as the obstacles placed in the path of understanding. The bird is much in keeping with the abstraction that allows the existence of the possible through the infinite. Okigbo is also concerned with Eliot's importance of form to the prosaic message of understanding.

His poems confront this issue through literal translation of metaphor such as in "Lament of the Lavender Mist" in which the natural purification symbol of water is personified in the female subject. Okigbo also follows Eliot's linguistic lead by engaging in the art of juxtaposition. Okigbo uses the technique of grouping together contextually unrelated images to concretise a new meaning from disparity. The result may not be immediately logical, but it is creatively coherent. Discordant language and cacaphonous rhythms are used to apprehend the new sensation forged from the fragmented reality of original meaning.

Eliot and Okigbo both use this kind of juxtaposition and linguistic flourish to highlight the fact that language can act as a stranglehold on knowledge, while also possessing the ability to force interpretation as an act of enlightenment. Eliot's purposeful confusion of seasonal imagery "East Coker" exposes the mystifying disorder of contemporary society. His insistent desire to see how far he can alter the method by which language communicates ideas generates a further issue concerning the inherent deceptive qualities of how words can be used to transmit thought. The restrictions of verbal communication serve as a metaphor for the development of language and society, illustrated by the lines discussing how tradition is "removed, destroyed, restored or in their place/Is an open field, or a factory, or a by-pass".

Eliot also engages the idea of the subtle treachery of language in such lines as "Our only health is the disease" as a way of understating the twofold aspect of everything. Eliot's poetry revealed that it requires context for understanding language and this obviously is compounded with the language is introduced to a foreign audience either through the immigration or emigration of communicable ideas and concepts. It is the emigration of communicable ideas that stifles indigenous cultural concepts that forms the basis of the colonial mindset in which Christopher Okigbo set out to follow in the tradition of T. S. Eliot. Spiritual themes involving the fragmentation of tribal traditions, Christianity and the struggle between the two dominate much of Okigbo's writing. The themes of religious suppression, anti Christianity, religious revival, and literary struggle predominate.

Okigbo's poetic attempt to reveal the fragmentary construction of communication combines African traditions and the intrusion of Western academia. Mirroring Eliot's position as an American intruder into British society, Okigbo works from the perspective of an African writing in an almost post-colonial mindset rather than an embrace of a pure nativism. Okigbo's poetry winds up having a transformative effect that is completely in keeping with Eliot's move toward establishing the duality of language as a means to both illuminate and obstruct the ability to communicate. By fusing together traditional Africa and post-colonial attributes, he concretises a synthesis of European and Africa perspectives to create a new modernist approach that also inhabits the significantly diverse fields of literary endeavors that take into full consideration the spiritual rituals of indigenous polytheistic belief and Christianity.

Okigbo merges Christian and Igbo religious iconography to showcase the difficulties inherent to language, which Eliot had identified, while providing the promise of reconciliation. He also manages to get around the constrictions of adhering to outmoded tradition, as well as skirt many issues of the post-colonialist literature. "Before you, mother Idoto,/Naked I stand" summons the specter of the Igbo religious tradition while also invoking Christian imagery with the line "upon waters of the genesis." What Okigbo is actually doing is synthesising the symbolism of water that runs throughout all religions in a general sense by using specifics to defragment the chasm that separates the specifics.

This is an imagistic amalgamation that echoes much of the greatest work of Eliot and, indeed, modernism as a movement. This usage of African and colonial religious traditions was not intended to put them into total competition through juxtaposition, but to draw them into relief together to show evidence of a cooperative effect on language and communication. At the same time, Okigbo is also quite capable of using these divergent images as a force of collision between two warring factions. This may be most effectively accomplished in the Fragments poems that take full promise of the idols of worship. "And the ornaments of him,/And the beads about his tail;/And the carapace of her/And her shell, they divided" explicitly draws attention to the divisive potential that exists in the confrontation and competition of a duality that exists between two traditions.

Heavensgate exists as a text whose mission is to defragment African and European manners of language and communication in an attempt to synthesise a new paradigmatic whole by connect the oral history of Africa with the written tradition of the West. Dramatic evolution is at the centre of this poetry, and throughout Okigbo is quite careful about the utilisation of voice. Okigbo accomplishes very much of the same thing in Limits and regularly adds another poetic dimension to the work in terms of the mood and ambience that pervades each of the poems. The same dependence on fragmented imagery exists, but the overall emotional mood is a bit more somber and possibly the target of the criticism of pessimism directed toward him. In these poems, there is an encroaching sensation of isolation; a sense of an isolated hero facing down the wasteland.

T.S. Eliot's poem "The Waste Land" describes a modern society overwhelmed by alienation and disorder, knocked off its bearings by the inexorable tide of progress arriving at double speed. For Eliot, industrialisation is the culprit; for Okigbo the sinister agent threatening to turn his society into a wasteland is colonialism, essentially a synonym for industrialisation. Throughout "The Waste Land" Eliot powerfully questions whether industrialisation and the consequences of urbanisation have resulted in positive effects on culture and society. He engages the same modernist techniques of discontinuity and fragmentation of language to underscore the confusion and chaos that is the topic of the poem. In the poems contained in Limits Okigbo recognises that the introduction of Christian religion is a metaphor for the European colonial designs at large.

Okigbo reveals quite explicitly in "Limits X" the full extent of the waste laid to his people through the symbolism of the invaders into the pristine land of his ancestors. Tellingly, these invaders are not just colonialists but also Christian missionaries. The missionaries, though imbued with the sense of savior in their own minds, are in fact little more than apologists for the devastation to come. This devastation is given poetic flight in the killing of the sacred sunbird before entering the jungle. There two different gods are present, metaphors for the indigenous ways and the new Christian path that is set to fragment those ancient traditions. The suggestion of death and rebirth connotes the unavoidable acceptance of

Christian iconography, but Okigbo wisely chooses juxtaposition as his greatest poetic tool. This juxtaposition of the old and the new, the indigenous and the forced reaches a state of ultimate artistic triumph with the image of the rite of fertility. Here, the pagan sacrifice of one of his own gods is utilised to upend the religious significance of the act and reveal it instead as an aggressive attempt to exterminate tribal rites and annihilate pre-colonial identity.

If Eliot might be termed a revolutionary artist in the sense that he was attempting to revolt against style and substance by enacting a sacrificial death and resurrection of the medium poetry, there can be no doubt that Okigbo was not attempting an actual revolution against the forces of spiritual colonialism. Okigbo ultimately comes down on the side of recognition. The defeat of the tribal tradition has a tremendous impact and there is an authentification of the sense of having lost something valuable to the psyche. Eliot's poetry forces the reader to recognise the potential threat of industrialisation and the loss of myth, whereas for Okigbo it is enough to merely recognise what has been lost and to move onward.

Despite these apparent differences in intention, both T.S. Eliot and Christopher Okigbo openly confront the issues they posit and defy easy explanations. Their dense, allusive language may at first appear to be merely adding to the obstacles that Eliot insist language presents to communication, but the real intention is to force the reader to polish his skills for interpretation and to understand that the simplistic declarative language he so often confronts is loaded with ambiguous connotations. Modernism as a general rule recognised that it is not the simplicity of language that assures communication and understanding.

Genuine communication is reached only through the contextual decoding of the fragmented cultural contributions of an increasingly diverse population. Understanding is not facilitated through common ideas of ease and direct discourse. Both Eliot and Okigbo position themselves as the translators that are necessary to full decode and then recode the transmission of signals, symbols and signs. Poetry serves that purpose best because it is the medium of literature that relies least upon the standard convictions of simplistic, stripped-down language. The irony is that though the poems of Eliot and Okigbo may be more dense and difficult than others, their many contextual clues actually make them better vehicles for communicating ideas those that are less dense. It is specifically this absence of simple clarification that turns the poetry of Eliot and Okigbo into things both beautiful and menacing to so many readers.

On The Waste Land

Cleanth Brooks

The bundle of quotations with which the poem ends has a very definite relation to the general theme of the poem and to several of the major symbols used in the poem. Before Arnaut leaps back into the refining fire of Purgatory with joy he says: "I am Arnaut who weep and go singing; contrite I see my past folly, and joyful I see before me the day I hope for. Now I pray you by that virtue which guides you to the summit of the stair, at times be mindful of my pain." This theme is carried forward by the quotation from Pervigilium Veneris: "When shall I be like the swallow." The allusion is also connected with the Philomela symbol. (Eliot's note on the passage indicates this clearly.) The sister of Philomela was changed into a swallow as Philomela was changed into a nightingale. The protagonist is asking therefore when shall the spring, the time of love, return, but also when will he be reborn out of his sufferings, and—with the special meaning which the symbol takes on from the preceding Dante quotation and from the earlier contexts already discussed—he is asking what is asked at the end of one of the minor poems: "When will Time flow away."

The quotation from "El Desdichado," as Edmund Wilson has pointed out, indicates that the protagonist of the poem has been disinherited, robbed of his tradition. The ruined tower is perhaps also the Perilous Chapel, "only the wind's home," and it is also the whole tradition in decay. The protagonist resolves to claim his tradition and rehabilitate it. The quotation from The Spanish Tragedy—"Why then Ile fit you. Hieronymo's mad againe"—is perhaps the most puzzling of all these quotations. It means, I believe, this: The protagonist's acceptance of what is in reality the deepest truth will seem to the present world mere madness. ("And still she cried... 'Jug jug' to dirty ears.") Hieronymo in the play, like Hamlet, was "mad" for a purpose. The protagonist is conscious of the interpretation which will be placed on the words which follow—words which will seem to many apparently meaningless babble, but which contain the oldest and most permanent truth of the race:

Datta. Dayadhvam. Damyata.

Quotation of the whole context from which the line is taken confirms this interpretation. Hieronymo, asked to write a play for the court's entertainment, replies:

Why then, I'll fit you; say no more.
When I was young, I gave my mind
And plied myself to fruitless poetry;
Which though it profit the professor naught
Yet it is passing pleasing to the world.

He sees that the play will give him the opportunity he has been seeking to avenge his son's murder. Like Hieronymo, the protagonist in the poem has found his theme; what he is about to perform is not "fruitless." After this repetition of what the thunder said comes the benediction:

Shantih Shantih Shantih

The foregoing account of The Waste Land is, of course, not to be substituted for the poem itself. Moreover, it certainly is not to be considered as representing the method by which the poem was composed. Much which the prose expositor must represent as though it had been consciously contrived obviously was arrived at unconsciously and concretely.

The account given above is a statement merely of the "prose meaning," and bears the same relation to the poem as does the "prose meaning" of any other poem. But one need not perhaps apologize for setting forth such a statement explicitly, for The Waste Land has been almost consistently misinterpreted since its first publication. Even a critic so acute as Edmund Wilson has seen the poem as essentially a statement of despair and disillusionment, and his account sums up the stock interpretation of the poem. Indeed, the phrase, "the poetry of drouth," has become a cliché of left-wing criticism. It is such a misrepresentation of The Waste Land as this which allows Eda Lou Walton to entitle an essay on contemporary poetry, "Death in the Desert"; or which causes Waldo Frank to misconceive of Eliot's whole position and personality. But more than the meaning of one poem is at stake. If The Waste Land is not a world-weary cry of despair or a sighing after the vanished glories of the past, then not only the popular interpretation of the poem will have to be altered but also the general interpretations of post-War poetry which begin with such a misinterpretation as a premise.

Such misinterpretations involve also misconceptions of Ellot's technique. Eliot's basic method may be said to have passed relatively unnoticed. The popular view of the method used in The Waste Land may be described as follows: Eliot makes use of ironic contrasts between the glorious past and the sordid present—the crashing irony of

But at my back from time to time I hear
The sound of horns and motors, which shall bring
Sweeney to Mrs. Porter in the spring.

But this is to take the irony of the poem at the most superficial level, and to neglect the other dimensions in which it operates. And it is to neglect what are essentially more important aspects of his method. Moreover, it is to overemphasize the difference between the method employed by Eliot in this poem and that employed by him in later poems.

The basic method used in The Waste Land may be described as the application of the principle of complexity. The poet works in terms of surface parallelisms which in reality make ironical contrasts, and in terms of surface contrasts which in reality constitute parallelisms. (The second group sets up effects which may be described as the obverse of irony.) The two aspects taken together give the effect of chaotic experience ordered into a new whole, though the realistic surface of experience is faithfully retained. The complexity of the experience is not violated by the apparent forcing upon it of a predetermined scheme.

The fortune-telling of "The Burial of the Dead" will illustrate the general method very satisfactorily. On the surface of the poem the poet reproduces the patter of the charlatan, Madame Sosostris, and there is the surface irony: the contrast between the original use of the Tarot cards and the use made by Madame Sosostris. But each of the details (justified realistically in the palaver of the fortune-teller) assumes a new meaning in the general context of the poem. There is then, in addition to the surface irony, something of a Sophoclean irony too, and the "fortune-telling," which is taken ironically by a twentieth-century audience, becomes true as the poem develops—true in a sense in which Madame Sosostris herself does not think it true. The surface irony is thus reversed and becomes an irony on a deeper level. The items of her speech have only one reference in terms of the context of her speech: the "man with three staves," the "one-eyed merchant," the "crowds of people, walking round in a ring," etc. But transferred to other contexts they become loaded with special meanings. To sum up, all the central symbols of the poem head up here; but here, in the only section in which they are explicitly bound together, the binding is slight and accidental. The deeper lines of association only emerge in terms of the total context as the poem develops—and this is, of course, exactly the effect which the poet intends.

The poem would undoubtedly be "clearer" if every symbol had a single, unequivocal meaning; but the poem would be thinner, and less honest. For the poet has not been content to develop a didactic allegory in which the symbols are two-dimensional items adding up directly to the sum of the general scheme. They represent dramatized instances of the theme, embodying in their own nature the fundamental paradox of the theme.

We shall better understand why the form of the poem is right and inevitable if we compare Eliot's theme to Dante's and to Spenser's. Eliot's theme is not the statement of a faith held and agreed upon nor is it the projection of a "new" system of beliefs. Eliot's theme is the rehabilitation of a system of beliefs, known but now discredited. Dante did not have to "prove" his statement; he could assume it and move within it about a poet's business. Eliot does not care, like Spenser, to force the didacticism. He prefers to stick to the poet's business. But, unlike Dante, he cannot assume acceptance of the statement. A direct approach is calculated to elicit powerful "stock responses" which will prevent the poem's being read at all. Consequently, the only method is to work by indirection. The Christian material is at the centre, but the poet never deals with it directly. The theme of resurrection is made on the surface in terms of the fertility rites; the words which the thunder speaks are Sanscrit words.

We have been speaking as if the poet were a strategist trying to win acceptance from a hostile audience. But of course this is true only in a sense. The poet himself is audience as well as speaker; we state the problem more exactly if we state it in terms of the poet's integrity rather than in terms of his strategy. He is so much a man of his own age that he can indicate his attitude toward the Christian tradition without falsity only in terms of the difficulties of a rehabilitation; and he is so much a poet and so little a propagandist that he can be sincere only as he presents his theme concretely and dramatically.

To put the matter in still other terms: the Christian terminology is for the poet a mass of clichés. However "true" he may feel the terms to be, he is still sensitive to the fact that they operate superficially as clichés, and his method of necessity must be a process of bringing them to life again. The method adopted in The Waste Land is thus violent and radical, but thoroughly necessary. For the renewing and vitalizing of symbols which have been crusted over with a distorting familiarity demands the type of organization which we have already commented on in discussing particular passages: the statement of surface similarities which are ironically revealed to be dissimilarities, and the association of apparently obvious dissimilarities which culminates in a later realization that the dissimilarities are only superficial—that the chains of likeness are in reality fundamental. In this way the statement of beliefs emerges through confusion and cynicism—not in spite of them.

Joseph Frank

In the Cantos and The Waste Land, however, it should have been clear that a radical transformation was taking place in aesthetic structure; but this transformation has been touched on only peripherally by modern critics. R. P. Blackmur comes closest to the central problem while analyzing what he calls Pound's "anecdotal" method. The special form of the Cantos, Blackmur explains, "is that of the anecdote begun in one place, taken up in one or more other places, and finished, if at all, in still another. This deliberate disconnectedness, this art of a thing continually alluding to itself, continually breaking off short, is the method by which the Cantos tie themselves together. So soon as the reader's mind is concerted with the material of the poem, Mr. Pound deliberately disconcerts it, either by introducing fresh and disjunct material or by reverting to old and, apparently, equally disjunct material."

Blackmur's remarks apply equally well to The Waste Land, where syntactical sequence is given up for a structure depending on the perception of relationships between disconnected word-groups. To be properly understood, these word-groups must be juxtaposed with one another and perceived simultaneously. Only when this is done can they be adequately grasped; for, while they follow one another in time, their meaning does not depend on this temporal relationship. The one difficulty of these poems, which no amount of textual exegesis can wholly overcome, is the internal conflict between the time-logic of language and the space-logic implicit in the modern conception of the nature of poetry.

Aesthetic form in modern poetry, then, is based on a space-logic that demands a complete reorientation in the reader's attitude toward language. Since the primary reference of any word-group is to something inside the poem itself, language in modern poetry is really reflexive. The meaning-relationship is completed only by the simultaneous perception in space of word-groups that have no comprehensible relation to each other when read consecutively in time. Instead of the instinctive and immediate reference of words and word-groups to the objects or events they symbolize and the construction of meaning from the sequence of these references, modern poetry asks its readers to suspend the process of individual reference temporarily until the entire pattern of internal references can be apprehended as a unity.

It would not be difficult to trace this conception of poetic form back to Mallarmé's ambition to create a language of "absence" rather than of presence—a language in which words negated their objects instead of designating them; nor should one overlook the evident formal analogies between The Waste Land and the Cantos and Mallarmé's Un Coup de dés. Mallarmé, indeed, dislocated the temporality of language far more radically than either Eliot or Pound has ever done; and his experience with Un Coup de dés showed that this ambition of modern poetry has a necessary limit. If pursued with Mallarmé's relentlessness, it culminates in the self-negation of language and the creation of a hybrid pictographic "poem" that can only be considered a fascinating historical curiosity. Nonetheless, this conception of aesthetic form, which may be formulated as the principle of reflexive reference, has left its traces on all of modem poetry. And the principle of reflexive reference is the link connecting the aesthetic development of modern poetry with similar experiments in the modern novel.

Grover Smith

The Waste Land summarizes the Grail legend, not precisely in the usual order, but retaining the principal incidents and adapting them to a modern setting. Eliot's indebtedness both to Sir James Frazer and to Jessie L. Weston's From Ritual to Romance is acknowledged in his notes. Jessie L. Weston's thesis is that the Grail legend was the surviving record of an initiation ritual. Later writers have reaffirmed the psychological validity of the link between such ritual, phallic religion, and the spiritual content of the Greek Mysteries.

Identification of the Grail story with the common myth of the hero assailing a devil-dragon underground or in the depths of the sea completes the unifying idea behind The Waste Land. The Grail legend corresponds to the great hero epics, it dramatizes initiation into maturity, and it bespeaks a quest for sexual, cultural, and spiritual healing. Through all these attributed functions, it influenced Eliot's symbolism.

Parallels with yet other myths and with literary treatments of the "quest" theme reinforce Eliot's pattern of death and rebirth. Though The Tempest, one of Eliot's minor sources, scarcely depicts an initiation "mystery," Colin Still, in a book of which Eliot has since written favorably), had already advanced the theory in 1921 that it implies such a subject." And Tiresias is not simply the Grail knight and the Fisher King but Ferdinand and Prospero, as well as Tristan and Mark, Siegfried and Wotan. In his feminine role he is not simply the Grail-maiden and the wise Kundry but the sibyl, Dido, Miranda, Brünnhilde. Each of these represents one of the three main characters in the Grail legend and in the mystery cults—the wounded god, the sage woman (transformed in some versions of the Grail legend into a beautiful maiden), and the resurrected god, successful quester, or initiate. Count rparts to them figure elsewhere; Eliot must have been onscious that the "Ancient Mariner" and "Childe Roland" had analo ues to his own symbolism.

In adopting fertility symbolism, Eliot was probably influenced by Stravinsky's ballet Le Sacre du printemps. The summer before writing The Waste Land he saw the London production, and on reviewing it in September he criticized the disparity between Massine's choreography and the music. He might almost have been sketching his own plans for a work applying a primitive idea to contemporary life:

In art there should be interpenetration and metamorphosis. Even the Golden Bough can be read in two ways: as a collection of entertaining myths, or as a revelation of that vanished mind of which our mind is a continuation. In everything in the Sacre du Printemps, except in the music, one missed the sense of the present. Whether Stravinsky's music be permanent or ephemeral I do not know; but it did seem to transform the rhythm of the steppes into the scream of the motor horn, the rattle of machinery, the grind of wheels, the beating of iron and steel, the roar of the underground railway, and the other barbaric cries of modern life; and to transform these despairing noises into music.

In The Waste Land he imposed the fertility myth upon the world about him. Eliot's waste land suffers from a dearth of love and faith. It is impossible to demarcate precisely at every point between the physical and the spiritual symbolism of the poem; as in "Gerontion" the speaker associates the failure of love with his spiritual dejection. It is clear enough, however, that the contemporary waste land is not, like that of the romances, a realm of sexless sterility. The argument emerges that in a world that makes too much of the physical and too little of the spiritual relations between the sexes, Tiresias, for whom love and sex must form a unity, has been ruined by his inability to unify them.

The action of the poem, as Tiresias recounts it, turns thus on two crucial incidents: the garden scene in Part I and the approach to the Chapel Perilous in Part V. The one is the traditional initiation in the presence of the Grail; the other is the mystical initiation, as described by Jessie L. Weston, into spiritual knowledge. The first, if successful, would constitute rebirth through love and sex; the second, rebirth without either. Since both fail, the quest fails, and the poem ends with a formula for purgatorial suffering, through which Tiresias may achieve the second alternative after patience and self-denial—perhaps after physical death. The counsel to give, sympathize, and control befits one whom direct ways to beatitude cannot release from suffering.

Stephen Spender

Conrad's Heart of Darkness is of course one of the "influences" in TheWaste Land. It seems to me, though, much more than this. Conrad's story is of the primitive world of cannibalism and dark magic penetrated by the materialist, supposedly civilized world of exploitation and gain; and of the corruption of the mind of a man of civilized consciousness by the knowledge of the evil of the primitive (or the primitive which becomes evil through the unholy union of European trade and Congolese barbarism). The country of them as described by Conrid is a country of pure horror. Eliot is usually thought of as a sophisticated writer, an "intellectual." For this reason, the felling of primitive horror which rises from depths of his poetry is overlooked.

Yet it is there in the rhythms, often crystallizing in some phrase which suggests the drums beating through the jungle darkness, the scuttling, clawing, shadowy forms of life in the depths of the sea, the spears of savages shaking across the immense width of the river, the rough-hewn images of prehistoric sculptures found in the depths of the primeval forest, the huge cactus forms in deserts, the whispering of ghosts at the edge of darkness. Probably this is the most Southern (in the American sense) characteristic of Eliot, reminding one that he was a compatriot of Edgar Allan Poe and William Faulkner. And Conrad's Heart of Darkness is a landscape with which Eliot is deeply, disquietedly, guiltily almost, familiar, and with which he contrasts effects of sunlight, lips trembling in prayer, eyes gazing into the heart of light or hauntingly into the eyes, a ship answering to the hand on a tiller as a symbol of achieved love and civilization.

Eloise Knapp Hay

The Waste Land, Eliot's first long philosophical poem, can now be read simply as it was written, as a poem of radical doubt and negation, urging that every human desire be stilled except the desire for self-surrender, for restraint, and for peace. Compared with the longing expressed in later poems for the "eyes" and the "birth," the "coming" and "the Lady" (in "The Hollow Men," the Ariel poems, and "Ash-Wednesday"), the hope held out in The Waste Land is a negative one. Following Hugh Kenner's recommendation, we should lay to rest the persistent error of reading The Waste Land as a poem in which five motifs predominate: the nightmare journey, the Chapel, the Quester, the Grail Legend, and the Fisher King. The motifs are indeed introduced, as Eliot's preliminary note to his text informs us, but if "the plan and a good deal of the incidental symbolism of the poem were suggested by Miss Jessie L. Weston's book on the Grail legend," the plan can only have been to question, and even to propose a life without hope for, a quest, or Chapel, or Grail in the modern waste land. The themes of interior prison and nightmare city—or the "urban apocalypse" elucidated by Kenner and Eleanor Cook—make much better sense when seen as furnishing the centripetal "pl n" and "symbolism," especially when one follows Cook's disc ssion of the disintegration of all European cities after t e First World War and the poem's culminating vision of a new C rthaginian collapse, imagined from the vantage point of India's holy men. A passage canceled in the manuscript momentarily uggested that the ideal city, forever unrealizable on eart, might be found "in another world," but the eference was purely sardonic. Nowhere in the poem can one find convincing allusions to any existence in another world, much less to St. Augustine's vision of interpenetration between the City of God and the City of Man in this world. How, then, can one take seriously attempts to find in the poem any such quest for eternal life as the Grail legend would have to provide if it were a continuous motif—even a sardonic one?

It seems that only since Eliot's death is it possible to read his life forward—understanding The Waste Land as it was written, without being deflected by our knowledge of the writer's later years. Before Eliot's death the tendency was to read the poem proleptically as if reflecting the poems f the later period. This is how Cleanth Brooks, writing he first fully elucidative essay on The Waste Land, read it, st essing the Grail legends, the longing for new life, rather than he purely negative aspects of the theme.

Thus Brooks interpreted the Sibyl's appeal for death at the beginning of the poem as exactly parallel to the Magus's appetite for deat in the Ariel poems (the Magus's, of course, filled with the pain of knowing that Christ had subjected himself to weak mortality and not knowing yet the Resurrection). To make the Sibyl and the Magus parallel was to read Eliot's development backward—perhaps an irresistible temptation when the pattern in his life was so little known and when (as then in 1939) Brooks was acquainted with the man at work on Four Quartets, who had recently produced the celebrated Murder in the Cathedral. It was also irresistible, in a culture still nominally Christian, to hope that The Waste Land was about a world in which God was not dead. But the poem was not about such a world.

Within ten years after finishing The Waste Land, Eliot recognized that the poem had made him into the leader of a new "way." His own words of 1931, however, require us to read the poem as having pushed this roadway through to its end—for him. It was no Grail quest. Those who followed him into it, and stayed on it, he said in "Thoughts After Lambeth," "are now pious pilgrims, cheerfully plodding the road from nowhere to nowhere." There could be no more decisive reference to the negative way he had followed till 1922, and also to the impasse where it ended.

A good reading of The Waste Land must begin, then, with recognition that while it expressed Eliot's own "way" at the time, it was not intended to lay down a way for others to follow. He did not expect that his prisonhouse would have corridors connecting with everyone else's. "I dislike the word 'generation' he said in "Thoughts After Lambeth"), which has been a talisman for the last ten years; when I wrote a poem called The Waste Land some of the more approving critics said that I had expressed the 'disillusionment of a generation,' which is nonsense. I may have expressed for them their own illusion of being disillusioned, but that did not form part of my intention." Dismay at finding his personal, interior journey (which he later called "rhythmic grumbling") converted into a superhighway seems to have been one of the main impulses toward his discovery of a new way after 1922.

If we listen attentively to the negations of The Waste Land, they tell us much about the poem that was missed when it was read from the affirmative point of view brought to it by its early defenders and admirers. Ironically, it was only its detractors—among them Eliot's friend Conrad Aiken—who acknowledged its deliberate vacuity and incoherence and the life-questioning theme of this first venture into "philosophical" poetry on Eliot's part. Aiken considered its incoherence a virtue because its subject was incoherence, but this was cool comfort either to himself or to Eliot, who was outraged by Aiken's opinion that the poem was "melancholy." It was far from being a sad poem—like the nineteenth-century poems that Eliot had criticized precisely because of their wan melancholias, based as he said on their excesses of desire over the possibilities that life can afford. Neither Aiken, who found the poem disappointing, nor I. A. Richards, who was exhilarated by its rejection of all "belief, " spotted the poem's focus on negation as a philosophically meditated position

Michael H. Levenson

Levenson quotes the opening four lines

Who speaks these lines? – presumably whoever speaks these next lines: Since the subject-matter (the life of the seasons) persists, as does the distinctive syntactic pattern (the series of present participles) and the almost obsessive noun-adjective pairings ("dead land," "spring rain," "little life," "dried tubers"). The second sentence, of course, introduces a new element, a narrating personal consciousness. But surely this need not signal a new speaker; it suggests rather that there is and has been a speaker, the unspecified "us," who will receive greater specification in the next several lines.

Certainly we want to identify the "us" that winter kept warm with the "us" that summer surprised, and with the "we" who stop, go on, drink coffee and talk. That is how we expect pronouns to behave: same referents unless new antecedents. But if the pronouns suggest a stable identity for the speaker, much else has already become unstable. Landscape has given way to cityscape. General speculation (April as the "cruellest month") resolves into a particular memory: the day in the Hofgarten. And the stylistic pattern shifts. The series of participles disappears, replaced by a series of verbs in conjunction: "And went... And drank... And talked." The adjective-noun pattern is broken.

What can we conclude so far? — that a strain exists between the presumed identity of the poem's speaker and the instability of the speaker's world. If this is the speech of one person, it has the range of many personalities and many voices — a point that will gain clarity if we consider the remaining lines of the sequence:

The line of German aggravates the strain, challenging the fragile continuity that has been established. Here is a new voice with a new subject-matter, speaking in another language, resisting assimilation. Is the line spoken, overheard, remembered? Among the poem's readers no consensus has emerged. Nor is consensus to be expected. In the absence of contextual clues, and Eliot suppresses such clues, the line exists as a stark, unassimilable poetic datum.

And yet, after that line a certain continuity is restored. The first-person plural returns; the pattern of conjunction reappears: "And when... And I... And down." Even that startling line of German, let us notice, had been anticipated in the "Hofgarten" and "Starnbergersee" of the previous lines. Discontinuity, in other words, is no more firmly established than continuity. The opening lines of the poem offer an elaborate system of similarities and oppositions, which might be represented in the following manner:

The diagram should indicate the difficulty. Lines 1-6 are linked by the use of present participles, lines 5-18 by personal pronouns, lines 8-12 by the use of German, lines 10-16 by the reiteration of the conjunction "and." The consequence is that in any given line we may find a stylistic feature which will bind it to a subsequent or previous line, in this way suggesting a continuous speaker, or at least making such a speaker plausible. But we have no single common feature connecting all the lines: one principle of continuity gives way to the next. And these overlapping principles of similarity undermine the attempt to draw boundaries around distinct speaking subjects. The poetic voice is changing; that we all hear. Certainly we hear it when we compare one of the opening lines to those at the end of the passage. But the changes are incremental, frustrating the attempt to make strict demarcations. How many speak in these opening lines? "One," "two" and "three" have been answers, but my point is that any attempt to resolve that issue provokes a collision of interpretive conventions. On the one hand, the sequence of first-person pronouns — an "us " that becomes a "we," a "me" an "I," and then "Marie" — would encourage us to read these lines as marking the steady emergence of an individual human subject. But if the march of pronouns would imply that

Marie has been the speaker throughout, that suggestion is threatened in the several ways we have considered: the shift from general reflection to personal reminiscence, from landscape to cityscape, from participial connectives to conjunctions, the disappearance of the noun-adjective pattern, the use of German. Attitudes, moreover, have undergone a delicate, though steady, evolution. Can the person who was "kept... warm... in forgetful snow... " be that Marie, who prefers to "go south in winter?" Can the voice which solemnly intones the opening and explosive paradox: April is cruel, utter such conversational banalities as: "In the mountains, there you feel free"? Perhaps — but if we insist on Marie as the consistent speaker, if we ask her to lay hold of this complexity, we can expect only an unsteady grasp. The heterogeneity of attitude, the variety of tone, do not resolve into the attitudes and tones of an individual personality. In short, the boundaries of the self begin to waver: if we can no longer trust our pronouns, what can we trust? Furthermore, though we find it difficult to posit one speaker, it is scarcely easier to posit many, since we can say with no certainty where one concludes and another begins. Though the poem's opening lines do not hang together, neither do they fall cleanly apart. Here, as elsewhere, the poem plays between bridges and chasms, repetitions and aggressive novelties, echoes and new voices.

In the opening movement of The Waste Land, the individual subject possesses none of the formal dominance it once enjoyed in Conrad and James. No single consciousness presides; no single voice dominates. A character appears, looming suddenly into prominence, breaks into speech, and then recedes, having bestowed momentary conscious perception on the fragmentary scene. Marie will provide neither coherence nor continuity for the poem: having been named, she will disappear; her part is brief. Our part is larger, for the question we now face is the problem of boundaries in The Waste Land.

Eliot, as we have already seen, rejects the need for any such integrating Absolute as a way of guaranteeing order. His theory of points of view means to obviate that need. Points of view, though distinct, can be combined. Order can emerge from beneath; it need not descend from above. And thus in the Monist he says of Leibniz' theory of the dominant monad: "I contend that if one recognizes two points of view which are quite irreconcilable and yet melt into each other, this theory is quite superfluous." And in the dissertation he writes that "the pre-established harmony is unnecessary if we recognize that the monads are not wholly distinct."

My italics are tendentious, dramatizing the repetitions in phrase. But the repetition is more than a chance echo; it identifies a problem which both the philosophy and the poetry address. How can one finite experience be related to any other? Put otherwise, how can difference be compatible with unity? Moreover, the poetic solution is continuous with the philosophic solution: individual experiences, individual personalities are not impenetrable. They are distinct, but not wholly so. Like the points of view described in the dissertation, the fragments in The Waste Land merge with one another, pass into one another.

Madame Sosostris, for instance, identifies the protagonist with the drowned sailor ("Here, said she/Is your card, the drowned Phoenician Sailor"). But the sailor, Phlebas, is also identified with Mr Eugenides: recall Eliot's phrase, "the one-eyed merchant, seller of currants, melts into the Phoenician Sailor." But, as Langbaum has shown, if the protagonist is identified with Phlebas and Phlebas with Eugenides, then it is difficult to escape the conclusion that the protagonist and the Smyrna merchant are, themselves, "not wholly distinct." What, then, do we make of these lines?

Levenson quotes lines from "Under the brown fog of a

winter noon" to "Followed by a weekend at the Metropole." The protagonist, as Langbaum points out, "stands on both sides of the proposition," and such a conclusion will unnerve us only if we hold fast to traditional concepts of self, personal identity, personal continuity and the barriers between selves.

But in The Waste Land no consistent identity persists; the "shifting references" alter our notions of the self. The characters are little more than aspects of selves or, in the jargon of Eliot's dissertation, "finite centres," "points of view." Here are the concluding lines of "The Fire Sermon":

Lines from Augustine alternate with lines from the Buddha, and, as Eliot tells us in the footnote: "the collocation of these two representatives of eastern and western asceticism, as the culmination of this part of the poem, is not an accident." Of course it is not. It is the way the poem works: it collocates in order to culminate. It offers us fragments of consciousness, "various presentations to various viewpoints," which overlap, interlock, "melting into" one another to form emergent wholes. The poems is not, as it is common to say, built upon the juxtaposition of fragments: it is built out of their interpenetration. Fragments of the Buddha and Augustine combine to make a new literary reality which is neither the Buddha nor Augustine but which includes them both.

But at my back from time to time I hear
The sound of horns and motors, which shall bring
Sweeney to Mrs. Porter in the spring.

The echo from Marvell passes into an echo from Day: the poetic effect depends on amalgamating these distinct sources, on recognizing them as not wholly distinct. For we know, argues Eliot, "that we are able to pass from one point of view to another, that we are compelled to do so, and that the different aspects more or less hang together." The movement of The Waste Land is just such a movement among points of view: Marvell and Day, the Buddha and St Augustine, Ovid and Virgil.

We find ourselves in a position to confront a problem, which, though distant, is not forgotten: the problem of the poem's unity, or what comes to the same thing, the problem of Tiresias. We may begin to see how Tiresias can serve the function of "uniting all the rest," without that obliging us to conclude that all speech and all consciousness are the speech and consciousness of Tiresias. For, if we rush too quickly to Tiresias as a presiding consciousness, along the lines established by Conrad or James, then we lose what the text clearly asks us to retain: the plurality of voices that sound in no easy harmony. What Eliot says of the Absolute can be said of Tiresias, who, also, "dissolves at a touch into... constituents." But this does not leave us with a heap of broken fragments; we have seen how the fragments are constructed into new wholes. If Tiresias dissolves into constituents, let us remember the moments when those constituents resolve into Tiresias. Tiresias is, in this sense, an intermittent phenomenon in the poem, a subsequent phenomenon, emerging out of other characters, other aspects. The two sexes may, as Eliot suggests, meet in Tiresias, but they do not begin there.

"The life of a soul," writes Eliot in the dissertation, "does not consist in the contemplation of one consistent world but in the painful task of unifying (to a greater and less extent) jarring and incompatible ones, and passing, when possible, from two or more discordant viewpoints to a higher which shall somehow include and transmute them." Tiresias functions in the poem in just this way: not as a consistent harmonizing consciousness but as the struggled-for emergence of a more encompassing point of view. The world, Eliot argues, only sporadically accessible to the knowing mind; it is a "felt whole in which there are moments of knowledge." And so, indeed, is The Waste Land such a felt whole with moments of knowledge. Tiresias provides not permanent wisdom but instants of lucidity during which the poem's angle of vision is temporarily raised, the expanse of knowledge temporarily widened.

The poem concludes with a rapid series of allusive literary fragments: seven of the last eight lines are quotations. But in the midst of these quotations is a line to which we must attach great importance: "These fragments I have shored against my ruins." In the space of that line the poem becomes conscious of itself. What had been a series of fragments of consciousness has become a consciousness of fragmentation: that may not be salvation, but it is a difference, for as Eliot writes, "To realise that a point of view is a point of view is already to have transcended it." And to recognize fragments as fragments, to name them as fragments, is already to have transcended them not to an harmonious or final unity but to a somewhat higher, somewhat more inclusive, somewhat more conscious point of view. Considered in this way, the poem does not achieve a resolved coherence, but neither does it remain in a chaos of fragmentation. Rather it displays a series of more or less stable patterns, regions of coherence, temporary principles of order the poem not as a stable unity but engaged in what Eliot calls the "painful task of unifying."

Within this perspective any unity will be provisional; we may always expect new poetic elements, demanding new assimilation. Thus the voice of Tiresias, having provided a moment of authoritative consciousness at the centre of the poem, falls silent, letting events speak for themselves. And the voice in the last several lines, having become conscious of fragmentation, suddenly gives way to more fragments. The polyphony of The Waste Land allows for intermittent harmonies, but these harmonies are not sustained; the consistencies are not permanent. Eliot's method must be carefully distinguished from the methods of his modernist predecessors. If we attempt to make

The Waste Land conform to Imagism or Impressionism, w miss its strategy and miss its accomplishment. Eliot wrenched h s poetry from the self-sufficiency of the single image and the s ngle narrating consciousness. The principle of order in Th Waste Land depends on a plurality of consciousnesses, an eve -increasing series of points of view, which struggle towards n emergent unity and then continue to struggle past that unity.

Calvin Bedient

This might be as fair a place as any to take the pulse of the notion of a single and unifying protagonist in The Waste Land.

Again, the argument is that this notion has not been sufficiently entertained and tested in earlier commentary on Eliot. Stanley Sultan's few pages on the subject in Ulysses, The Waste Land, and Modernism form—as will be more fully noted—the one substantial, and neglected, exception.

As has perhaps been demonstrated, part I presents no obstacles to reading the poem in this light. On the contrary, the hypothesis of a single speaker and performer adds shadow, depth, drama, and direction to everything in the movement. It discovers a poem of far more seriousness, profundity, and complexity than Edward Said (among others) regards it as being: namely, "a collection of voices repeating and varying and mimicking one another and literature generally."

Certainly the original working title, "He Do the Police in Different Voices," implies the presence of a single speaker in the poem who is gifted at "taking off" the voices of others—just as the foundling named Sloppy in Dickens's Our Mutual Friend is, according to the doubtless biased and doting Betty Higden, "a beautiful reader of a newspaper. He do the police in different voices." This speaker has a flair for tones of criminality, sensationalism, and outrage—the whole gamut of abjection and judgment; or so the title implies. He shows a relish for such tones, he is virtuosic at rendering them. The working title was thus itself a harsh judgment on the protagonist (whom it travesties). All speech is abjection? The very impulse to perform voice is suspect? A complicity in the fascination of crime—say, murder? To create and to murder are near akin? These severe intimations are of a piece with the contemptus mundi of the poem.

The hypothesis of an all-centering, autobiographical protagonist-narrator is not only consistent with the working title; it explains the confident surfacing, in the latter part of the poem, of an unmistakable religious pilgrim. Unless this pilgrim can be shown to develop (to inch, scramble, flee) out of a waste land that is, or was, himself, the poem splits apart into two unequal sections, a long one constituted by what Lyndall Gordon calls "the Voices of Society" and a shorter one on a lone pilgrim to elsewhere. Neither Gordon nor A. D.

Moody—each so admirable on The Waste Land—connects what they concur in regarding as a pilgrim with what they might agree to call the Voices of Society. But there is no difficulty in the way of positing the former as the "doer" of the latter—as one of the social voices, yet he who surpasses them in being able to do and place them in an ironic relation to other voices, including his own.

Gordon's valuable suggestion that the poem belongs in the religio-literary category of "the exemplary life" is in fact better served by this more unifying reading. "In the lives Eliot invokes," Gordon comments, "—Dante, Christ, Augustine, the grail knight, Ezekiel—there is always a dark period of trial, whether in a desert, a slough of despond, or a hell, followed by initiation, conversion, or the divine light itself." The protagonist is not merely one among others in hell (and the "conversation" between him and Stetson, who were alive and comparatively heroic together so long ago, only makes sense in a dimension of hell); hell is not merely others; the protagonist is hell, and it is out of this hell, at once his own and collective, that, through conversion, he must climb toward the divine light. If he does the voices of others, it is because in the first instance his ears are whores to them; he dramatizes, thus, his own abjection.

He is not merely one of the denizens of the waste land; he is their sum, he is sin upon sin, even sinner upon sinner—or so his self-multiplying and self-shading ventriloquism suggests. Not that he does the voices altogether helplessly; on the contrary, he gathers them in his fist like a rattlesnake's severed coils and shakes them so as to disturb his own and his readers' war-dulled, jazz-dulled, machine-dulled ears. But, in any case, he demonstrates thus—he confesses—his own hellish entanglements with secularism and the flesh. The first three parts of the poem present the equation the others = me, if in a way that proves the equation a little false (it involves a sick self-belittlement). The rest of the poem clarifies the actual opposition of others/me that endows the first three parts with insidious drama. The protagonist both suffers from and exploits this essential theatricality of voice. His nature is a poet's nature, at once powerfully secretive and helplessly "open"—empathetic, susceptible, yours for the asking. The protagonist is, in a phrase Delmore Schwartz applies to Eliot himself, a "sibylline listener." He listens in on others with the mercilessness of one who fails to hear "the silence" in their speech yet with the full dramatic sympathy of his empathic nature, too—with a tenth of that capacity for sympathy which also, at its fullest and subtlest stretch, enables him to detect the ethereal presence of an attendant "hooded" figure, or look into the heart of light.

Eliot's prose poem "Hysteria" was about just such a protohysterical, protosalvational empathy. "As she laughed, I was aware of becoming involved in her laughter and being part of it... I was drawn in by short gasps, inhaled by each momentary recovery, lost finally in the dark caverns of her throat, bruised by the ripple of unseen muscles." Laughter is hysteria, empathy with voice is hysteria-in-the-making, acting is controlled hysteria. The protagonist "acts" the voices of others as if he had little choice in the matter, and even his "own" voice is, to him, theater, the voice of Hieronymo as he plots a Babel of other voices, plots the crash of Babel itself.

Almost helplessly many, almost incapacitated by his capacity for openness, the protagonist will nonetheless find in this susceptibility to otherness and outsidedness (a susceptibility that, largely "sympathy," makes them inward, his) his virtú and virtue, his identification with what is pure and utter: so Other that sympathy with it minimalizes his abjection, which becomes no more than a clot of sound that he must cough up, a phlegm of speech. By imbuing his protagonist with his own auditory and vocal genius of participation in the abjectness of his times and in approaches to the Absolute (for "the silence" must be heard, and speech must edge it), Eliot made his poem a barometer sensitive both to the foggy immediate air and to the atmospheric pressure high and far off, the "thunder of spring over distant mountains". A group or medley of voices cannot attend to a charged, remote silence; for that a single protagonist was necessary, one who could both "do" the group and find in himself the anguish and strength to leave it, repressing the fatal impulse (as Moody puts it) "towards a renewal of human love" and seeking, instead, the Love Omnipotent.

John Xiros Cooper

The Waste Land does not merely reflect the breakdown of an historical, social, and cultural order battered by violent forces operating under the name of modernity. For Eliot the disaster that characterized modernity was not an overturning, but the unavoidable, and ironic, culmination of that very order so lovingly celebrated in Victoria's last decade on the throne. Unlike the older generation, who saw in events like the Great War the passing of a golden age, Eliot saw only that the golden age was itself a heap of absurd sociopolitical axioms and perverse misreadings of the cultural past that had proved in the last instance to be made of the meanest alloy. The poem's enactment of the contemporary social scene in "The Burial of the Dead," "A Game of Chess," and "The Fire Sermon" exhibits the "negative liberal society" in which such events and people are typical. Eliot's choice of these events and people—Madame Sosostris, the cast of characters in "A Game of Chess," and the typist—as representative of a particular society is susceptible, of course, to a political analysis, which is to say, their representativeness is not self-evident, though they are presented as if it is.

The "one bold stare" of the house-agent's clerk, put back in the bourgeois context where staring is one of the major lapses in manners, does not hold up the mirror to a simple gesture, but illuminates the underlying conditions that make a mere clerk's swagger possible. What is exposed is the "fact" that clerks in general no longer know their place. What we are to make of this fact is pointedly signaled by the disgust that the specifics of the rendering provoke and the social distance generated by the Tiresian foresufferance....

As its social critique was aimed negatively at the liberal ethos which Eliot felt had culminated in the War and its disorderly aftermath, The Waste Land could not visibly adopt some preliberal code of values. In the same way, the poem could not propose a postliberal, historicist or materialist ethic without an historicizing epistemology. The poem's authority rested instead on other bases that provided, not a system of ideas as the primary form of legitimation, but a new lyric synthesis as a kind of experiential authenticity in a world in which the sacred cosmologies, on the one hand, had fallen prey to astrologers and charlatans, while, on the other, the cosmology of everyday life, i.e. the financial system (the "City" in the poem), had fallen into the soiled hands of racially indeterminate and shady importers of currants and the like, among them, of course, the pushing Jews of the plunderbund....

The poem attempts to penetrate below the level of rationalist consciousness, where the conceptual currencies of the liberal ethos have no formative and directive power. Below that level lay the real story about human nature, which "liberal thought" perversely worked to obscure, by obscuring the intersection of the human and the divine at the deepest levels of consciousness. That stratum did not respond to the small-scale and portable logics of Enlightenment scientism, but to the special "rationality" of mythic thought. Its "logic" and narrative forms furnish the idiom of subrationalist, conscious life. To repeat: if not on the conventional rationalist basis, where does Eliot locate the authority of The Waste Land, and authority that can save the poem from mere eccentric sputter and give it a more commanding aspect? I think it was important for Eliot himself to feel the poem's command, and not simply to make it convincing to skeptical readers; Lyndall Gordon's biography makes this inner need for strength in his own convictions a central theme in Eliot's early life. But to answer our question: the authority the poem claims has two dimensions.

The first is based on the aesthetics of French symbolisme and its extension into the Wagnerian music-drama. Indeed the theoretical affinites of Baudelaire et al. and Wagner, which Eliot obviously intuited in the making of The Waste Land, can be seen now as nothing short of brilliant. Only in our own time are these important aesthetic and cultural connections being seriously explored. From symbolisme Eliot adopted the notion of the epistemological self-sufficiency of aesthetic consciousness, its independence from rationalist instrumentality, and thus its more efficacious contact with experience and, at the deeper levels, contact with the divine through its earthly language in myth. From his French and German forebears, Eliot formulated a new discourse of experience which in the 1920s was still very much the voice of the contemporary avant-garde in Britain and, in that sense, a voice on the margins, without institutional authority.

But here the ironic, even sneering, dismissal of the liberal stewardship of culture and society reverses the semiotics of authority-claims by giving to the voice on the margins an authority the institutional voices can no longer assume since the world they are meant to sustain has finally been seen through in all those concrete ways the poem mercilessly enacts. The Waste Land is quite clear on that point. We are meant to see in "The Fire Sermon," for example, the "loitering heirs of City directors" weakly giving way to the hated métèques, so that the City, one of the "holy" places of mercantilism, has fallen to profane hands, The biting humour in this is inescapable. The second dimension of the authority on which The Waste Land rests involves the new discourse on myth that comes from the revolutionary advances in anthropology in Eliot's time associated with the names of Émile Durkheim, Marcel Mauss, and the Cambridge School led by Sir James Frazer and Jane Harrison.

We know that Eliot was well acquainted with these developments at least as early as 1913-14. The importance of these new ideas involved rethinking the study of ancient and primitive societies. The impact of these renovations was swift and profound and corresponds, though much less publicly, to the impact of On the Origin of Species on the educated public of midcentury Victorian life. Modernist interest in primitive forms of art (Picasso, Lawrence, and many others), and, therefore, the idioms and structures of thought and feeling in primitive cultures, makes sense in several ways. Clearly the artistic practices of primitive peoples are interesting technically to other artists of any era. Interest in the affective world or the collective mentality of a primitive society is another question altogether. That interest, neutral, perhaps, in scholarship, becomes very easy to formulate as a critique of practices and structures in the present that one wants to represent as distortions and caricatures of some original state of nature from which modernity has catastrophically departed. Eliot's interest in the mythic thought of primitive cultures, beginning at Harvard, perhaps in the spirit of scientific inquiry, takes a different form in the argument of The Waste Land. There it functions pointedly as a negative critique of the liberal account of the origins of society in the institutions of contract, abstract political and civil rights, and mechanistic psychology.

The anthropologists rescued the major cultural production of primitive societies—myth—from the view that saw these ancient narratives either as the quaint decorative brio of simple folk or, if they were Greek, as the narrative mirrors of heroic society. Instead myth, and not just the myths of the Greeks, was reconceived as the narrative thematics of prerationalist cosmologies that provided an account of the relationship between the human and the divine. Myth was also interpreted psychologically, and Nietzsche is crucial in this development, as making visible the deeper strata of the mind.

If the concept is the notional idiom of reason, myth is the language of unconscious life. What Eliot intuited from this new understanding was that myth provided a totalizing structure that could make sense, equally, of the state of a whole culture and of the whole structure of an individual mind. In this intuition he found the idiom of an elaborated, universalizing code which was not entirely the product of rationalist t ought. In addition, this totalizing structure preserved he sacred dimension of life by seeing it inextricably entwine with the profane. For the expression of this intuition in he context of an environment with a heavy stake in the elabo ated codes of a rationalist and materialist world view hich had subordinated the sacred to the profane, Eliot adapted for his own use the poetics of juxtaposition. The textual discontinuity of The Waste Land has usually been read as the technical advance of a new aesthetic. The poetics of juxtaposition are often taken as providing the enabling rationale for the accomplishment of new aesthetic effects based on shock and surprise. And this view is easy enough to adopt when the poem is read in the narrow context of a purely literary history of mutated lyric forms. However, when the context is widened and the poem read as a motivated operation on an already always existing structure of significations, this technical advance is itself significant as a critique of settled forms of coherence. Discontinuity, from this perspective, is a symbolic form of "blasting and bombardiering."

In the design of the whole poem, especially in its use of contemporary anthropology, the broken textual surface must be read as the sign of the eruptive power of subrational forces reasserting, seismically, the element totalities at the origins of culture and mind. The poem's finale is an orgy of social and elemental violence. The "Falling towers," lightning and thunder, unveil what Eliot, at that time, took to be the base where individual mind and culture are united in the redemptive ethical imperatives spoken by the thunder. What the poem attempts here, by ascribing these ethical principles to the voice of nature and by drawing on the epistemological autonomy posited by symbolisme, is the construction of an elaborated code in which an authoritative universalizing vision can be achieved using a "notional" idiom uncontaminated by Enlightenment forms of rationalism.

Powerful as it is in the affective and tonal programme of the poem, functioning as the conclusion to the poem's "argument," this closural construction is, at best, precarious when seen beyond the shaping force of the immediate social and cultural context. This construction, achieved rhetorically, in fact is neither acceptable anthropology, nor sound theology, nor incontestable history, but draws on all these areas in order to make the necessary point in a particular affective climate. The extent to which the poem still carries unsurpassable imaginative power indicates the extent to which our own time has not broken entirely with the common intuitive life that the poem addressed 60 years ago.

Louis Menand

All the difficulties with the late-nineteenth-century idea of style seem to be summed up in The Waste Land. It is, to begin with, a poem that includes an interpretation—and one "probably not in accordance with the facts of its origin"—as part of the poem, and it is therefore a poem that makes a problem of its meaning precisely by virtue of its appare t (and apparently inadequate) effort to explain itself. We ca not understand the poem without knowing what it meant to i s author, but we must also assume that what the poem meant to its author will not be its meaning.

The notes to The Waste Land are, by the logic of Eliot's philosophical critique of interpretation, simply another riddle—and not a separate one to be solved. They are, we might say, the poem's way of treating itself as a reflex, a "something not intended as a sign," a gesture whose full significance it is impossible, by virtue of the nature of gestures, for the gesturer to explain."And the structure of the poem—a text followed by an explanation—is a reproduction of a pattern that, as the notes themselves emphasize, is repeated in miniature many times inside the poem itself, where cultural expressions are transformed, by the mechanics of allusion, into cultural gestures. For each time a literary phrase or a cultural motif is transposed into a new context—and the borrowed motifs in The Waste Land are shown to have themselves been borrowed by a succession of cultures—it is reinterpreted, its previous meaning becoming incorporated by distortion into a new meaning suitable to a new use.

So that the work of Frazer and Weston is relevant both because it presents the history of religion as a series of appropriations and reinscriptions of cultural motifs, and because it is itself an unreliable reinterpretation of the phenomena it attempts to describe. The poem (as A. Walton Litz argued some time ago) is, in other words, not about spiritual dryness so much as it is about the ways in which spiritual dryness has been perceived. And the relation of the notes to the poem proper seems further emblematic of the relation of the work as a whole to the cultural tradition it is a commentary on. The Waste Land is presented as a contemporary reading of the Western tradition, which (unlike the "ideal order" of "Tradition and the Individual Talent") is treated as a sequence of gestures whose original meaning is unknown, but which every new text that is added to it makes a bad guess at.

The author of the notes seems to class himself with the cultural anthropologists whose work he cites. He reads the poem as a coherent expression of the spiritual condition of the social group in which it was produced. But the author of the poem, we might say, does not enjoy this luxury of detachment. He seems, in fact, determined to confound, even at the cost of his own sense of coherence, the kind of interpretive knowingness displayed by the author of the notes. The author of the poem classes himself with the diseased characters of his own work—the clairvoyants with a cold, the woman whose nerves are bad, the king whose insanity may or may not be feigned. He cannot distinguish what he intends to reveal about himself from what he cannot help revealing: he would like to believe that his poem is expressive of some general reality, but he fears that it is only the symptom of a private disorder.

For when he looks to the culture around him, everything appears only as a reflection of his own breakdown: characters and objects metamorphose up and down the evolutionary scale; races and religions lose their purity ("Bin gar keine Russin, stamm' aus Litauen, echt deutsch"); an adulterated "To His Coy Mistress" describes the tryst between Sweeney and Mrs. Porter, and a fragmented Tempest frames the liaison of the typist and the young man carbuncular; "London bridge is falling down." The poem itself, as a literary object, seems an imitation of this vision of degeneration: nothing in it can be said to point to the poet, since none of its stylistic features is continuous, and it has no phrases or images that cannot be suspected of—where they are not in fact identified as—belonging to someone else. The Waste Land appears to be a poem designed to make trouble for the conceptual mechanics not just of ordinary reading (for what poem does not try to disrupt those mechanics?) but of literary reading. For insofar as reading a piece of writing as literature is understood to mean reading it for its style, Eliot's poem eludes a literary grasp.

Carol Christ

In The Waste Land Eliot, with a desperate virtuosity, presents various ways of constituting the male and female, as if in search of a poetic figuration and voice that place him beyond the conflicts that characterize his earlier poetic stances. The early sections of the poem, up to the entry of Tiresias, develop the strategy of "Portrait of a Lady." They juxtapose the meditations of a male voice with a number of female portraits: Mme. Sosostris, the wealthy woman and the working-class woman in "A Game of Chess," Marie, the hyacinth girl, and, in Eliot's rough draft of the poem, Fresca. In this collage Eliot gives the women of the poem the attributes of traditional literary character.

They inhabit settings, they exist in dramatic situations, they have individual histories, and they have voices. They constitute most of the identified speakers in the first three sections of the poem, and they contain among them a number of figures for the poet: the sibyl of Cumae; Mme. Sosostris with her Tarot deck; Fresca, who "scribbles verse of such a gloomy tone/That cautious critics say, her style is quite her own"; and La Pia, who can connect "nothing with nothing." One might appropriately object that these are for the most part satiric portraits (indeed, some of them savagely satiric), but they are nonetheless the ways in which the poem locates both verbal fluency and prophetic authority.

In contrast, the male voice through which Eliot presents these women has none of the definitional attributes of conventionally centered identity. It resists location in time and space, it conveys emotion through literary quotation, and it portrays experience only through metaphoric figuration: the cruel April at the poem's beginning, the desert landscape, the rat's alley, where "dead men lost their bones." Eliot thus turns the shifting figuration that appears as unsurety in "Portrait of a Lady" to a poetic strength. The very lack of location and attribute seems to place the speaker beyond the dilemmas of personality, as if Eliot had succeeded in creating the objective voice of male tradition. But for all this voice seems to offer, the early parts of the poem imagine men as dead or dismembered: the drowned Phoenician sailor, whose eyes have been replaced by pearls, the one-eyed merchant, the fisher king, the hanged man, the corpse planted in the garden. Thus Eliot allows us to read the sublimation of body and personality that mark the poem's voice as a repression of them as well, an escape from dismemberment by removing the male body from the text. The one place where Eliot attaches a specific historical experience to the speaking voice of the poem — the episode of the hyacinth girl — supports such a reading. The episode begins with the speaker's quoting a woman who addressed him, recalling a gift he gave her: "You gave me hyacinths first a year ago." The speaker then describes his own consciousness of that moment in their relationship.

When they came back from the Hyacinth garden, her arms full and her hair wet, he could not speak and his eyes failed, he was neither living nor dead, and he knew nothing, "looking into the heart of light, the silence." Perhaps in recognition of the special status that this episode has by virtue of its attachment to the poet's "I," many critics have found in it the emotional centre of the poem. The moment offers some revelation of spiritual and erotic fullness ("the heart of light"), but the speaker portrays himself as unequal to it. Speech and vision fail him, and he ends the passage by borrowing the articulation of another poem ('Oed' und leer das Meer'), a ventriloquized voice that is not his own, that reveals him at a loss for words. We have here a Tiresias who, at the moment of sexual illumination, loses not only his sight but his voice as well, a seer who does not gain prophetic power from sexual knowledge. As in his early poetry, Eliot represents the moment of looking at a woman as one that decomposes his voice.

Eliot's use of visual imagery in "A Game of Chess" sustains this sense of a moment of vision evaded. For all the elaborate description of the woman's dressing table and chamber, the passage avoids picturing the woman herself, unlike its source in Antony and Cleopatra, The long opening sentence of the description — seventeen lines long — carefully directs the eye around what is presumably the woman sitting in the chair, but she only appears at the end of the passage, in the fiery points of her hair, which are instantly transformed into words. The passage thus finally gives the reader only a fetishistic replacement of the woman it never visualizes, a replacement for which he immediately substitutes a voice. A number of the images in "A Game of Chess" reinforce this concern with the desire to look and its repression the golden Cupidon that peeps out while another hides his eyes behind his wing, the staring forms leaning out from the wall, the pearls that were eyes, the closed car, the Pressing of lidless eyes, and in the second section, Albert's swearing he can't bear to look at Lil. All of the eyes that do not look in this section of the poem are juxtaposed to images of a deconstituted body, imagined alternately as male and as female: the change of Philomel, withered stumps of time, the rat's alley where dead men lost their bones, and the teeth and baby Lil must lose. As the men in the section resist looking, so they do not speak. Albert is gone, and the speaker cannot or will not answer the hysterical questions of the lady.

The poem changes its figuration of gender with the introduction of Tiresias. Eliot states in a note to the passage that "the two sexes meet in Tiresias. What Tiresias sees, in fact, is the substance of the poem" — a declaration that critics have tended to view rather skeptically. But what Tiresias sees is the sight that the poem has heretofore evaded: the meeting of the sexes, a meeting that Tiresias experiences by identifying with the female. As the typist awaits her visitor, Tiresias asserts, "I too awaited the expected guest," and at the moment when the house agent's clerk "assaults" her, he states, "And I Tiresias, have foresuffered all," a position assumed again in the lines spoken by La Pia.

Paradoxically, when the poem assumes the position of the female, male character becomes far more prominent: in the satiric portrait of the house agent's clerk, which is the first extended satiric male portrait in the poem, in the image of the fishermen, and in the extended fisherman's narrative that originally began Part IV and concludes with the death of Phlebas. As if repeating the doubleness of identification that Tiresias represents, that death affords at once the definitive separation of male identity and a fantasy of its separation of male identity and a fantasy of its dissolution as "He passed the stages of his age and youth/Entering the whirlpool."

In the final section of the poem, Eliot changes its representation of gender dramatically. He drops the strategy of character that had been the principal way in which the poem had up to this point centered its emotion and develops a voice and figuration for the speaker that remains separate from categories of gender. He accomplishes this by using both specifically religious allusions and natural images that for the most part avoid anthropomorphization. He seeks to evoke a poise from natural elements, as in the water-dripping song, which he gives a religious rather than a sexual resonance. Through the song Eliot moves the power of articulation in the poem from character to nature. The hermit-thrush sings in the pine trees, and the sound of the water for which he yearns is finally realized in the last line of the section: "Drip drop drip drop drop drop drop." As if in recognition of its separation from gender, this temporary poise immediately issues in the appearance of the third figure, "who walks always beside you./ ... hooded/I do not know whether a man or woman."

When the sexual concerns of the poem return, in the next passage, they assume a very different form than they have heretofore. Eliot does not locate them in relation to particular female characters or voices, although the image of the woman who "drew her long black hair out tight" does recall the woman in "A Game of Chess"; he evokes them through a sexual fantasy that represents the collapse of civilization as an engulfment within an exhausted and blackened vagina, suggested in the images of empty cisterns, exhausted wells, and bats "with baby faces" crawling "head downward down a blackened wall." This passage develops the technique of "Prufrock" in displacing images of sexual anxiety onto elements of the poem's landscape, such that the world itself rather than the characters within it locates its sexual malaise. These feminized images now possess the power of music and song that had been given to the water and the thrush; the woman fiddles "whisper music" on the strings of her hair, the bats whistle, and voices sing out of the cisterns and wells. Despite what would seem the movement of the power of articulation to the feminine, Eliot's figurative technique here opens the way both for the poem's resolution and for the transfer, through nature, of the power of music and song to the male poet.

By shifting to a poetic mode that expresses emotion through landscape rather than through character, Eliot can achieve sexual potency in purely symbolic terms, as, in the decayed hole, the cock crows, and the damp gust comes, bringing rain. The very way in which these images resist, because of their natural simplicity and the literary allusions with which Eliot surrounds them, what would seem to be their obvious sexual symbolism is precisely their virtue, for they enable the poem to resolve its sexual conflict at the same time that it arrives at a figuration that places the poet beyond it. At the moment when the cock crows, Eliot transfers the power of articulation to the landscape, as the thunder speaks, giving the power of translation to the poet. When the poet interprets the commands of the thunder, he once again describes human situations, but he articulates them in abstract and ungendered terms, as if only a language free from the categories of gender allows him to imagine human fulfillment.

Michael North

The typist who appears next in the passage is a worker named metonymically for the machine she tends, so merged with it, in fact, that she is called a "typist" even at home. In The Education, Henry Adams proclaims his astonishment at the denizens of the new American cities: "new types, — or type-writers, — telephone and telegraph-girls, shop-clerks, factory hands, running into millions on millions.... " Eliot's point here seems very close to Adams's. Eliot's woman is also a "type," identified with her type-writer so thoroughly she becomes it. She is a machine, acting as she does with "automatic hand." The typist is horrifying both because she is reduced by the conditions of labour to a mere part and because she is infinitely multiple. In fact, her very status as a "type" is dependent on a prior reduction from whole to part. She can become one member of Adams's faceless crowd only by being first reduced to a "hand."

The typist is the very type of metonymy, of the social system that accumulates its members by mere aggregation. Yet this "type" is linked syntactically to Tiresias as well. In fact, the sentence surrenders its nominal subject, Tiresias, in favour of her. The evening hour "strives/Homeward, and brings the sailor home from sea,/The typist home at teatime, clears her breakfast, lights/Her stove, and lays out food in tins." The typist shifts in mid-line from object to subject, from passive to active. Does the evening hour clear her breakfast, or should the reader search even farther back for an appropriate subject, to Tiresias himself. Though this would hardly clarify the syntax, Tiresias could function logically as both subject and object, seen and seer, because, as the notes tell us, he is the typist: "All the women are one woman, and the two sexes meet in Tiresias." The confused syntax represents this process of identification, erasing ordinary boundaries between active and passive, subject and object.

On what basis can the typist merge with all other men and women to become part of Tiresias? In other words, what is the figurative relationship between the whole he represents and the part acted by the typist? The process of figurative identification seems similar to that in "Prufrock," where women are also represented as mere "arms" and where all women are also one woman. As in "Prufrock," the expansion to "all" depends on a prior reduction of individual human beings to standardized parts, just as Prufrock has "known them all already, known them all," Tiresias has "foresuffered all." His gift of prophecy, however, depends on the supposition that human behaviour is repetitive, that "all" is in fact the mere repetition of a single act into infinity, enacted "on this same divan or bed." What, therefore, is the real difference between the industrial system, in which "all the women are one woman" and the identification represented by Tiresias? In which case is the typist less of a type?

The poem itself suggests that there may be no difference because Tiresias and the "human engine" are one and the same: North quotes from the line beginning "When the human engine" to the line ending "throbbing between two lives."

By means of this intricate chiasmus, Eliot links the human engine that waits to Tiresias who throbs through the middle term of the taxi, which both waits and throbs. In so doing, Eliot suggests a link between the reduced conditions of the modern worker and the mythical hermaphrodite who includes all experience. The passage contains within itself a representation of this link in Tiresias's throbbing "between two lives." Tiresias appears here almost as a metaphor for metaphor, throbbing between two lives as the common term that joins them. But the activity of joining, the throbbing that seems to evoke human longing, is in fact the noise of the taxi engine, the drumming of its pistons a travesty of human sexual activity. In this way, the passage mocks its own insertion of Tiresias between two lives by positioning the taxi as the true medium between individual and race, present and eternity.

Even stylistically, the passage undermines its own assertion of metaphorical identification by merely juxtaposing the two elements that both terms share: There is no "between" between throbbing and waiting, no comma or other punctuation, and yet this is where the all important connection between Tiresias and the modern worker is accomplished. Read in this, way, the passage suggests that the process by which Tiresias represents all men and women is no different from the process by which the modern industrial machine conglomerates them into one mass, that what looks like metaphorical representation is but the additive accumulation typical of industrialism.

The typist, that is to say, is just as much a type within the "inclusive human consciousness" represented by Tiresias as she is within the routines of her office. The same thing is true of the typist's lover. Tiresias is able to understand the young man carbuncular, "one of the low," because he has "walked among the lowest of the dead." He is able to understand human beings, in other words, only insofar as they are types. The uniformity of modern industrialized life is therefore but one instance of the uniformity of all human life. Adorno makes this point when he says of Kafka, "The absence of choice and of memory which characterizes the life of white collar workers in the huge cities of the twentieth century becomes, as later in Eliot's 'Waste Land', the image of an archaic past." That archaic past is not the one the Victorians fondly identified with Athens but one in which human beings are "driven together like animals." Adorno may well be thinking of Tiresias, in whom a sterile conglomeration of male and female represents an ancient situation still repeated in the modern city, inside, in the loveless sex of the typist and her young man, and outside, in the inorganic relationships of the crowd.

Tiresias was certainly at one point to have served the very function Eliot assigned to modern literature in his early essays. As an observing eye that is both of the crowd and outside it, he is to reconcile individual and community, part and whole, freedom and necessity. The directions Eliot included in his notes to the poem suggest that Eliot hoped even after the poem was written that Tiresias could fill this role. But the Tiresias he has actually portrayed in the poem itself is instead the incarnation of the failure of reconciliation, a mere juxtaposition of part and whole that dramatizes the gulf between them. As a dramatic figure, Tiresias demonstrates two equal but opposite fears that both gripped Eliot, a fear of fragmentation and loneliness and a fear of featureless uniformity. In the modern world, it seems, freedom cannot be had without fragmentation and loneliness, and community cannot be had without coercion and conformity.

Margot Norris

Lewis' Nietzschean derision of "the crowd" in Blast was widely echoed in modernist representations of patriotic enthusiasm, as in Yeats's elegy for Major Robert Gregory, and the blind obedience of massed armies and the mass casualties they produced, as in Eliot's "A crowd flowed over London Bridge, so many/I had not thought death had undone so many." But in Blast Lewis doubly politicizes the crowd by naming its desire as suffrage, echoing Nietzsche's excoriation in Ecce Homo of women's democratic movements as bids for cattle voting rights: "Their attitude is as though these universal crowds wanted some new vague Suffrage". Of Cantleman, his alter ego in Blasting and Bombardiering running with the crowds at the Olympiad, Lewis writes, "he was very stupid. He was a suffragette." In "The Code of a Herdsman" Lewis writes, "As to women: wherever you can, substitute the society of men. Treat them kindly, for they suffer from the herd".

This feminization of the crowd brings modernism's contradictory discourse of population control into sharper focus, and exposes the logical strategy that lodges control with art. The 1915 war issue of Blast blasts "Birth-Control" and blesses "War Babies". The logic of the etymological play—the blighting of birth control as enabling the breaking out of the embryo—is clearer than the political logic of a polemic that simultaneously despises the crowd produced by overpopulation and inveighs against the contraception that would reduce its size and proliferation.

The issue is clearly the investiture of control: the indiscriminate population control by war preferred to the discriminate population control by democratic female suffrage, because the violence of the war at least releases energy and creates a vortex while feminism empowers the herd. Modernism ultimately enacted, in its own textual strategies, the function of the war as an imperfectly self-correcting machine that disciplined the masses and thereby institutionalized itself as the war's cultural counterpart.

The modernist text that becomes most conspicuously identified with the contradictory effects of this project is, of course, Eliot's The Waste Land. Canonized as the premier address to "the unprecedented death toll of the First World War," its historical reference encloses the illogical nexus of maritial and feminist discourses of population control in order to sublate them wholly to the mythology of sacral fertility.

Upon the editorial pruning by Pound, the poem's opening introduces a montage of displaced historical codes for the outbreak and aftermath of World War I: the post-war haunting of watering places by the dislocated German aristocrats from eastern Europe, the ethnic chauvinisms and tensions of the Hapsburg Empire displaced from the Balkans to the Baltic, and the figure of the arch-duke careening downhill on a sled nearly out of control: "Bin gar keine Russin, stamm' aus Litauen, echt deutsch./And when we were children, staying at the arch-duke's/My cousin's, he took me out on a sled,/And I was frightened." The challenge of the poem may be sited in the insomniac reading of the baroness: "I read, much of the night, and go south in the winter."

What does one read after the catastrophe of a war that murders sleep, and what a writing replaces the peace foreclosed by historical nightmare? "Falling towers/Jerusalem Athens Alexandria/Vienna London." The fall and dispersal of the Austro-Hungarian Empire opens the text, and the deferred twilight of the British Empire, ingesting the religion of its colonies along with India's tea and spices, closes it in a cacophony of indigested and untranslated quotations that textually foreclose geopolitical peace. The poem's tacit attempt to reconstitute a third empire of polyglot and polymath a culture—what Eagleton describes as "an alternative text which is nothing less than the closed, coherent, authoritative discourse of the mythologies a which frame it"—becomes no more than another haunting, another invasion of the poem by the dead. "Eliot celebrates the voices of the dead," Maud Ellmann writes, "but he comes to dread their verbal ambush in The Waste Land."

Ellmann's elegant rhetorical summation of the poem's compulsive attempt to remember and resurrect the dead through a doomed prosopopoeia—"The Waste Land strives to give a face to death"—endows the impossibility of representing the mass death and destruction of World War I with a compelling figure of poetic performativity. But one might argue that there are two kinds of dead trying to appear in the poem, and that they are not equal: the poetic dead voices of the literary tradition, whose eloquence is the louder for the fragmentariness of their utterance, and the voiceless war dead. Indeed, even the figure of the spared, the demobbed of returning soldier who gives the poem its most direct and specific historical reference, is not detachable from the repulsiveness of the mob.

His wife, in fact, is given a face, or gives herself a face ("pulling a long face"), and it is the face of an anti-Helen; the face that launched a thousand ships becomes the young version of Pound's "old bitch gone in the teeth." Lil is a young bitch gone in the teeth, whose toothless face creates universal aversion: "He said, I swear, I can't bear to look at you./And no more can't I, I said." In fattaching Lil's supreme ugliness to the unwholesomeness of her class, Eliot tracks highly specific causalities—the toothlessness of calcium deficiency from the multiparity of six pregnancies before the age of thirty-one "You ought to be ashamed, I said, to look so antique./(And her only thirty-one)"—back to the pullulating breeding of the masses.

The poem reverses the flow of the war dead to return them, by way of London Bridge, to the teeming slums from which they came. Eliot, like Lewis, tropes the war as a bridge between home and front, between living and dead—"The bridge, you see, is the war" —and this bridge crosses, too, the discourses of population control that have cast their contradictory shadows upon other modernistic war writing. Reversing Gaudier's "good mouth," Lil's toothless head is carved into the barren landscape like a giant dead skull: "Dead mountain mouth of carious teeth that cannot spit" to be traversed by "the hooded hordes swarming/Over endless plain, stumbling in the cracked earth."

But in spite of the industrial and urban pollution ("The river sweats oil and tar") they produce along with the "White bodies naked on the low damp ground/And bones cast in a little low dry garret," the poem blasts Birth-Control for the masses as surely as did Blast. "You are a proper fool," says Lil's interlocutor of her botched abortion, and Lil replies, "The chemist said it would be all right, but I've never been the same." As a form of population control, the war too was a botched abortion—of the sort that reduced her progeny, but left Lil ill, disfigured, and prematurely aged. World War I may have reduced some of Europe's unwanted masses, but at the price of leaving her countries weak, disfigured, and spiritually dessicated.

The conversation in the pub that retells the conversation with Lil is Eliot's Arnoldian demonstration that the discourse of the Populace is impervious to poetry because it lacks the porosity of other parts of the poem that let quotation leak in. For discourse to become art like sculpture requires the scission of metaphoric teeth. "I didn't mince my words," the speaker says, and her narrative is conspicuous in its seamless wholeness, unchopped by the parataxes that segment the poem's other speech. The masses produce a nearly perfect redundancy of citation, the episode suggests; culture and tradition are replaced by verbatim or unmasticated reproduction of earlier verbatim reproductions.

This pullulation or regurgitation of trivial discourse—the speaker telling us what she told Lil Albert had said before he left—reproduces endless Heideggerean Gerede or idle talk deprived of teeth, "You have them all out, Lil, and get a nice set,/He said." The conversation's twice-told and triangular structure, whose parenthetical asides make a confidante of the poem's addressee, restores the implied reader herself to the masses. It is among the poem's projects to break up this mindless abulia of the masses by using the text's erudition to babelize its readership, carving its homeogeneous philistinism into polyglottal segments and cultural elites. By refusing to translate or reference many of its citations, the poem's cultivation creates borderlines of incommunication and minefields of incomprehension that recreate the conditions of geopolitical war and class revolution. The unified empire of culture the poem conjures up in its referenced appeal to the cosmopolitanism of Cambridge anthropology and the archetypalism of comparative religion becomes no more than a bogus sublation of the poem's politics into a myth of universal order that its own textual babelization ritually destroys.

Tim Dean

My account of impersonality shifts the critical debate away from closet logic toward a different way of conceptualizing sexuality's impact on Eliot's poetry. Sexuality in Eliot involves hiddenness not as a mode of concealment, but as an occult mode of access with erotic implications. His impersonalist theory of poetry compels Eliot—even in the face of his own conscious intentions—to embrace a passivity and openness that renders him vulnerable to what feels like bodily violation. Hence his propensity for embodying these qualities in women and sexually ambiguous youths, such as Saint Sebastian and Narcissus. Eliot imagines figures for the ideal impersonalist poet as eminently rapable, and he conceives this violation as the paradoxical precondition for that "inviolable voice," which, in The Waste Land, he attempts not merely to represent but actually to approximate. The raped and wounded figures in his poetry represent not abject bodies that Eliot repudiates as a means of shoring up his precarious masculine heterosexual identity, as recent critics have claimed. On the contrary, these violated figures represent Eliot's poetic ideal. Rejecting the terms of revelation and concealment that have dominated Eliot criticism, I shall argue that from his impersonalist practice something fundamental remains to be learned about the relation between transhistorical conceptions of poetic utterance and modern forms of sexuality.

A rather different way of reading Eliot's gestures of renunciation stems from recognizing in the modernist use of masks a technique of self-dispossession that entails a structural rather than a psychological form of masochism. By this I mean that impersonal masking—the speaking in a voice other than one's own—involves the poet in a suspension or diminuition of self that tends to accompany the poetic medium itself, irrespective of his or her own preferences. While modernist impersonality is readily grasped as entailing the use of personae, we need not understand masking as solely or even primarily a technique of concealment. Persona originally referred to the mask worn by actors in Greek drama, but the word etymologically derives from the Latin phrase per sonare, meaning "to sound through." Rather than designating the visual form hiding the actor's face, persona initially denoted the mask's mouthpiece or a reed device inserted into it for amplifying the actor's voice. Thus in the first place a persona was less a means of visual concealment than of vocal channeling; it entailed a form of speaking through rather than of speaking falsely. More than a mode of camouflage, impersonation may represent a way to inhabit other existences—a way to transform oneself by becoming possessed by others. This distinction furnishes us with a rationale for approaching modernist impersonality as a strategy not of dissimulation but of access to regions of voice beyond the self's.

Eliot's ideas about occult transmission are dramatized in The Waste Land. While Madame Sosostris stands as the poem's best known medium, she is not the only figure associated with clairvoyance. Both the Sibyl, whose words compose the poem's epigraph, and Tiresias, who supposedly unites the poem, are second-sighted. Given that Eliot derived Madame Sosostris's name from a fortune-teller called Sesostris in Aldous Huxley's Crome Yellow (a novel published only in November 1921), biographer Lyndall Gordon is justified in claiming that the Sosostris scene must have been a significant late addition to the poem; her pack of cards "is a unifying device," Gordon suggests, "a late attempt to draw the fragments together with a parade of the poem's characters." Madame Sosostris is thus in one respect a modern incarnation of Tiresias, himself "the most important personage in the poem, uniting all the rest," according to Eliot's note. It is not only as mediums but also as ostensibly unifying consciousnesses that Tiresias and Sosostris represent surrogates for the impersonalist poet.

Although associated with femininity and so-called passive homosexuality, the experience of self-dispossession cannot be understood as the prerogative of any psychological identity because it represents the loss of identity as such. Self-dispossession is rendered intelligible by psychoanalytic theories of masochism—or by cultural stereotypes about heterosexual women and effeminate homosexuals—but may in fact be a structural entailment of the poetic medium as much as a psychological impulse. "he poet has... no identity... he has no self," argued Keats, in a formulation suggesting that the poet's identity consists in the loss of identity or, as he put it in the same letter, in self-annihilation. In this transhistorical conception of poetic utterance, which stretches back to Plato's Ion, the suspension of individual identity, by whatever means, is deemed necessary for poetic making. With Bersani's account in mind, we could say that the "appeal of powerlessness" concerns aesthetic pleasure as much as it does erotic Jouissance, because the medium requires a self-shattering or impersonalization that is synonymous with poetic practice itself.

An Ode of Rejeuvenation in T.S. Eliot's "The Wasteland"

"April is the Cruellest Month..."

In T. S. Eliot's "The Wasteland", he seems to be saying that out of death and winter comes spring and new life. In order for there to be healing and happiness, first a pain must occur. The opening of his poem portrays this concept clearly while the rest of the poem seems to briefly brush upon that notion. At the time the poem was written, World War I had just ended placing the world in an era of depression, loss, and ultimately death looming over everyone. Eliot's own life was going through a dry spell where he was not receiving any inspirations or new ideas to write about. The world was a wasteland, and his life was a wasteland, but there still seemed to be a hope in the midst of it all. In order for things to improve, this feeling of pain and desolation had to be dealt with and pushed aside. Once that was accomplished healing and new beginnings could occur.

The world would be capable of savoring the happy times after having gone through such terrible times. Eliot compares this era of new beginnings to spring, since spring generally is symbolic of new life. However, unlike Chaucer, he does not imply that spring is necessarily a happy time, or that beginnings are happy. He simply says that spring is a necessity when dealing with pain that will enable things to become fully alive again. Eliot says that "April is the cruelest month" which mixes "memory and desire". Mixing memory and desire can be interpreted many ways. Often for something new, living, and less painful to happen there needs to be a desire for life. The desire is there because the memories of life in the past prevail. Gregory Jay says in his article that memories can also block the past, but April and a season of new life comes. As it arrives the life awakens passion pulling out the coldness. He calls this an "ode of dejection" that shows a form of hurt and feeling coming after the initial pain. Therefore, in his essay Jay argues that Eliot has taken Chaucer's celebration of life, and turned it into an ode of dejection. Another way of looking at Eliot's "ode of dejection" is that this "celebration of life" was written realistically to reflect Eliot's time. Eliot wrote "The Wasteland" during the modernist movement in the early twentieth century. An element of the modern philosophy led to poems being written about or with a sense of loneliness, dejection, and despair. This sense of dejection reflects his time, which was quite different from the medieval ideas implied by Chaucer in The Canterbury Tales.

Most writers choose to write about issues that are of great concern to them at the moment. For example, Europe was in shambles at the time Eliot was writing. Many had died in the war, so life was not being celebrated. The poem may have been about dejection or celebration as it was something everyone was in need of. Eliot wanted to show people it was possible for them to handle all the death they had experienced. A healing process must occur in order for people to continue on with life. In line five Eliot writes, "Winter kept us warm, covering Earth in forgetful snow". This is a line which implies that people had not begun to come to terms with the death they had experienced. It still comforted people to feel depressed and cold, both feelings winter brings to mind. More confirmation that winter does not have life in it is found in the line that says, "A little life with dried tubers". Winter was the time right after the war, the time in people's lives where there was not much hope, yet it was a comfortable place to be in. David Spurr writes that "forgetful" and "snow" are compared nature. Giving snow a human quality makes the image stronger in Spurr's case showing a type of consciousness that pursues disorder in an inner world.

He says Eliot never unifies the disorder, but uses the inner imagination and looks out to the desolate sea the poem seems to display. This modernist idea of desolation supports the idea of the world being in disarray after the war, in this time of winter. After winter the discomfort truly begins to be noticed, the soothing feeling of depression is gone with the sharp sting of the thaw. Dull roots begin to stir in the rain, the lilacs begin to blossom, and life begins again. This is a cruel process according to Eliot. It is the healing process after the war that is painful, but brings people back to a similar existence they had before the war, one with less pain and more life. Edmund Wilson claims that the poem exhibits a "post-War world of shattered institutions, strained nerves and bankrupt ideals where life no longer seems serious or coherent" (Smith 138). Eliot may show in his poem that these things happened after the war, but he also seems to show that the shattered fragments of institutions and ideals can be rebuilt and reunified. As April, or this new season in time, begins the healing process can start, and these things can be reestablished.

"The Wasteland" portrayed "high hopes raised by the idealism of Woodrow Wilson", according to Maurice Bowra, a critic of the 1930s. Grover Smith, who quotes Bowra, claims it was Stalin's idealism and not Wilson's sense of hope. However, whoever's idealism it was is not as important as the new hopes they had to try and rebuild countries and bring life to them again. These were desires determined after the war and are portrayed in the poem by the first few opening lines. The mixing of memory and desire is clearly seen here. The way the world was in the past is now being desired again for the future. There is hope that the world can go back to how it was according to Spurr. Smith also writes about Malcolm Cowley wrote in Exile's Return "The Wasteland" was "socially divisive to its time". Cowley said the poem was stating that the past was dignified and the present was barren of emotion. Most critics do not agree with this argument, so many people tend to pay attention to other critics who saw hope in the future coming about. Eliot might be saying that the past was dignified and the present is barren, but he is also saying it does not need to stay that way. He perhaps means that the healing process has begun, and things will go back to the dignified past, once the winter is gone, and the pain is dealt with. The memory and desire are mixing "Stirring dull roots with spring rain". The lines "stirring dull roots with spring rain" is once again another image of the healing process as roots grow deeper in the spring rain.

They must break through the hard ground in order to grow, but the rain softens the ground and nourishes the plants helping them grow. Not only are these references to growth and life about recovering after the war, but Gregory Jay also believes it is referring to Eliot's own personal life. He writes that Eliot had come to a standstill in his writing career at this point. He was having a hard time thinking of things to write about and was afraid that he would never have another good idea again. He alludes to this in some of his own writings, so there is a death that has occurred in his brain when it comes to ideas. The "death" does not last long, and though perhaps painful Eliot thinks of new ideas, and this new creation he has made is the beginning of a new season.

April represents the awakening of ideas and passions he was holding inside as the past he held was blocking his ability to write new works. The reference to "Dull roots" in this case can mean that his ancestry was dull. The winter and forgetful snow was a "secure oblivion that seduces and comforts those who do not presume to begin writing again". Gregory Jay was saying that Eliot was in a state of fear that he might never be able to get out of because it felt comfortable to him. Eliot explains in these lines that he overcame his fear of having nothing to write about by merely writing.

Then it can be possibly stated that because of the fear that he would never write again, he was able to force himself to write this poem. There are many different interpretations and possibilities as to why Eliot wrote about April being a cruel month. Most of them make sense, and are correct in their own way. He apparently wrote the poem quite rapidly. Martin mentions in an essay that no one really knows what the poem is about and that no one probably ever will be able to determine it. His collection of essays therefore gives different interpretations as every critic does. Martin explains how the poem was originally received, in a variety of ways. Some people thought it was puzzling, some a hoax, and one person said Eliot just did not know how to write poetry.

These sometimes conflicting interpretations are dealt with as the entirety of the poem is studied by critics. Continuing on with the next couple lines of the poem Eliot left more images about the seasons to be understood. He had mentioned winter and spring, but he went on to talk about summer. He never concludes with autumn, however, but just continues with the story the poem tells ending with summer. "Summer surprised us...with a shower of rain" implies things are still not always perfect, but the life is there making things easier. "And went on in sunlight" shows that despite the rain life continues after the rain and there is sunlight again. Summer is the result of the pain and healing process that spring takes people through. Eliot is suggesting in his poem that the world can overcome difficulties and barrenness.

Through a healing process that may hurt life can be restored once again to the world. The world after the war went through years and years of healing. It was never completely restored before there was another World War that left the land devastated once again. The cruelness occurred for a long time, but after the Second World War lilacs blossomed out of the dead land. It was a very long healing process, longer than Eliot probably imagined, but it was necessary.

In the end seasons of summer came. The world has not seen another major war since then which suggests that summer has arrived again. Eliot did not know all this was going to happen, of course, but he was giving people a type of hope in the midst of the fragments and wasteland left behind after the war. He had no idea the healing process would take long, but he had struggled with a similar situation in his own life. His writing had come to a desolate lonely place, but he began again and brought the world "The Wasteland". Just by writing his poem he was proving that after the cruel process of getting things to grow out of dead land the results can be glorious. Lilacs and other plants that must grow in desolate lands become hearty after breaking through the ground. Plants bear the wind and weather in order to blossom and live. The opening of "The Wasteland" is now quite different from the original "Boston night-town scene" he originally planned. It is understandable why a poem entitled "The Wasteland" would begin with a depiction of a desolate land, or a place in need of a thaw.

The winter Eliot begins with makes the reader think of a barren wasteland where everything is dead. This mod rn sense of despair is there and continues even through the healing process. The thawing of winter into spring and the growth of the lilacs shows that the land is not going to be bare anymore. There is a growing and replanting that is happening throughout the dead land. The land so badly in need of life is now developing slowly and cruelly into the long desired summertime where life is abundant. "The Wasteland" has been interpreted by a great assortment of literary critics with an array of differing opinions. The opening lines of the poem are clearly about new beginnings whether they are beginnings after a war, in Eliot's career, or in nature. Eliot is saying that in order for the new life generally associated with summer the pain that comes with April and spring must be dealt with after winter. Though it is not necessarily a "celebration of life" like Chaucer's Canterbury Tales, it is not quite the "ode of dejection" Jay also refers to it as. Rather it is perhaps an ode of rejuvenation, a bringing about of life through a cruel process after a lifeless time.

Tennyson's Influence on T.S. Eliot

George P. Landow Professor of English and Art History, Brown University Tennyson provides a major influence on Eliot's poetry throughout his career, and of all his poems In Memoriam had the most pervasive effect, as its wasteland imagery, style, subject, and experimental structure appear again in The Wasteland. Indeed, The Wasteland in many ways appears a spiritual rewriting of Tennyson's In Memoriam. Although Eliot imitated Tennyson in his first poems, by the time he set out on his own path, he tended to denigrate his predecessor in critical essays, but as he matured, he increasingly acknowledged Tennyson's mastery.

In his fine book on Eliot's Victorian inheritance, David Ned Tobin describes how pervasive was Tennyson for young poets at Harvard:

The subject of "Tennyson at Harvard" suggests a paradox: Tennyson was the compromising arch-Victorian, or the unread, dead Great Poet, or the misread Master — but in all cases his poetry was still impossible to avoid, still a living voice. Eliot's Harvard poems, like those of his peers, echo the voice of Tennyson.... A young man writing poetry in the first decade of this century would find it impossible to avoid the shadow of Tennyson. It wasn't necessary to "discover" him, or cultivate a special enthusiasm for him. One simply knew Tennyson, Tennysonian diction, Tennysonian nuance, Tennysonian themes. Eliot's early poems bear this out.

The older he became, the more secure his reputation as a major poet, the more Eliot found himself able to praise Tennyson. As Tobin shows, in succeeding iterations of remarks on his Victorian predceessor, Eliot made his praise less and less equivocal until by 1936 he could write: "Tennyson is a great poet, for reasons that are perfectly clear. He has three qualities which are seldom found together except in the greatest poets: abundance, variety, and complete competence". Eliot, Tobin points out, "no longer had to cloud his appraisal of Tennyson with defensiveness"

By this point in his career, the modern poet unequivocably praises his predecessor's great experimental elegy:

Its technical merit alone is enough to ensure its perpetuity. While Tennyson's technical competence is everywhere masterly and satisfying, In Memoriam is the most unapproachable of all his poems. Here are one hundred and thirty-two passages, each of several quatrains in the same form, and never monotony or repetition.... We may not memorize a few passages, we cannot find a "fair sample"; we have to comprehend the whole of a poem which is essentially the length that it is.... It is unique: it is a long poem made by putting together lyrics, which have only the unity and continuity of a diary, the concentrated diary of a man confessing to himself. It is a diary of whiich we have to read every word.

Some of Eliot's highest praise of In Memoriam comes, Tobin demonstrates, during the years he is composing The Four Quartets, another major work with strong parallels to the elegy. Anyone interested in the rich, complex relatinship between the two poets — each perhaps the most influential of his age — should read Tobin's valuable book.

"Such a Vision of the Street as the Street Hardly Understands"

Jonathan Swift, T. S. Eliot, and the Anti-Pastoral

The following four poems, one by Jonathan Swift and three by T. S. Eliot, are all poems of morning in the city. I use the term "anti-pastoral" in the title of this paper to draw attention to the urban settings and themes of these poems and to suggest that Swift and Eliot were explicitly rejecting the pastoral genre. In Swift's poem, the anti- or mock-pastoral is perhaps most clear in the lines "The Turnkey now his Flock returning sees,/Duly let out at Night to steal for Fees." Here the pastoral shepherd becomes a jailer who releases inmates at night to steal money for bribes. Each of these poems gives us an unromanticized, naturalistic vision of the working- and lower classes in the city, as opposed to the romanticized images of rural folk characteristic of the pastoral genre. In "A Description of Morning," the apprentice is slipshod, the chimney-sweep is shrill, and Brickdust Moll screams through half the street. Far from the harmonious pastoral idyll, we are presented a scene of chaos, noise, and corruption.

I first became interested in the Swift-Eliot comparison when I read Swift's "A Description of Morning" and immediately thought of Eliot's "Preludes." I saw that by weaving the lines of these poems together we might say that Swift's "A Description of the Morning" represents "the thousand sordid images" of which Swift's soul is constituted. Likewise, the image of Betty discomposing her own bed after leaving her master's bed, along with the catalogue of hypocrisies throughout the poem, could be characterized as the "masquerades that time resumes" each morning. We might also say that Swift had "such a vision of the street as the street hardly understands."

Jonathan Swift, 1709
"A Description of the Morning"
Now hardly here and there an Hackney-Coach
Appearing, show'd the ruddy Morns Approach.
Now Betty from her Master's Bed had flown,
And softly stole to discompose her own.
The Slipshod Prentice from his Masters Door
Had par'd the Dirt, and Sprinkled round the Floor.
Now Moll had whirl'd her Mop with dext'rous Airs,
Prepar'd to Scrub the Entry and the Stairs.
The Youth with broomy Stumps began to trace
The Kennel-Edge, where Wheels had worn the Place.
The Smallcoal-Man was heard with Cadence deep,
Till drown'd in shriller Notes of Chimney-Sweep.
Duns at his Lordships Gate begin to meet,
And Brickdust Moll had Scream'd through half the Street.
The Turnkey now his Flock returning sees,
Duly let out at Night to steal for Fees.
The watchful Bailiffs take their silent Stands,
And School-Boys lag with Satchels in their Hands.

T.S. Eliot

Prelude II
The morning comes to consciousness
Of faint stale smells of beer
From the sawdust trampled streets
With all the feet that press
To early coffee stands.
With all the other masquerades
That time resumes,
One thinks of all the hands

That are raising dingy shades
In a thousand furnished rooms.
Prelude III
You tossed a blanket from the bed,
You lay upon your back and waited;
You dosed, and watched the night revealing
The thousand sordid images
Of which your soul is constituted;
They flickered against the ceiling.
And when all the world came back
And the light crept up between the shutters
And you heard the sparrows in the gutters,
You had such a vision of the street
As the street hardly understands;
Sitting along the bed's edge, where
You curled the papers from your hair,
Or clasped the yellow soles of feet
In the palms of both soiled hands.
Morning at the Window
They are rattling breakfast plates in basement kitchens,
And along the trampled edges of the street
I am aware of the damp souls of housemaids
Sprouting despondently at area gates.
The brown waves of fog toss up to me
Twisted faces from the bottom of the street,
And tear from a passer-by with muddy skirts
An aimless smile that hovers in the air
And vanishes along the level of the roofs.
1917

It is well known that T. S. Eliot had a great appreciation for certain Restoration and Augustan poets and playwrights, as well the metaphysical poets. Thus, it should not be surprising to find that Eliot borrowed from, "stole," or modeled some of his work on seventeenth- and early-eighteenth-century authors. Richard Turner makes a good case for Eliot's borrowing a phrase from Swift's A Tale of a Tub in his poem "Burbank With A Baedeker: Bleistein With A Cigar." Turner argues that with this borrowing "Eliot puts himself in the tradition of Swift as those who see into the forces that corrupt civilization". Nicholas Joost and Ann Risdon also cite Eliot's borrowings from Ben Jonson, among others. It appears that Swift and Eliot each saw himself inhabiting a corrupt, (crumbling civilization-as opposed to the harmony of the pastoral idyll. In addition, their work indicates that they found urban settings conducive to good poetry-a poetry filled with tension, ambiguity, and vivid imagery. Placed aside to the energy, confusion, and noise of the city, the pastoral landscape must have seemed quite dull to these two poets. The concept of the "anti-pastoral" comes to mind when we consider Eliot's view that at the root of mediocre English poetry, as represented by the 1920 Georgian Anthology, is the idea that "It is necessary to pretend that England is a green and pleasant land". "Green and pleasant" pastoral England is set against Eliot's hard, stony Waste Land, of which we see a preview in the "Preludes" and the "Morning at the Window." Yet Eliot is just as contemptuous of popular American poetry. In commenting on the 1920 anthology entitled Some Contemporary Poets edited by Harold Munro, Eliot writes, "The conventional literature of America is either wretchedly imitative of European culture, or ignorant of it, or both". Eliot characterizes contemporary American literature as a "literature without any critical sense; a poetry which takes not the faintest notice of the development of French verse from Baudelaire to the present day and which has perused English literature with only a wandering antiquarian passion".

It has been well documented that Eliot admired Swift for, among other traits, his sense of "disgust." Eliot classified "Dryden as the great master of contempt, Pope as the great master of hatred, and Swift as the great master of disgust" (Johnson 310). Maurice Johnson notes that in 1924, seven years after the publication of "Preludes" and "Morning at the Window," Eliot wrote that he had earlier planned an essay on Swift as a poet to be included in a series of essays on seventeenth- and eighteenth-century English authors; however, as far as I am aware Eliot's only published statements on Swift are in the nature of asides, such as the remark about his sense of disgust. Eliot claimed that Swift's writings successfully represent the objective correlative of Swift's sense of disgust; that is to say, Swift was able to externalize, or give objective representation to, his emotions of disgust in the language of his poetry. Maurice Johnson writes: "There is in Swift's own life, according to Eliot, an objective correlative for the disgust he famously expressed in his poetry and prose.". Johnson goes on to state that "in Eliot's opinion, deep and intense emotion, terror, passion, bitter personal feeling, and tortured talent will be felt through satire that is 'Swiftian' and great". Eliot also claimed that Dryden "has not the passion of his cousin Swift" (Johnson 313). Evidently, Eliot felt a powerful attraction for and seems to have identified with Swift, and they do seem to have had similar temperaments-at least in Eliot's opinion, if not in fact. Again quoting Maurice Johnson, "Eliot characterized Gullivers Travels as a 'work of cynicism and loathing,' which manifests 'the progressive cynicism of the mature and disappointed man of the world.' This was written not in censure but in praise, for a sense of personal disgust was for Eliot a distinguishing characteristic of great 'Swiftian' satire". It is unlikely that Eliot would have expressed such a keen interest in Swift if he had not felt that he and Swift had certain traits in common. I should note, however, that the poems by Eliot that I have selected for this paper are not satirical, and the satire aspect is not the main thrust of my argument. My primary concern in this paper is the connection between Swift and Eliot's views on the middle classes and how these views were expressed in their poetry.

Eliot's own sense of disgust is clearly expressed in his "London Letters," which he composed from 1921-22 as a correspondent for The Dial. The main source of Eliot's disgust, as expressed in the "London Letters," was the English and American "insurgent middle class, the General Reading Public" along with the poets who appeal to middle-class audiences. Eliot claims that "the Middle Class finds itself on the side more and more of what used to called the Lower Class". The April 1922 "London Letter" is devoted to a critique of two new poetry anthologies: Methuen and Company's Anthology of Modern Verse and Untermeyer's Modern American Poetry. Eliot speaks of the

instinct for safetywhich seems to make the English poet take refuge in just those sentiments, images, and thoughts which render a man least distinguishable from the mob, the respectable mob, the decent middle-class mob ....

We have, then, a large number of writers giving the public what it likes; and a large body of reviewers telling it that it is right to like what it likes; and the Morning Post to tell it that everything new is a symptom of Bolshevism; and the London Mercury to tell it that it is already such an enlightened public that what it does not like cannot be really good.

Judging by his "London Letters," Eliot found the middle classes dull, insipid, and completely lacking in "culture." He speaks, on one occasion, of "this great middle class public which consumes Georgian poetry" (70: 451-52). In his April 1922 "London Letter" Eliot writes, "There is certainly, in the atmosphere of literary London, something which may provisionally be called moral cowardice". In his November 1922 "Letter" Eliot goes as far as to state that "the middle classes are morally corrupt".

It is important to recognize, however, that Eliot's scorn was directed against the middle classes, not the working or lower classes, and the most salient parallel is these four poems by Swift and Eliot is that their subjects come primarily from the lower social strata-such as, in Prelude II, the population that resides in "a thousand furnished rooms." It appears that both Swift and Eliot were more kindly disposed to the working and lower classes. Arno Löffler notes that

Swift's manners were habitually easy with common peopleSwift's attitude was certainly exemplary in his time: There was an increasing interest in the 'common people': this enlightened view interest was-partly at least-based on the observation that among the 'common people' there were to be found specimens that possessed outstanding talents and abilities and were able to make the best of them.

This type of native talent is evident in the first Moll, who "whirl'd her mop with dext'rous airs," as well as in the singing Small-Coal Man, whom I discuss at greater length below. In a significant parallel, Eliot's primary complaint against the middle-classes was that they stamped out all individuality, the culture of mass production being inimical to genius. Yet this does not necessarily mean that Eliot expressed great benevolence toward the lower classes, as some critics have implied. Joost and Risdon, for instance, claim that in his "London Letters" Eliot "is never snobbish or lacking in sympathy for the ordinary working man and woman, quite the contrary".

The evidence, however, does not support the claim that Eliot was particularly well disposed toward the lower classes, and indeed there is plenty of snobbishness in the "London Letters." It might be more accurate to suppose that Eliot was friendlier toward the lower classes because they posed no immediate threat to high culture. In November 1922, Eliot writes, "The middle classes, in England as elsewhere, under democracy, are morally dependent upon the aristocracy, and the aristocracy are morally in fear of the middle class which is gradually absorbing and destroying them". Lumping the middle an lower classes together, in the March 1921 "Letter," Eliot writes, "Both the middle and lower classes are finding safety in Regular Hours, Regular Wages, Regular Pensions, and Regular Ideas. In other words, there will soon be only one class, and the second Flood is here". It is interesting that in Joost and Isdon's quote of the above statement b

Eliot, they leave out the words "Bothand lower class," along with the final ominous sentence, thus making Eliot appea friendlier toward the lower classes than he may have been. hile a student at Harvard, Eliot developed a fondness for urlesque and vaudeville, and in London he loved to atte d the musical-hall comedies. Eliot wrote that "in the music-h ll comedians the lower class find the artistic expression and dignity of their own lives".

Thus, Eliot, who is a notorious as a snob and an elitist, in his younger years had an appreciation for "vulgar" pleasures. Recalling Swift's famously vulgar "excremental vision," Eliot applauded a London production of Ben Jonson's Volpone which refused to expurgate any "indecencies." In the June 1921 "London Letter" Eliot wrote: "The sense of relief, in hearing the indecencies of Elizabethan and Restoration drama, leaves one a better and a stronger man". Joost and Risdon write:

There is obviously a direct parallel between enjoyment of the bawdy of the Jacobean comedy and of the frank and sometimes crude humour or the music-hall performers. In contrast to his disgust with the inanities of contemporary 'Georgian' literature, is his pleasure in the openness and frankness of both the music hall and Jonson's play.

The connection between social class structures and the "anti-pastoral," or Swift's and Eliot's rejection of the pastoral, is that the middle classes would have been the prime consumers of pastoral poetry, both in the early eighteenth and the early twentieth centuries. Furthermore, the readership that favored contemporary texts and modern ideas, whom Swift mocked in The Battle of the Books, A Tale of a Tub, and elsewhere, would have been come largely from the middle classes.And while it is true that Swift himself was a member of the middle class, he, unlike some other eighteenth-century authors (e.g., Defoe, Fielding, Richardson) wrote primarily for an aristocratic audience and resented middle-class encroachments.

Looking at two of these poems more closely, in Swift and Eliot's mention of gates we have a concrete manifestation of the desire to keep the social classes apart in both the early-eighteenth and the early-twentieth centuries. In Swift's poem we have: "Duns at his Lordships Gate begin to meet." And from Eliot's "Morning at the Window": "And along the trampled edges of the street/I am aware of the damp souls of housemaids/Sprouting despondently at area gates." In other words, the working and lower classes are waiting outside the gates of the upper classes. Only this physical structure separates the rich from the lower classes. From the above lines, "duns" are creditors, which implies that even his Lordship is in financial trouble, and nothing is as it appears. In fact, "his Lordship," given that he lives in the city, would actually have been a member of the upper-middle class, as opposed to the landed nobility-and the same can be said of the master who sleeps with his servant Betty. Hence, it is the upper-middle class characters who serve as the target of Swift's satire, rather than the lower classes, whom Swift treats much better - witness the first Moll and the Small-Coal Man.

Perhaps the first thing the reader notices on a first reading of these four poems is that there is dirt, dust, and mud everywhere; it's a collection of sordid, soiled images. From Eliot: "One thinks of all the hands/That are raising dingy shades/In a thousand furnished rooms"; you "clasped the yellow soles of feet/In the palms of both soiled hand"; "From the sawdust trampled street/With all its muddy feet"; "The brown waves of foga passer by with muddy skirts," and so on. And from Swift: "The slipshod 'prentice from his master's door,/had pared the dirt, and sprinkled round the floor./Now Moll had whirled her mop with dextr'ous airs,/Prepared to scrub the entry and the stairs./The Youth with broomy Stumps began to trace/The Kennel-Edge, where wheel has worn the place." Swift's poem is filled with dirt, coal, brickdust, as well as a bit of moral dirt. Of course, there is much more of this sort of imagery in Swift "Description of a City Shower," but for this paper I chose to limit myself to poems which describe morning in the city.

In reading these four poems one generalization we can make is that these are all poems of disorder. The city, in contrast with the romantic pastoral idyll, is disorderly. In an important respect, this is the disorder of different social classes coming together-the city being the place where members of various social strata come together most visibly. Frederick Smith makes the point that, in Swift's poetry, "the order of the world has been disturbed". In Swift's poem most of the people, from the Betty to the bailiffs, are going about putting things in order, although the order is inevitably a masquerade-the "masquerade that time resumes" each morning. Ironically, the servant Betty, who awakens in her master's bed, preserves appearances by discomposing her own bed-Betty's disturbed bed thus maintaining the facade of decorum, which rests on the separation of the social classes. It is noteworthy that in eighteenth-century England the word "promiscuous" was used to refer to the mixing of social classes - social promiscuity being, for conservatives anyway, a bad thing. The disorder of these poems, then, reflects the threatened breakdown of strict class divisions. In other words, the Great Chain of Being, in all its manifestations, was quite vulnerable in post-Cromwellian England.

A. B. England comments on the disorder or apparent randomness of the elements Swift has collected into this poem, and he refers to the line "Such Order from Confusion sprung" in Swift's poem "The Lady's Dressing Room." Yet, in departing from the conventional interpretation, which assumes an order at the heart of the poem, England argues that disorder actualiy represents the truth of the poem and that whatever order we may find is imposed on the poem by the reader. In other words, any order we perceive in Swift's poem simply represents our desire to find order in chaos; it is a f nction of reader-response. Despit

the fact that a number of critics (Manlove; Real & Vi nken; Smith) have found order underlying the disorder of Sw ft's "Description of Morning" and other of his poems, I don't believe Swift was that naïve or optimistic, and any statement about "order from confusion sprung" should be taken as ironic. A. B. England writes that "Swift was well aware of the human mind's impulse to find order in apparently random sequences, and he capitalized on this with his poetry so as to create a 'revolutionary realism'". The conventional reaction, the ordering impulse, might therefore be seen as the reader's effort to get past or deny the initial discomfort associated with the perception of disorder.

In the works of Swift and Eliot there is a dynamic interplay of order and disorder. There is disorder in Eliot's Waste Land with its jarring juxtaposition of different languages, themes, and imagery. And in this jarring, clashing style, Eliot appears to have been influenced by the music of Igor Stravinsky. In a "London Letter" in which Eliot comments on Stravinsky's ballet Le Sacre du printemps, which was notorious for provoking a riot at its 1913 Paris debut, Eliot writes of the clashing of modern noises that somehow makes a revolutionary, modern kind of music: "Stravinsky's musicdid seem to transform the rhythm of the steppes into the scream of the motor horn, the rattle of machinery, the grind of wheels, the beating of iron and steel, the roar of the underground railway, and the other barbaric cries of modern life; and to transform these despairing noises into music". In Swift's "A Description of Morning" there is plenty of noise as well, along with some music: "The Smallcoal-Man was heard with Cadence deep,/Till drown'd in shriller Notes of Chimney-Sweep./Duns at his Lordships Gate begin to meet,/And Brickdust Moll had Scream'd through half the Street." In the above lines, the Smallcoal-Man is of some interest. In a recent article, Arno Löffler, who identifies the "Smallcoal-Man" as one Thomas Britton, writes:

In the years about 1700 one particular sonorous voice often towered above the diffused and dissonant street cries of the trading mob, the bass of the coal merchant Thomas Britton (1654?-1714) .... However, Britton was well-known in London not only as a coal dealer. He was held in high esteem also as a collector of books and as a virtuoso, but, first of all, as a talented amateur musician and as a pioneer of the public concert .... Jonathan Swift could, therefore, be certain that his London readers would be able to understand his allusion to Britton. Thomas Britton's voice must not, therefore, be lumped in among the harsh noises of the London morning. Indeed, his deep cadence is music that is drowned out by the shrill notes of the Chimney Sweep. Löffler continues:

In Swift's poem Britton stands out from the uncleanly, shabby urban scene as a dominant figure, and he is introduced without any tinge of satire. Satirical mockery would have been amiss anyway, as Britton possessed a completely stainless image. Already during his lifetime, he was held in high repute as an upright, honest, industrious man without snobbish attitudes and social aspirations.

In the juxtaposition of Thomas Britton and the Chimney Sweep, we have the type of revolutionary clash spoken of by

Eliot. The city, from Swift's time to Eliot's and into the twenty-first century, is perhaps most distinctive as environment were all types, degrees, and levels of humanity - and non-humans - come together. In Eliot's third "Prelude," for instance, we have the sound of "the sparrows in the gutters" - a pleasant sound, but set amid the dirt of the rooftop gutters.

I believe that the disorder Eliot and Swift created in their poetry may be characterized as a type of "revolutionary music" created from the sounds, sights, and smells of their respective urban realities. This theme of disorder, which in Eliot's case was thoroughly Modernist and avant garde, also relates to Eliot's interest in the work of Pablo Picasso, whom he mentions along with Stravinsky, in his "London Letters." Picasso's revolutionary paintings are in some ways quite similar to Eliot's verse with its strange juxtapositions and odd perspectives. And returning to Swift, despite the fact that he sided with the Ancients, his work is actually quite Modernist in the twentieth-century sense of that term. Swift scatological references are quite Joycean, in fact-or it might more accurate to say that James Joyce's scatological references are quite Swiftian.

In closing, I believe that it's possible to gain a greater understanding and appreciation of Jonathan Swift by studying T. S. Eliot, as well as other twentieth-century Modernists - strange as this may sound. We might also gain insight into Eliot's work by studying Swift, along with other poets of the seventeenth and eighteenth centuries whom Eliot is known to have admired. It seems to me that Eliot was answering questions posed by Swift two centuries earlier, and if we can we get a sense of what Eliot's answers were, we might gain some insight into Swift's questions.

Mary Butts's "Unrest Cure" for The Waste Land

In 1928, Lost Generation writer Mary Butts published Armed with Madness, a novel that utilized Arthurian grail-quest mythology to comment on the conditions of modernity. She was, of course, not the first to connect these themes: T. S. Eliot's celebrated long poem, The Waste Land, had been published in 1922. In a journal entry from 1927, Butts half-jokingly complains that Armed with Madness "might well have been called 'The Wasteland.' Eliot always anticipates my titles.... Eliot and I are working on a parallel," she says, "but what is interesting is that he is working on the San c Grail on its negative side" ("Selections" 172). A simultaneous reading of Eliot's The Waste Land and Mary Butts's Armed with Madness is fascinating precisely because these contemporary works have so much in common, and yet manage to present such different visions. Working from an understanding of the grail myth similar to Eliot's own and even utilizing elements of his topography, Armed with Madness is nevertheless nothing like a mere reiteration of The Waste Land. Through its suggestion of readily available cures for the condition of barrenness and sterility illustrated in Eliot's poem, Butts's novel subtly critiques both Eliot and The Waste Land.

Those who knew both Butts and Eliot might have anticipated the nature of Butts's response to The Waste Land. Even the physical presences of these two authors would have suggested critical differences in vision and tone. In her memoir Shakespeare & Company, Sylvia Beach describes a Mary Butts who "bounced in and out... in the Paris of the twenties, with her red cheeks and red hair, and wasn't melancholy at all". The Eliot of the same period showed artistic Bloomsbury "a face tinted green with powder to look cadaverous" (Gordon 5). Butts seems to have known nearly every artistic personality of Paris and London in the 191 Os and 1920s. Her friends and admirers included Ezra Pound, Ford Madox Ford, E. M. Forster, H.D., and Marianne Moore (Blondel xv). Nevertheless, her situation as a writer, in the late 20s, differed significantly from Eliot's. By this time, Eliot was "established... at the centre of London's literary society" (Gordon 1).

A "member of the underground" living mostly in Paris, Butts was much less well known, despite the fact that her individual stories, her first collection of stories (Speed the Plough, 1923), and her first novel (Ashe of Rings, 1925) had all received critical acclaim. While the conservatively clad Eliot prayed on the London subway during his daily commute to the offices of Faber and Faber (Gordon 6), Mary Butts was pub-crawling through Paris by night, squandering her meager income on opium and penniless men.

Eliot and Butts knew each oth :r, although they were never close friends. In 1920, Ovid Press, run by Butts's then-husband, John Rodker, had published Eliot's second book of poetry, Ara Vos Prec. In the 1927 journal entry in which she describes the "parallel" between Armed with Madness and The Waste Land, Butts indicates her sense of her relationship with Eliot. "T.S. Eliot... the only writer of my quality, dislikes me and my work, I think," she says (qtd. in Blondel 186).

She then describes the incident that "made her after years 'see through' T.S. Eliot (not to lose an ounce of... admiration for his poetry)." She recalls a time when " said: 'that - in some such a way - the mandarins who went to M. Bergson's lectures at the Sorbonne may have been said to have been using their minds.'" An admirer of Eastern philosophy and culture, Butts claims that the "provincialism" of this racist comment is what "at last... decided her" against Eliot ("Selections" 172). Her decision against him easily could have been influenced by other factors as well, including Eliot's refusal to write an introduction for Ashe of Rings, despite his pronounced esteem for this work (Blondel 416). In his post as editor of The Criterion, Eliot had also rejected a number of Butts's stories in 1925 (Blondel 141).

The extent to which Eliot actually disliked either Mary Butts or her writing is unclear. Virginia Woolf's few recorded comments about Butts, however, seem to indicate a marked dislike, which was probably shared by at least some other members of her circle. Butts's abandonment of John Rodker seems to have played a part in triggering Bloomsbury's aversion (Wagstaff 44). Her brother Anthony, well known to the Woolfs as writer William Plomer's companion, also seems to have done much toward turning Bloomsbury against his sister. Although their personal situations and personalities differed significantly, Butts and Eliot have a number of similarities as writers.

Both authors are difficult. Butts, who also wrote poetry, writes very poetic prose. It has been called "some of the most elliptical prose in English," prose that "reveals the space between things, inciting the reader to fill the space or begin to commune with what is there already, in between" (West vii). Like Eliot, Butts is given to splicing borrowed quotations into her work without warning or explanation. And like Eliot's poetry, her prose requires a fairly high level of intellectual as well as emotional engagement.

Eliot and Butts also share a large number of scholarly interests and were clearly influenced by some of the same authors, especially in the writing of their modernist grail texts. Butts's journals and memoir reveal that she possessed an intimate familiarity with Sir James Frazer's The Golden Bough and Jessie Weston's From Ritual to Romance, works cited by Eliot as his chief influences in the endnotes to The Waste Land. Although in recent years questions have been raised about the importance of these texts to the actual production of The Waste Land, we can assume that in 1927, Mary Butts would have taken Eliot's endnotes at face value.

Because understanding how her grail novel functions as a critique of Eliot requires some understanding of Weston and Frazer, a brief synopsis of these influential texts serves as a useful prologue to further analysis of the connections between Armed with Madness and The Waste Land. The basic premise of Jessie Weston's From Ritual to Romance is that the grail stories, composed mostly between 1180 and 1230 CE, contain elements of earlier myths and religious cult practices, although these have been reduced to vague, confused, and jumbled forms in the texts. Weston claims that "at the root of the grail story lies the record, more or less distorted, of an ancient Ritual, having for its ultimate object the initiation into the secret of the sources of Life, physical and spiritual". She shows how the grail and bleeding lance of the story are symbolic objects from an ancient rite, representative of male and female generative powers.

The vegetation or fertility ritual that Weston sees embedded in the grail saga is also the topic of the "Adonis,"

"Attis," and "Osiris" sections of Frazer's The Golden Bough, which describe a group of similar myths and ritual practices that revolve around seasonal and growth-cycle changes. Adonis, Attis, and Osiris are all mythological figures beloved of a powerful goddess. Their untimely deaths and miraculous resurrections are celebrated annually with public rituals. Because the deaths of these vegetative "dying gods" often involve castration or injuries to the groin or thigh, Weston sees a connection between the Adonis-type figures of Frazer's discussion and the Fisher King of grail legend, who languishes from a groin or thigh wound. In the grail saga, the condition of this wounded king is related to the condition of the surrounding lands, which are similarly disabled and infertile. Both the King's wound and the wasted land are curable only if a young questing knight performs the proper ritual act at the proper moment of his quest.

Interpretations of The Waste Land informed by knowledge of The Golden Bough and From Ritual to Romance assume that Eliot is associating the decay, sterility, and decadence of modernity with the blighted land of the grail myth. They suggest the possibility that Eliot sees himself as the Fisher King of this same legend, the impotent representative or microcosm of an impotent land. Weston- and Frazer-centered readings tend to analyse, image by image, how The Waste Land creates a portrait of disintegration and impotence. They demonstrate how Eliot's is a ruined world where once a fertility ritual may have been effectively enacted, where once the seasonal changes could be counted on to bring new life, but now there is only "A heap of broken images, where the sun beats/And the dead tree gives no shelter, the cricket no relief,/and the dry stone no sound of water"

Readers who interpret The Waste Land through the lens of Frazer and Weston nearly always point to a partial reenactment of a vegetation ritual occurring at the end of "The Burial of the Dead." In this scene, one of the deathly inhabitants of the "Unreal City" stops another, named Stetson, and enquires:

You who were with me in the ships at Mylae!

That corpse you planted last year in your garden,
Has it begun to sprout? will it bloom this year?
Or has the sudden frost disturbed its bed?
O keep the Dog far hence, that's friend to men,
Or with his nails he'll dig it up again!

The reference here is to the "Adonis" section of The Golden Bough, where Frazer explains the ancient practice of ceremonially planting a corpse or constructed human figure representing the sacrificial god, in order that new life and new crops might spring out of the sacrificed body.

That the planted corpse in Eliot's poem will "sprout," bringing new life, seems uncertain, however, since "sudden frost" might have "disturbed its bed," or a dog might "dig it up again." The poetic speaker also seems ambivalent as to whether this sprouting would be desirable, should it occur. The "Dog" of the passage is surely meant as a double reference to both an earthly canine and the Dog Star, Sirius, associated, in Frazer, with Isis, the summer solstice, and the celebration of vegetative renewal and abundance (Frazer 429-30). When the speaker tells Stetson that the "Dog" might dig the corpse up again, the encoded message is that the corpse might bloom at the solstice.

In telling Stetson to "keep the Dog far hence," the speaker demonstrates repulsion at the prospect of a blooming corpse. The same sort of repulsion at - or resistance to - rejuvenation can be found in the poem's opening lines, "April is the cruellest month, breeding/Lilacs out of the dead land," and throughout the poem, particularly in the sequences depicting vacuous sexual relations between men and women. The repulsion toward sex and rejuvenation that Mary Butts would have noticed throughout The Waste Land is even more clearly visible in the longer original drafts published in 1971. More recent publications of Eliot's letters and of Lyndall Gordon's biography, Eliot's New Life, have also reinforced what critic Robert Alter terms "one's darker suspicions about ": that "Eliot lived a cramped, painfully impaired emotional existence" and that "the rejection of the body and a visceral horror of women constituted a fundamental pattern in Eliot's life". Indeed, contemporary biographical and psychoanalytic critics tend to find everywhere in Eliot's work evidence of the author's sexual neuroses and misogyny. Some even see a suppressed homosexuality underlying Eliot's homosocial behaviour.

At the time when Butts was writing Armed with Madness, Eliot was a celebrity in England, and his personal circumstances were not a secret to others in the literary and arts community. Butts would have had knowledge of the strained relationship between Eliot and his wife Vivienne, and of his psychological and physical retreat from the nightmare of his marriage into the comparative safety and comfort of a strict, ascetic Christian practice. An understanding of Eliot's personality and personal circumstances would have colored Butts's interpretation of The Waste Land, a poem that Eliot himself once described as "only the relief of a personal and wholly insignificant grouse against life."

Just as The Waste Land was undoubtedly born of Eliot's personal circumstances, so the composition of Armed with Madness seems linked to patterns of Butts's personal life. Mary Butts was repeatedly attracted to men who were depressed or physically unwell, "underhanded, unstable, lost, homosexual, and unavailable" (Blaser, Afterword 75). In fact, she found it difficult to write unless she was simultaneously working on "curing" a "psychically sick" man (Hanscombe 110). Her treatment of her adopted psychic invalids involved wrenching them out of their withdrawal and immersing them in life. According to a good friend, the composer Virgil Thomson, Butts referred to herself as an "unrest cure" (qtd. in Hanscombe 106). In a journal entry from May 2, 1927, Butts records that she has always had an incomparable pleasure in finding someone psychically sick, and learning about it, and seeing if there is a way out. This feeling very much mixed up with sex - bed not necessary, but it makes things work better. That is, any power I have seems to work better in that relation. I've always wanted to make my lovers well, sense powers liberated in them, fears in the dustbin, raw life taken in and coming out translated. ("Selections" 171)

Butts's desire to heal "psychically sick" men seems

intimately linked with her vision of her purpose as an artist. In the same journal entry, she also writes: Up to now I am an unsuccessful writer, lover, dubious mother, of no social distinction.... Well, I can write and I want to, should never want to do much else. What for?... In the old cant phrase I want to show people beauty - soundness. Now the best work cannot be made up wholly from the ugly and unsound. And our world is both.... What apart from the specific work of writing is what interests me? Nothing but spiritual development, the soul living at its fullest capacity. That is the lever, the new synthesis, or vision or faith. I have not got it yet, but I am beginning to know what is wrong with the times. ("Selections")

Butts seems to have seen her writing as part of a general effort to heal her world. In her journal, she says that she wants to come to a full understanding of "what is wrong with the times," an understanding of what in Armed with Madness she calls the "dis-ease" of modernity. She wants to fight against this "dis-ease" by "showing people beauty - soundness," and by finding a "new synthesis, or vision or faith" that will allow human souls to finally " at fullest capacity."

Butts clearly read Eliot's The Waste Land as a text about the "dis-ease" of modernity, a text reflecting the thoughts and feelings of a "psychically sick" author. And while she may have had no opportunity to apply her "unrest cure" directly to Eliot himself, Butts was able to write her prescription in the form of a novel. Armed with Madness focuses on the interactions within a group of six artistic young people gathered for an indefinite stay at the Taverner family home in Dorsetshire. As the novel opens, siblings Felix and Scylla Taverner and their friend Ross are about to receive an American visitor, Dudley Carston.

Not long after Carston's arrival, friends Picus and Clarence also come to stay, since the well at their cottage has run dry. Of this group of five men and one woman, only the solidly grounded, nature-loving Ross seems entirely free of the "psychic sickness" that Butts would have associated with Eliot and his The Waste Land. Other members of the novel's cast are, to varying degrees, underhanded, unstable, lost, depressed, or physically unwell. Felix displays the sort of repulsion toward women and the life cycle suggested by and embodied in The Waste Land. Clarence is a war veteran, suffering from posttraumatic stress disorder.

While Armed with Madness, like The Waste Land, gives a fair portrait of "psychic sickness," it goes one step beyond, in that it simultaneously points toward a number of cures for this condition. One potential cure is suggested through the portrayal of Ross, whose Taoist simplicity and close connection to nature seem to inoculate him against this "dis-ease." Even Scylla, who is herself frequently associated with nature, expresses her admiration and envy for this man who "never wants anything that he not get," never wants anything but "something to eat and drink, to embrace and paint". "Wherever he touched it life grew," we are told. "Plants and dogs and children. Eggs hatched. And men? They were there to make him laugh. If they found rest in him, he was indifferent as Nature, and in general as kind".

Ross is, as Scylla says, a "very sensual man". Throughout, Butts's novel seems to propose sensuality and soulful sexuality as antidotes to the "dis-ease" of modernity. It especially stresses the curative power of sexual relationships between men and women. Early in Armed with Madness, while the men are trying to solve the water shortage problem at Tollerdown cottage, they discover a mysterious grail-type object in the well, "shrunk by drought, yielding nothing but dead hedgehogs". This cup is removed with a fishing spear, a symbolic act since, in Weston's From Ritual to Romance, cup and spear together represent heterosexual union. Shortly afterward, Picus, who has been feeling unwell, is restored to health. "We got over there,"

Felix tells Scylla and Carston, and found Picus saying he was ill and Clarence doing all the work. As usual. So, after tea with soda water, I went down in the bucket. The others hung on to the windlass and Picus strolled out. Got a fishing spear with him, because he said high hedgehogs aren't things to handle.... I raised that cup along with the corpses. We were looking at it, and Picus began to whistle. You must hear him whistle; it's like Mozart. Said he was perfectly well again. After the finding of the cup, rains come pouring down: "For an hour it rained, through sheet lightning and thunder like a departing train, the hills calling to one another". During this rejuvenating rainstorm, Picus and Scylla make love for the first time, beginning a relationship that will evolve into the successful marriage depicted in a later novel, Death of Felicity Taverner.

Armed with Madness thus overtly connects sexual practice, health, and landscape conditions. This connection, as Butts must have noticed, is also present in The Waste Land. Here, though, descriptions of sterile and repulsive sexual encounters are mirrored in descriptions of an unrelievedly barren and grotesque landscape. No grail is found, no healing rainstorm occurs. Inscribed on the land is a parade of Freudian images suggesting aversion toward and fear of female sexuality. Critics Robert Alter and Wayne Koestenbaum have identified images of the Freudian vagina dentata in other Eliot poems of the same period (Alter 35-37; Koestenbaum 116). The Waste Land itself contains numerous images of mouths, caves, pits, wells, doorways, and churches, and continuously beckons us to come and look into these orifices to see just how barren and horrifying they are. We are made to gaze into a "decayed hole among the mountains" (line 386), the "doors of mudcracked houses" where "red sullen faces sneer and snarl", and an "empty chapel, only the wind's home" that "has no windows". We cannot help but recognize in the "dead mountain mouth of carious teeth that cannot spit" a grotesque and frightening image of female sexuality. Nor can we avoid associating this grotesque mountain mouth with the mouth of the woman named Lil from "A Game of Chess," whose husband urges her to purchase false teeth, saying, "You have them all out, Lil, and get a nice set/... I swear, I can't bear to look at you".

In light of Freud's association of vermin and small animals with children, the poem's images of hollow spaces filled with bones and rats become interpretable as nightmare images of pregnancy and female reproductivity. The "little low dry garret,/Rattled by the rat's foot only, year to year" becomes a vagina/womb-like space. We see an image of grotesque childbirth in the passage that reads: "A rat crept softly through the vegetation/Dragging its slimy belly on the bank". The connection between women, vermin, and childbirth becomes perhaps most intriguing in a passage from "What the Thunder Said" where "bats" (flying rodents) are given "baby faces":

A woman drew her long black hair out tight
And fiddled whisper music on those strings
And bats with baby faces in the violet light
Whistled, and beat their wings
And crawled head downward down a blackened wall
And upside down in air were towers
Tolling reminiscent bells, that kept the hours
And voices singing out of empty cisterns and
exhausted wells.

The downward movement of these bats is something like a grotesque reenactment of childbirth. The witch-like woman here, with her "long black hair," seems responsible for the motion of these bats, as well as for the frightening sound of "voices singing out of empty cisterns and exhausted wells," which evoke female reproductive spaces.

In Armed with Madness, bats and a rat appear, early on in the story, while Scylla is entertaining Carston on the patio. The appearance of such animals is not alarming here, however, since they are simply a natural part of a quietly fecund setting:

So they ate together; an eatable meal, fresh-tasting wine, and the inevitable whisky after. A rabbit crossed the lawn. A rat came under the verandah and stole a piece of bread. Two bats flew in.... Nothing went on happening: the delicate quiet waited on them.

Just as the significance of bats and rats is altered in the landscape of Butts's novel, so too is the significance of a witch-woman's presence. When we are first introduced to Scylla, Felix, and Ross, the three together are described in positive terms as a witch figure. Sitting out on the shoreline, conspiring over the arrival of Carston, these three become "a triple figure, like Hecate the witch, amused, imaginative".

Armed with Madness counters The Waste Land's uniformly bleak vision, both through offering such alternative readings for Eliot's figures of the grotesque and through descriptions of a dual-natured landscape, both lovely and grotesque. Heavily influenced by the thought of Blake and Nietzsche and very much attracted to Taoism, Butts typically depicts a world characterized equally by forces of dissolution and regeneration. Armed with Madness constantly illustrates her notion that "in the world there is a fifty-fifty deal of pleasure and grief", and that thus "the best artistic work cannot be made up wholly from images of the ugly and unsound" ("Selections" 171). When Felix, Scylla, and Ross are first introduced, they are "lying out naked on a rock-spit which terminate s their piece of land."

"The sea at the moment," we are told, "was something for the men to swim in, an enormous toy". Later, however, the same sea, in a more violent mood, sinks a ship, and Felix, who works with the rescue team, is traumatized by a vision of "twenty-three dead men," "singularly drowned with their wounds shewing - where the fish gnawed". In the opening sequences of Armed with Madness, the Taverner land is depicted as simultaneously "marvelously noisy," and so silent that "not many nerves can stand it". About the Taverners' two closest neighbors we are told that "the fisherman was a gentleman, and a fine carver in wood. The shepherd was a troglodyte. He came home drunk in the moonlight spinning round and yelling obscene words to the tune of old hymns". The Taverners, who themselves want "everything and nothing," are "equally friends with both" the Dionysian shepherd and the Apollonian fisherman.

With its potential to embody opposing impulses, the grail itself finds a comfortable home in Butts's dual-natured landscape. A hybrid symbol with both pagan and Christian heritage, the grail can represent equally both the passion of the Christian dying god and the fertile womb of an earlier pagan earth goddess. It forms part of a death tableau when described as the container in which Joseph of Arimithea caught the falling blood of the crucified savior. The grail figures as a source of life when depicted as a cornucopia or an icon with magical healing powers. Its shape (most frequently a cup or bowl) and nearly invariable pairing with a magical, blood-dripping spear, point toward its role as a symbol of female sexuality and reproductivity, yet its hollow interior makes it a ready symbol for emptiness. In Armed with Madness, Butts thoroughly exploits the complexity of this symbol. While all grail-shaped objects mentioned in The Waste Land (the "empty cisterns" and "exhausted wells," for instance) seem to possess roughly the same symbolic content, the meaning of grail-objects constantly shifts throughout

Armed with Madness. Butts promotes a proliferation of grail meanings because she wishes to show both how opposing forces can coexist within a single object, and how the yield of a symbolic container is affected by what is brought to and placed inside that container. When, early on in Armed with Madness, the Taverner friends play the "Freud game" in order to explain the Sanc Grail to Carston, their new visitor, each group member produces a comment or recollection about the grail that is mediated by individual character, position, and interests. Robin Blaser notes how Scylla Taverner's comments during the "Freud game" promote the romance between herself and Picus.

Carston's comment that "the girl who carried it" might have been "the female spirit of life" shows him to have "perhaps the most twentieth-century and anthropological" view of the grail (Blaser, "Here Lies the Woodpecker" 183). The doctor, by contrast, associates the grail with Christian ceremony and Wagner's Parsifal. Clarence, who only voices a distaste for "those awful pre-Raphaelite pictures" is, Blaser says, "attached to the merely stylish and mannered." He is "a voice out of the twenties" who can "dismiss in the name of a newer, more geometric art, pre-Raphaelite, art nouveau and symbolist alike".

The specific cup found by the Taverner group in Tollerdown well itself has multiple uses and identities. It might be the Sanc Grail, but it might also be an Indian rajah's poison cup. We are never sure. While it once may have held the blessed sacrament, the cup has also, more certainly and more recently, served as a dying mistress's spittoon. Unsure not only whether the specific cup in question is holy or unholy, but also whether it is authentic or a hoax, we see the Taverner clan making uneasy jokes while using their grail as an ash tray and a glass for whisky and soda. With its confusion of potential meanings and uses, its links to processes of both healing and destruction, the Taverner grail breeds unrest. Within a week of its discovery, the gathering of friends at the Taverner home is dispersed. Driven away variously by jealousy, anxiety, and curiosity, Scylla, Felix, Clarence, Picus, and Carston all set off on individual quests, only to be reunited at the novel's end. In this, Armed with Madness structurally parallels Thomas Malory's Le Morte d'Arthur, clearly an important source for Butts. In Malory's version of the grail saga, Quest du Sanc Graal, the appearance of the grail disperses the Round Table. Malory's narrative then moves back and forth between tales of the scattered questers. As Butts traces the paths of her questers, images of grails, grail maidens, and grail rituals multiply, just as they do in Le Morte d'Arthur.

More

Articles of Interest

Travels in "The Waste Land.".(Critical Essay)

Disciplining 'The Waste Land', or how to lead critics into temptation Understanding "The Waste Land"; Why Eliot's famous poem resists... "Brightness falls": magic in the short stories of Mary Butts - Critical Essay

Armed with questions: Mary Butts's sacred interrogative

Like Malory's Quest du Sanc Graal, Armed with Madness is the story of an entire grail cycle. Butts's grail appears and has its effects. It brings confusion, violence, and anger, but also the potential for moments of self-realization, healing, and love. At the novel's end, Scylla Taverner is nearly crucified by Clarence, her lover's recently abandoned companion. This moment of sacrifice, however, reminiscent of the ceremonies discussed in Frazer's Golden Bough, seems to trigger a sort of restoration of harmony among the friends. When the Taverner grail is thrown back into the well, its work is done: all characters are forever changed. A new cycle has begun. Butts's novel is, thus, epic in its scope, unlike the more lyric The Waste Land, which uses its collage of materials to create a picture of a single psychological state and shows only "the Sanc Grail on its negative side," as Butts says in her journal. Eliot describes no healing of his land and prescribes no true cure for its inhabitants, though he does suggest potential coping strategies available to wasteland dwellers. We can, for instance, Eliot's poem suggests, attempt a saintlike "burning burning burning burning" (line 308) away of our sexually polluted flesh (Gordon 14). We can sustain ourselves with memories of times past when we were still capable of impulsively giving ourselves to others (lines 401-09). We can "think of the key, each in his prison," despite the fact that "thinking of the key" only "confirms a prison". Like the still-maimed Fisher King of the poem's conclusion, we can try to "at least set our lands in order", even if we are impotent to do much else.

Armed with Madness moves beyond offering such coping strategies and points to potential cures for the wasteland and its inhabitants. Butts reinforces the healing power of empathetic connection with and care for the natural world, of love relationships that are simultaneously deeply sexual and spiritual, and of living within a community of like minds. Rather than retreat into a saint-like asceticism or comforting dogmatism, Butts's characters take chances with their feelings, bodies, minds, and lives. They actively seek; they create quests. Rather than resent the fact that the life force might best be embodied in the form of a laughing, changeable, trickster god, they emulate their deity. In a world full of fragments, a world in flux, they learn to live with chaos, and even sometimes to thrive on it.

Armed with Madness received mixed reviews when it was published in 1928. It is uncertain whether T. S. Eliot ever read it and, if he did, what he thought of it. An anonymous New York Times reviewer who enjoyed Armed with Madness but seems to have understood little of it, expressed his relief that at least Butts had this time "herself admitted the madness of her characters" which "permitted one to stop seeking her novel's esoteric meanings and motives, and enjoy the book as a sophisticated and most exquisitely written fantasy" ("Sophisticated" 9). A New York Herald Tribune reviewer enjoyed Butts's "beautiful and admirable prose" and her "asides" with their "Rabelaisian unashamedness," though he found these same asides basically meaningless. Understanding little beyond the Freudian sexual symbolism of the novel's grail and spear, his review mostly expressed shock at Butts's "frank" treatment of sexual themes. "No average reader would put up with the implications of the story," he thought.

More

Articles of Interest

Travels in "The Waste Land.".(Critical Essay)

Disciplining 'The Waste Land', or how to lead critics into temptation Understanding "The Waste Land"; Why Eliot's famous poem resists... "Brightness falls": magic in the short stories of Mary Butts - Critical Essay Armed with questions: Mary Butts's sacred interrogative. Though Armed with Madness fell victim to a number of such shallow reviews, much of Butts's work, and especially her later work, actually fared quite well with reviewers. In fact, Mary Butts seems to have been well on her way to etching a permanent place for herself in English letters when she died suddenly in 1937, of a perforated ulcer and peritonitis. She was 46 at the time, living alone in a cottage in Cornwall, and hard at work on a seventh novel about Julian the Apostate. Her 40s had been an incredibly productive period for her. She had published three novels, a collection of short stories, two pamphlets, and a vast number of reviews and articles. Her notebooks were brimming full of ideas. She was in the process of searching out a publisher for a recently completed memoir of her childhood. T. S. Eliot had just offered to publish a collection of her stories with Faber.

It is unfortunate that this collection was in fact never published; the reason why is unknown. Four days after Mary Butts's death, Eliot wrote a letter to inform her that the stories he had requested had not yet arrived. When Butts's literary executor, Angus Davidson, wrote back explaining the circumstances, Eliot expressed the appropriate shock and remorse (Blondel 425). But the Faber volume never appeared. The collected stories intended for Faber were edited by Butts's friend, the novelist Bryher, and published by Brendin Publishing in 1938. "Had Faber published a volume of Mary Butts's stories," as biographer Nathalie Blondel notes, "there is no doubt that her reputation, albeit posthumously, would have been secured". As it was, Butts's passing was commemorated in a number of journals, and her posthumously published memoir, The Crystal Cabinet, actually proved to be her most popular book (Blondel 426). But Mary Butts never really experienced the "poet's success" that she "looked forward to" on The Little Review's 1929 questionnaire. In the years following her death, her works quickly became unavailable. Already in 1943, she was mentioned only in passing in W. J. Entwhistle and E. Gillett's The Literature of England AD 500-1942, where she was dismissed as "among other women writers who have written workmanlike and, at times, satisfying fiction" (qtd. in Blondel 433).

Although Mary Butts has perhaps always maintained something of a small cult following, much of her writing had never been republished until very recently. During the past decade, McPherson & Company has been reissuing her entire oeuvre and has also published an excellent biography by Nathalie Blondel and a critical and commemorative volume edited by Christopher Wagstaff. Today's reader, no longer likely to be offended by either Butts's "frankness" or her experimental style, may find a great deal of interest and relevance in this modernist writer's works. Butts was an adamant campaigner for ecological preservation and for the preservation of historical landmarks. She saw a deep connection between the internal and external, the past and the present, the social and the spiritual. Almost all of her works, like Armed with Madness, show us a bountiful world infused with spirit, one simultaneously requiring and offering profound care. "Why catch up with the Holy Spirit when He is hovering over Asia and saying 'Shantih'?" Mary Butts would quip in a 1932 letter to her friend, Eliot critic Hugh Ross Williamson. "He is in a nut in a Glastonbury thicket.

Bibliography

The Flesh and the Word: Eliot, Hemingway, Faulkner, Floyd C. Watkins (Vanderbilt Univ Press, 1971).

T.S. Eliot: A Collection of Criticism, Ed. Linda Welshimer Wagner (McGraw-Hill, 1974).

T. S. Eliot, Stephen Spender (Viking Press, 1976).

Eliot's Early Years, Lyndall Gordon (Oxford University Press, 1977).

"*Ulysses,*" "*The Waste Land,*" and Modernism: A Jubilee Study, Stanley Sultan (Associated Faculty Press, 1977).

A Half-Century of Eliot Criticism, Mildred Martin (Associated Univ Press, 1979).

Thomas Stearns Eliot, Poet, Anthony David Moody (Cambridge University Press, 1979).

T.S. Eliot: An Introduction, Northrop Frye (University of Chicago Press, 1981).

T. S. Eliot: The Critical Heritage, Ed. Michael Grant (Routledge Kegan & Paul, 1982).

T.S. Eliot and the Poetics of Literary History, Gregory S. Jay (Louisiana State University Press, 1983).

T. S. Eliot: A Life, Peter Ackroyd (Simon & Schuster, 1984).

The Matrix of Modernism: Pound, Eliot, and Early Twentieth-Century Thought, Sanford Schwartz (Princeton Univ Press, 1985.)

The Poetics of Impersonality: T. S. Eliot and Ezra Pound, Maud Ellmann (Harvard Univ Press, 1987).

T.S. Eliot's the Waste Land, Harold Bloom (Chelsea House, 1988).

The American T. S. Eliot: A Study of the Early Writings, Eric Sigg (Cambridge University Press, 1989).

Skepticism and Modern Enmity: Before and After Eliot, Jeffrey M. Perl (Johns Hopkins Univ Press, 1989).

Reading "*The Waste Land*": Modernism and the Limits of Interpretation, Jewel Spears Brooker an l Joseph Bentley (Univ. of Massachusetts Press, 1990).

Harmony of Dissonances: T.S. Eliot, Romanticism, and Imagination, John Paul Riquelme (Johns Hopkins Univ Press, 1991).

The Savage and the City in the Work of T.S. Elliott, Robert Crawford (Oxford University Press, 1991).

T.S. Eliot: The Modernist in History, Ronald Bush (Cambridge University Press, 1991).

A Guide to the Selected Poems of T.S. Eliot, B. C. Southam (Harvest Books, 1996).

T.S. Eliot and the Ideology of Four Quartets, John Xiros Cooper (Cambridge University Press, 1996).

T.S. Eliot Anti-Semitism and Literary Form, Anthony Julius (Cambridge University Press, 1996).

T.S. Eliot and the Use of Memory, Grover Cleveland Smith (Bucknell Univ Press, 1996).

A Reader's Guide to T.S. Eliot: A Poem-By-Poem Analysis, George Williamson (Syracuse Univ Press, 1998).

T.S. Eliot and American Poetry, Lee Oser (Univ of Missouri Press, 1998).

T.S. Eliot: Comprehensive Research and Study Guide, Harold Bloom (Chelsea House, 1998).

Eliot's Dark Angel: Intersections of Life and Art, Ronald Schuchard (Oxford University Press, 1999).

T.S. Eliot and the Philosophy of Criticism, Richard M. Shusterman (iUniverse.com, 2000).

T.S. Eliot: An Imperfect Life, Lyndall Gordon (W.W. Norton & Company, 2000).

T.S. Eliot and Our Turning World, Ed. Jewel Spears Brooker (Palgrave Macmillan, 2001).

A Critical Reading of the Selected Poems of T.S. Eliot, Manju Jain (Oxford University Press, 2002).

Discovering Modernism: T.S. Eliot and His Context, Louis, III Menand (Oxford University Press, 2003).